PAROLE CHIEF

DAVID DRESSLER

Parole Chief

NEW YORK · 1951

THE VIKING PRESS

In the recital of the incidents in this book no
actual records or material of the New York State
Division of Parole have been referred to, made
available to, or utilized by the author. All incidents
have been taken from his personal recollections,
adapted to avoid any betrayal of confidence or
individual identification.

Acknowledgment is made to the following magazines in which excerpts from this book have appeared: *This Week*, Chapters XI and XII; *Saga*,
Chapter XVIII; *True Detective*, part of Chapter
VIII.

To

Belle, David Mark, and Joshua

who give me strength

Contents

Contents

PAROLE CHIEF

CHAPTER I

How I Began

I was eight years old, a willful, nasty-tempered brat, and I was mad. I was packing my belongings, preparing to run away from the orphanage, when I heard the matron say to her assistant, "That boy will wind up on the gallows some day!"

Infuriated, I walked out and away, much, I am certain, to the relief of the matron.

Her dire forebodings were partly justified. I haven't wound up on the gallows yet, but I did go into crime in a big way. My career in parole work in New York State, which went from the job of rookie parole officer to executive director of the Division of Parole, may have had its beginnings on that day.

As I recall it, there was a fundamental difference of opinion between me and the authorities at the Home. It had to do with theories of child training, on which we both had very definite notions. In those days, at least in Louisville, it was assumed a child of eight should be interested in playing with blocks. I wasn't. I didn't care for *any* big muscle activity. A puny, undersized kid, I overcompensated by a concentration on school, reading, imagining myself a pirate, a general, an executioner officiating at the decapitation of the Home's matron and staff. What I couldn't achieve by brawn, I was going to achieve by imagination.

3

The situation at the Home was aggravated by the fact that I was a gangster. The term wasn't in vogue then, and I think what the ladies called me was "hoodlum."

It happened this way. Whenever I passed a certain boy's house, he used to muss me up, punch me, call me a Jew bastard. I would cry in frustration but never dared fight back, not having developed those muscles. I couldn't bypass the scoundrel, for he lived right next door to the branch library. So I formed a Jewish army, composed of kids who lived in the neighborhood. I drilled them regularly, worked them into shape for D-Day. My plan was to deploy several contingents about the area, each led by a captain carrying a homemade Jewish flag and a whistle. If some part of the army came upon my enemy —or any other gentile boy who didn't look too tough—the captain was to blow his whistle, all forces were to converge and knock hell out of the hapless boy unfortunate enough to be a Christian. I even set a day when we were to begin our blitz. Thus all Christianity was to suffer for the sins of one villain. There is undoubtedly a moral here somewhere.

One afternoon I came back from some errand downtown to find the street blocked with boys standing in front of the Home, screaming, "David! Oh, David!" This was D-Day, and I'd forgotten about it. The matron now knew of our plans, and I had the devil of a time explaining.

The straw that broke the matron's back, however, had to do with my having developed a morbid interest in tobacco. An older boy rolled a Bull Durham cigarette for me and I took several puffs. The acrid taste didn't appeal to me at all, and I was deeply disappointed, for now I couldn't be a big fellow like some of the others. To make up for this loss of face I tried something else. I had noted that the really manly men, like truck drivers and saloonkeepers, kept a wad of chewing tobacco in their mouths.

One day I was sent to the grocery store for some bread. On the counter stood a big machine with a keen blade, used to cut plug tobacco into appropriate sizes. There was a scrap of plug lying on the machine. I put it in my mouth. While I was waiting my turn, I chewed vigorously. All might have gone well, except that I was ignorant of one thing—the truck drivers and saloonkeepers didn't *swallow* the stuff. I did—and was carried home in an ambulance.

The matron, fundamentally, was a kindly, well-disposed woman, really interested in children. But she had had enough. There was talk of sending me to a reformatory. I know now she didn't mean it; she was only trying to scare me. In fact, she couldn't have sent me away. The law didn't provide for the incarceration of juveniles who had committed no offense. But the prospect was so terrifying that I had a violent nightmare about being in a reformatory.

That settled it. Shaken, shocked, I decided it was the better part of wisdom to depart before the law caught up with me.

Perhaps what saved me from the gallows in ensuing years, as I knocked around Kentucky, Indiana, and Missouri, was religion. I developed an awful dose of it, became an Orthodox Jew in practice. I prayed in Hebrew when I arose, before and after each meal, and at night before retiring. I wouldn't carry even a handkerchief on Saturday.

I became an insufferable prig, eternally moralizing, preaching, insisting everyone must live as I did. Consequently I was completely law-abiding. As a matter of fact, even before I got religion I didn't often knowingly violate the law. I can remember stealing only twice. Once I took a picture postcard from a candy store—I don't know why. It showed a bosomy lady and a handsome man, and one of them, according to the caption, was saying, "Do you care for me still?" The other time I crept into the pantry of the orphanage, armed with a large carton, and unloaded about twenty pounds of graham crackers from the stock. These I hid in the backyard privy, since it was no longer in use. But now, with religion, I looked with loathing on anyone who would do a thing like that.

Then I met two elderly ladies who caused me great emotional distress. I was about ten and living in St. Louis. The ladies came across me sleeping in an empty tenement flat below their quarters. They were kindly souls, Catholic and deeply religious. They insisted on providing me with a bed in their place, and it was a month before I could escape. They set about converting me. Their eyes lighting up with that religious ecstasy only prophets experience, they lectured me on the one true faith. They assured me I would positively go to hell unless I came to Jesus. They got down on their knees and prayed for me. They had me so upset that I would cry in my room, in frustration at being unable to decide which religion was the true one. I became despondent and moody.

Then I resolved my conflict. I found the one certain answer. At night I would put on my skull cap, get into bed, and repeat Krishma, the Hebrew night prayer. Then I would get out of bed, take off my cap, kneel, and pray in English, the Catholic way. Upon finishing, I would wave an arm toward heaven and humbly plead, "Whichever is right, God, please take it!"

Apparently the good Lord was satisfied with this double dose of devotion, for things improved. I located an empty apartment in another building, moved in, and made friends with the janitor's son. Theretofore I had been dependent on odd jobs for a living—scrubbing floors, washing windows, rushing the growler for the policemen at the precinct house that abutted Columbus Park. But my new-found friend was a capitalist. He was also a sniveling, filthy-faced child of seven, an ugly sight indeed. So much so that parents enjoined their children from playing with him. He was happy to have as a friend a chap like me, who cared naught about a man's appearance so long as he had a heart of gold.

My friend not only had a heart of gold, he had nickels, which he shared with me. He also had a seemingly inexhaustible supply of sweet potatoes, which we roasted over a fire in the courtyard. He would hand me one and say, "Know why I give you this?"—sniffle, sniffle. "Coss why you play with me!"

Through my friend's generosity I built up enough capital to go into business. I made sandwiches which I sold at recess time in the schoolyard. If I sold out, my profit was fifteen cents. And usually I did sell out. I was becoming rich.

I was going to school regularly because I loved it. I gave a home address and hoped no one would check. No one did until I hit hard times. I lost my capital, had no sandwiches to sell, became hungry, and lived for a couple of days on lumps of sugar. I fainted in class, and someone took me "home." Soon after, I was put on a train for Louisville.

I got off in East St. Louis.

One way or another I got along, went through elementary and high school. I was back in Louisville, living in a furnished room, the envy of all my schoolmates because I had no rules to govern me. I worked after class, earned twenty-five dollars a week by the time I graduated.

As valedictorian of the class at Louisville Male High School, I was entitled to a scholarship. I chose the University of

Chicago because it had a school of social work. Why social work? Simple!

One man, Charles Nemser, the director of the Louisville YMHA, had demonstrated complete faith in me as I was growing up. He didn't consider me jail material or gallows bait. He befriended me, counseled me, became a father to me. He gave me faith in myself. He also gave me a job at the Y. I regarded him with the kind of respect and affection possible only to a hero-worshiping kid. I wanted to be like Charles Nemser.

He had a rolltop desk that I admired enormously. To me it represented the professional man, the man of status and stature. I wanted someday to own such a desk. So to get a rolltop desk I undertook the study of social work.

CHAPTER II

John McCooey and I

My selection of the particular social work specialization that was to become my career was just as haphazard as my choice of social service generally.

I had finished the University of Chicago's school of social work and decided it was time to eat. I became a caseworker, then a community-center director—like Charles Nemser. I was feeding regularly, had a rolltop desk, but was vaguely apprehensive that constant association with the male social workers I knew would make of me a very bright lad who smoked cork-tipped cigarettes and discussed humanism and D. H. Lawrence.

Working in New York, I ran into an aunt I had never met before. A forthright woman, she snorted when she heard what I was doing. "That's no job for a man! You're twenty-two. Before it's too late, get into something with a future."

"Like what?" I queried.

"Why not Civil Service?"

That, I have since discovered, is a reaction quite typical of the majority of citizens. They consider Civil Service a safe, secure, permanent haven, one in which you get promoted fast, earn better and better wages, and retire on a generous pension to some turkey farm.

My aunt suggested I read a local Civil Service paper that carried announcements of forthcoming examinations. The first

copy I bought headlined: PAROLE OFFICER EXAMINATION. New
York State, I read, had created an entirely new parole system.
It was going to hire some sixty parole officers, all through competitive examination. Persons with social-work experience were
particularly needed.

I didn't know what parole was, exactly. But in that depression year of 1930 an annual salary of three thousand dollars
sounded munificent. Moreover, I reasoned, the work would be
interesting and right in my line. I luxuriated a while in the
fantasy that a parole officer was quite a fellow. I visualized
myself walking down the corridor of a jail cell block, passing
out cigarettes to prisoners, delivering here and there a brusque
but confidence-inspiring word of advice. That's what I thought
parole was like.

I filed application, along with twelve thousand others. Then
I completely forgot about it and went on smoking cork-tipped
cigarettes until, some months later, I was called to the examination, with some twenty-five hundred other men and women
who had qualified.

Since Civil Service is always an austere and unhurried
mother of the career servant, the examination had a gestation
period of more than nine months before producing offspring.
It was a year before the results were published and I was offered a job, contingent upon the impression I would create in
an interview with the three members of the Parole Board.

The parole commissioners were Dr. Joseph W. Moore, an
eminent psychiatrist; Frank Hanscom, an affable ex-minister;
and Bernard J. Fagin, formerly chief probation officer of the
New York County Children's Court.

Mr. Fagin did most of the talking, and I was charmed. In
spite of his black-ribboned pince-nez, he was a jolly, informal

man. He wisecracked throughout the interview, and I figured I was getting along famously.

Then he looked at some papers and remarked, "Oh! I see you live in Brooklyn!"

I acknowledged that with none of the vehemence characteristic of a true Brooklynite. After all, I was born in Louisville.

"Well," said Mr. Fagin, chuckling, "I guess that means you know John McCooey."

"Who?" I asked, puzzled.

"You don't know John McCooey?"

"No. Should I?"

Mr. Fagin laughed. "If you don't know John McCooey, I guess that means you're not a Democrat. Heh! Heh!"

Then I caught on. McCooey was political boss of Brooklyn, the good right hand of Manhattan's Tammany Hall. I burned up. With all the dignity of my twenty-three years I arose and spat out, "No, I don't know John McCooey. And if I have to know John McCooey to get this job, you can have the job!"

"But—" spluttered Commissioner Fagin.

"When I took this examination," I continued, "I understood this was a new outfit, entirely out of politics. I'm not a Democrat and I'm not a Republican or anything else. If I have to have a party label, to hell with the job!" I started for the door, the living image of civic virtue.

Dr. Moore had listened to this exchange in silence. Now he stopped me, turned to Commissioner Fagin, and in quiet, courteous tones laid him out forty ways for Sunday. "We're not interested in this man's politics," he ended up. "This is not a political club."

Mr. Fagin cackled and assured me he hadn't meant to suggest any such thing. "I only thought—heh! heh!—living in Brooklyn you must know John McCooey. Heh! Heh! I thought everybody in Brooklyn knew John McCooey!" And he was convulsed with mirth at the thought of a Brooklynite not knowing good old John.

We finished the interview somehow. I left, convinced I'd be smoking cork-tipped cigarettes for a long, long time.

My reactions were not very different from what most aspiring or actual civil servants would have felt. Only they would have shown better judgment in expressing themselves. Most competitive class employees, I have since learned, don't want or like politics on the job. They fear it. They feel they can't get a fair deal under a political administration. They prefer to be beholden to no one, free to act on the merits of a case without regard to whom the "case" knows.

I am aware now that Mr. Fagin was the only member of that Parole Board who had any political background or leanings. And he was more than counterbalanced by the other two members, who didn't care a continental how a man voted.

Only because of this did I get the job.

CHAPTER III

I Enter the Squirrel Cage

My first month as parole officer in the New York State Division of Parole was one of utter confusion and perpetual amazement.

Forty of us arrived for work the same day and were put behind desks in one tremendous room. Each of us was given a stack of cards and told these were our cases, to get to work. We were to check on the activities of parolees, weed out those who were reverting to crime and return them to prison, help the rest to become stable citizens. That was that. There was no advance indoctrination, no in-service training. Here were the cards and here was the directive.

I had a hundred and sixty cases. My territory covered all of Manhattan, part of the Bronx, and a modest piece of Long Island. I didn't know a thing about any parolee. Records supposedly had been kept on each, but transcription was a year behind.

I looked around the room. It was obvious there were two vintages of officer. Most were young enthusiastic newcomers, eager to get started. A few were elderly men, long on the job, who smiled tolerantly as they gazed at the new recruits. A mere handful, these veterans had been blanketed into the new organization without examination by virtue of having been in state service a certain number of years. They viewed us with kindly commiseration or open hostility. We were the rah-rah boys who were going to revolutionize the world. We still believed we could help criminals become decent citizens.

On our side, we regarded the veterans with cautious reserve and, I am ashamed to say, some pitying contempt for their uneducated ways and defeatist views about "those bums," as they called their parolees. I didn't learn until later that most of these untrained, tired veterans had a lot they could teach to wet-behind-the-ears neophytes.

One old-timer particularly resented us. A shaggy fellow with a cartoonist's conception of an Irishman's face, he usually arrived at the office reeking of alcohol. He spent his time glaring at us and making audible comments, in a thick Irish brogue, the general tenor being that we were a bunch of "collegiates" who didn't know our elbows from a hole in the wall.

For days he didn't deign to say good morning to me, although I was seated next to him. He never spoke directly to me, only to some invisible comrade to whom, staring into space a little to the left of him, he would confide his opinions.

Once he overheard me interviewing a parolee at my desk. I was saying, "Now please don't forget to come in on Thursdays instead of Tuesdays from now on."

Mr. Mahoney shot a glance up at his noncorporeal pal. "How do ye like that collegiate?" he guffawed. " 'Please' he says to the bum!"

Some weeks later Mahoney broke down to the extent of asking me a direct question. He had been studying some prison reports on an inmate eligible for parole. He read out loud as a first-grader might, in a stumbling manner. His brow puckered. He studied a sheet, read it over twice. Then he came over to me, pointed to the heading on the paper, and asked, "Hey, you're a collegiate! What does it mean, 'pissychiatrists' report'?"

Another gentleman of the old school surprised me by introducing himself one day.

"I see you've taken over my cases. If I can be of any help, let me know."

"Thanks," I said, gratified.

"You don't want to be breaking your tail over these bastards," he counseled. "Check on 'em once a month or once a year, they won't change none. Besides, if you cover too much territory, it shows the rest of us up."

I nodded noncommittally.

"When you cover Long Island," he went on, "put on your expense account you went by train. Take Jamaica. You put you went by Long Island Railroad. You go by subway and keep the difference."

"But," I said, my bare face hanging out, "that isn't honest!"

He shot his head back as if he had received a blow on the jaw. "All right, smart guy!" he sneered. "All right! I been charging railroad, you're gonna charge subway. How does that make me look?" And he turned his back on me.

It should be said that the administration did not sanction such peculation, or drinking on the job, or laziness. It wanted to create a new atmosphere and a new deal. But that first year or so the Parole Board had its problems with the two schools of thought on the staff.

Not all the old-timers were rascals or malingerers. A number worked hard and sincerely. They were "naturals," doing a good job intuitively in spite of lack of formal training and education. They cared nothing about hours and they had a nonpolitical approach to their work. As time went on they became friendly toward us newcomers and very helpful in getting us to leaven our theory with a pinch of common sense.

The old-timers didn't have a corner on eccentricity either.

One new recruit, a charming, pleasant, and stimulating chap, believed implicitly in dreams. One day he came to the office in a blue funk.

"You know Jim ——, who was locked up yesterday for robbery with a gun?" he asked me.

"What about him?"

"He's innocent. I'm going to get him a lawyer who will take his case free. And I'm going to tell the judge he's innocent."

"*He's* innocent?" I asked. "The guy is caught with a gun ten minutes after a streetcar conductor is robbed. His pockets are loaded with nickels. The conductor picks him out of a lineup. He's *innocent?*"

"Yes."

"How do you know?"

"I had a dream last night. He's definitely innocent."

The first few weeks I did little besides find out who was and who was not a parolee charged to my supervision. In the confusion of organization, cases got mixed up, duplicated, lost in the shuffle. I had a feeble-minded parolee who had served a term in a New Jersey reformatory for the heinous offense of "larceny of a duck." We were supervising the lad for New Jersey. I visited his home, introduced myself, and asked him to report to me every Thursday. He grunted.

He didn't show up. I called on him again and slowly, simply, explained. I wanted him to report every Thursday. He grunted.

But he didn't report. I went to his home a third time and laid down the law. "Look here," I said, "I've told you twice now that I want you to report to my office every Thursday.

Every Thursday, you understand? Every *Thursday!* EVERY THURSDAY! Do you understand?"

His dull eyes lighted up with frustration and anger. "Okay!" he blurted out. "If that's what you say. But Jeezus! Monday night I report to Mr. Lappner. Tuesday night I report to Mr. Murphy. Wednesday night I report to Mr. Keleher. If you want me to report to you every Thursday, all right, I will. But I gotta have *one* night off!"

Four of us had been supervising one man, each officer oblivious of the contact of the others.

Another time I discovered that a parolee for whom I had a card hadn't reported to me all month. I found he no longer lived at the address given, nor did he work where the card said.

I went to my Dictaphone and began a violation report, which would lead to the issuance of a warrant for his arrest. I was down to the "respectfully submitted" when Mr. Lappner, who sat opposite me, came out of a brown study and asked, "*Who* is that you're declaring a parole violator?"

"John ——."

"Oh, he's been reporting to me all month. Lives in my territory now."

Once my supervisor sent me out to locate a man who, he said, was suspected of a burglary. The parolee, he told me, should have been assigned to me the first day, but there had been a slip-up. Now I was to go out and arrest him, so the police might question him.

I was scared. There is no other word for it. This would be my first arrest. I pictured myself entering a house, hearing the door slam behind me, being confronted by a snarling giant with a drawn gun. It didn't add to my comfort to discover that the parolee lived in an isolated section of Long Island. As I approached the address I noted there was no other house on the block, only vacant lots full of tall weeds.

I knocked on the door, my heart beating fast. A woman answered. Quaveringly I asked for Anthony.

"Are you a cop?" she asked.

Aha! The fusillade would follow hard upon . . . But possibly even a desperate, cornered man would hesitate to shoot a policeman. So I said I was a policeman.

"Then," the woman snapped, "*you* tell *me* what you done with Tony! The cops took him out of here last Tuesday and I ain't seen him since!"

I tipped my hat, bowed from the hip, heaved a big sigh of relief, and departed. A check revealed that, the Tuesday in question, two parole officers, on orders of the same supervisor who had sent me out, had arrested Anthony and put him in the Tombs.

I don't know who would have felt worse, Anthony or I, had I been forced to arrest him. My first sight of a man in handcuffs was a distinct shock to me.

A week after my wild-goose chase a colleague came into the office with a prisoner he was about to return to Sing Sing as a parole violator. The bedraggled man, a silver-haired Negro, had sad eyes, a despondent demeanor, and a stubble of beard on his chin. He looked disreputable and without hope as he sat at a desk, both wrists handcuffed.

I tried not to look at him, for that seemed discourteous, an underscoring of his predicament. I felt sorry for him and somehow ashamed of myself. I didn't know the prisoner had raped an eight-year-old girl, but in the state of my experience it probably wouldn't have made any difference if I had known.

I couldn't get over the feeling that this was a monstrous

thing, man's inhumanity to man, chaining him that way. Fascinated yet repelled, I kept looking at him surreptitiously. The officer went into another room for a while, and on an inexplicable impulse I dashed out to the cigar counter in the hall and bought two packs of cigarettes. Perhaps I was thus absolving society of the guilt it carried for producing such human derelicts. I strode back to the office, walked up to the prisoner, and said brusquely, "Here! Take these with you!"

The rapist looked at me wonderingly, compassionately. "Thank you, brother, no," he said. "I'm a religious man. If the good Lord wanted us to smoke, we'd be born with smokestacks."

Gradually I matured on the job, got used to the rough and tumble, and toughened enough to look on almost anything as part of the business.

I was intrigued by parolees and their families. But I was just as interested in my colleagues, and in the meaning of Civil Service.

I found that public workers have a grim faith in "doing it for the record." We did some things not because they added to the effectiveness of the work, but because they "covered" us in case of question. For example, we were expected to visit every parolee once a month. I argued for a time that some parolees needed more supervision than this, some less. To make a blanket regulation of this kind meant we saw more parolees, but none (considering our case loads) long enough to discover the true facts or to influence any one man to any extent. My supervisors, who undoubtedly understood the exigencies of public service better than I, agreed with my position but argued that if there was ever an investigation of parole, a criticism in the newspapers, we could always show we'd been active, overlooked no parolee. Today I feel this makes no sense from the standpoint of treatment of offenders, but makes right good sense from a public relations standpoint. If you don't bow to some extent to public opinion, there won't be *any* parole around.

I scoffed, too, at the then existing regulation (later modified) that parolees must be home by ten-thirty P.M. Some men, it seemed to me, could stay out all hours and be safe. Others were theoretical hazards even if tucked in at six o'clock. Besides, we deluded ourselves if we believed all parolees obeyed this rule. Sure, I was informed, but it looks better "on the record" if, when a gunman is arrested at one A.M. it can be shown we had at least warned him to be off the streets early.

Another, and much more understandable, preoccupation of public servants had to do with salary. Every parole officer felt he was entitled to a raise—but quick. The office had at that time a very inequitable policy on salaries. The jobs had been advertised at three thousand dollars. I received that on appointment, partly because I was one of the better-qualified men, in terms of education and experience, but mostly because, when asked, I refused less.

Others, however, had accepted at eighteen hundred or a little more. The money so saved went to buy additional staff, and the more people the Division of Parole could put on, the more effective the job would be. Nevertheless it has always struck me that from a morale standpoint one shouldn't have two people of the same title getting different salaries.

Be that as it may, one man became restless. He figured he deserved more, and he went to see the executive director, who listened to him sympathetically. Then the official told him that money had been provided in the budget for sixty men. In the confusion consequent on setting up the organization, sixty-four officers had already been appointed. And in spite of the difference in salary between one officer and another, the budget was already exceeded. Unless additional funds were scratched up somewhere, somebody in the administration was liable to go to jail.

The parole officer walked out with tears in his eyes and a slight voluntary pay cut.

It was some months before there was a semblance of order in the office, but gradually the Division settled down. Standards of work were established. Some supervision and training of officers became current. The administration was determined to create a service based on honesty and professional competence. It was a tough job, but before too long the New York State Division of Parole was rated by penologists the best in the country, a leadership it maintained for more than a decade.

I learned from experience and supervision. I began to live in a world theretofore foreign to me. First by emulation and then by reflex, I felt and acted a little tougher. I could take a drink with the best of them, use a choice and imaginative vocabulary of expletive and obscenity. I learned, too, to talk the lingo of the underworld. This was a necessity, even if it tended to ruin one's grammar. You don't ask a parolee if he served a sentence, I discovered. You ask him if he got dropped or did a rap. You advise him not to take it on the lam, to keep his nose clean, to refrain from packing a rod, to cease and desist going on a h'ist. As a matter of fact, talking the King's English to parolees and their families often leaves them befuddled.

I once heard a member of the staff interrogating a young woman who had come in to make a complaint against a parolee.

"Did you and he have sexual congress?" asked the officer.

She looked at him uncomprehendingly.

"Did you have sexual intercourse?"

"Huh?"

"Did you have sex relations?"

"I don't think so," she answered.

"Did he knock you up?" the officer asked in desperation.

Her face brightened. "Oh, yeah! Yeah! I didn't know what you meant, mister!"

Eventually we all fitted into a pattern, more or less. The squirrel cage quieted down. I lost the feeling of being on a Ferris wheel revolving at ninety miles an hour. I began to understand what parole is supposed to mean.

CHAPTER IV

Something About Parole

The aims of parole are not too well understood. Fact and fiction are very much intertwined in the thinking of the public. Parole is, or should be, a very vital public service. It deserves more understanding.

The Division of Parole that was created in New York in 1930 and activated in 1931 was the result of enlightened public pressure. The prison riots of 1929 had focused attention on the entire correctional system of the state. At Auburn Prison, inmates set fire to some buildings. Assaults on guards and serious rioting spread to other state penal institutions. The public wanted to know why.

Governor Franklin D. Roosevelt assigned to Lieutenant Governor Herbert H. Lehman the task of exploring the matter. What came to be known as the Lewisohn Commission was set up, to study all phases of the state's penal program.

One result of the work of this Commission was the recommendation that the parole system be entirely revamped, that paroles from all state prisons and the Elmira Reformatory should be the function of one central board of parole, instead of being administered separately by each institution. Money ought to be appropriated, the Commission felt, to make of parole something more than the "underfinanced moral gesture" it had been up to then. A career service was needed, parole officers who were qualified social workers entirely divorced from politics. Paroles should be granted solely on the basis of merit, and supervision of those released should be more than a routine.

At the request of Governor Roosevelt the legislature adopted the recommendations of the Commission, and the New York State Division of Parole came into being. Its program was in line with the most progressive thinking of the time.

Ideally, parole is a system for the conditional release of offenders before they have served their full sentences. The theory is that there comes a time when further incarceration is no longer beneficial (if it ever was). When an inmate has so changed in attitude and orientation as to lead to the belief that he would be a safe risk on the outside, he should be released, under supervision. He should be helped to get back into society as a decent citizen. But at any sign of reversion to crime, he should be returned to the institution.

To retain an inmate in an institution after he has reached that psychological moment when he is ready to go out is a mistake, it is argued. It serves only to harden and embitter him. He must eventually come out, unless he is a lifer. He should come out when best prepared for freedom, and while the state still has a hold on him by virtue of the unexpired portion of his sentence, hence can supervise his activities for a time.

The New York system was established on these principles. The staff, top to bottom, was in the competitive Civil Service, except for the parole commissioners, who were appointed for six-year terms by the Governor, with the advice and consent of the upper house of the state legislature.

The three members of the Parole Board met in the penal

institutions of the state to interview those inmates who by law
had become eligible for parole. The board decided who should
and who should not be released.

Parole has often been criticized as a device for freeing prisoners ahead of schedule. In New York a prison inmate can
never be considered for parole before he has served a certain
minimum called for by his sentence. Only then does he get a
parole hearing; and he doesn't have to be paroled. Frequently
he isn't paroled on the first hearing—at least this was so when
I was in the system. From the standpoint of time served, the
only effect the board can have on a sentence is to lengthen it
beyond the minimum. It can never shorten it.

For instance, there was a notorious thug in New York named
Joey Rao. For years he seemed to operate with almost complete impunity. He committed crimes, beat people up, even, it
was said, shot at cops, and still remained a free man and leader
of a band of hoodlums as bad as he. He did serve a term in the
New York County Penitentiary once, and it was discovered
he practically ran the place, carrying on his underworld business from the penitentiary, via carrier pigeon.

Finally Rao committed a crime that simply couldn't be overlooked or forgotten. He was sentenced to state prison for, as
I recall it, all of one to two years.

When he came out, two years later, some people demanded
to know how come such a vicious criminal was at large again
so soon after conviction. The answer was simple. Rao came
out because a judge had seen fit to give him a light sentence.

Rao could have been paroled in one year, but he wasn't. In
fact, he wasn't paroled at all. He was released by expiration of
his full term. In other words, parole operated here to lengthen

a sentence beyond what it might have been. The board refused to parole him, and he served all of his term, then walked out, scot free.

The majority of inmates, however, were and are released on the authority of the Parole Board while still owing time on their sentences. Prior to an appearance before the board, an inmate's background is investigated by a parole officer and a report furnished the commissioners. They give the prisoner a hearing. If they decide to parole him, the process known as parole supervision is set in motion.

Once released, parolees are supervised by parole officers, who are charged with the duty of helping those who need and want help. Officers try to influence and counsel parolees, to the end that they may not want to revert to crime.

The parolee meets his parole officer as soon as he is released, and he is given to understand what is expected of him and what will be done for him if he wishes—and as long as he behaves. The rules and regulations of parole are explained to him. They are designed to guide him so he does not engage in activity that may lead to further crime.

Some parolees take these rules seriously, some do not. I recall one man who was so impressed with the regulation that he must keep his parole officer informed of all his movements that he traveled over fifteen miles to come to the office to ask for permission to go to the Bronx Zoo, which was around the corner from his house. Permission was granted.

All parolees in New York State report to their parole officers regularly. There is some disagreement among workers in the field as to the value of these office reports. Those who question their utility ask, "Do you expect the parolee to tell you he's burglarizing homes?" The proponents of reporting retort that they do not, but the report of the parolee is the starting point of further investigation in the field. Besides, it proves that at that given moment the parolee is all in one piece, in one place.

Judging from office reports alone, I found my parolees adjusting remarkably well. When I asked what they did in their leisure time I discovered that ex-offenders *all* have only four forms of recreation. According to their stories, they "go to a movie, go for a walk, listen to the radio, or sometimes read a good book." It was downright inspiring how many even *said* it the same way. Of course, this was before the days of television. Today, I don't doubt, parolees have added a fifth form of recreation to their list—watching Hopalong Cassidy.

One evening a chap I'll call Eugene sat at my desk, reciting what he had done that week. He had worked very hard in a pickle factory. He had just come from there, was making his report, now would go home, probably to bed.

"Don't you ever go out of an evening?" I asked.

"No." Eugene smiled. "To tell de trut', Mr. Dressler, I'm so tired when I quit woik, all I care to do is get in bed and read a book, maybe listen to de radio . . ."

At this juncture the door flew open. A cloud of detectives burst into the room, descended on Eugene, and tore the pants right off him. Strapped inside his thigh was a revolver, which he had just used in a stickup. He had been injudicious enough to hold up a man who knew him by face and name. Having trussed up his victim, Eugene, being a conscientious parolee, decided to make his report to me at once—possibly to establish a near-airtight alibi.

In addition to receiving reports from parolees, officers go into the field to check on the activities of their charges. They visit homes, talk with members of the family, discover what, if anything, the officer can do to help parolees readjust into society. Jobs are checked without jeopardizing parolees' employment.

If an officer has reason to suspect a parolee of violating the law or the conditions of his parole, he investigates carefully and, if facts warrant, arrests the suspect. A parole commissioner reviews the case and may order the parolee returned to the institution as a parole violator. Here the Parole Board will determine what portion of the unexpired term the parole violator must serve.

The majority, however, finish their parole period without violation and are discharged from parole.

With local variations, this is about the general pattern of parole in the country.

Its theory is sound. Its administration has not always been so. And the theory often is lambasted because the public is thinking of the poor parole administration in a given state.

CHAPTER V

Jimmy Hines Keeps Me on the Staff

Later in my career, as I thought through some of the under-
lying philosophy of parole, I became rather respectful of public
service in general and parole in particular. But after a few
months on the job I still had the average "intellectual's" contempt for public servants and I determined to get out of public
work before long. I still suspected that political influence was
a factor in all government work, even though I saw little evidence of this around me. I was sure that was because I was an
underling, at the bottom of the ladder, not in the know.

But while I was a parole officer, a matter of a little over a
year, I was never directly approached by anyone in a manner
to suggest that the "bosses" wouldn't support me in some issue
because they would necessarily bow to politics. Other officers
with whom I associated whispered about this case and that, that
Joe Smith had better not be arrested because he knew Alder-
man Jones who knew Senator Bones who controlled Commissioner Tones. I wanted to believe this, but I had no basis for
doing so.

Then I was promoted.

In 1933 I became senior parole officer, in charge of a comple-
ment of officers. By then I had not especially endeared myself to
the commissioner who was the head of the New York District
Office. (One commissioner acted as head in New York, one

in Buffalo, one in Albany.) I was a hothead, a perfectionist, a stiff idealist, and an intellectual prig. If the book I had read in college said you did so and so, I insisted the whole world had to do so and so. Moreover, the commissioner was a man who set great store by "loyal" staff members, that is, officers who accepted the boss as omniscient, and I didn't think anyone was omniscient, except possibly myself. I didn't, therefore, rate high with the commissioner. He was the only board member who, rumor had it, was politically minded, and that too made him poison to me—something he must have sensed.

When I placed first on the promotion examination the commissioner had little choice but to appoint me senior parole officer. He wasn't happy about it. I became a thorn in his side, and I know I got a kicking around in the brief time he was in office.

On one occasion I ordered the arrest of a parolee who was known to have strong political ties. One charge the officer filed against him was that he was in the numbers racket. The commissioner sent for me and roared that the charge was flimsy and that I'd better get the hell over to the Tombs personally and release the parolee *at once.*

I did as ordered. With the connivance of the parole officer, I then followed the man to the subway and arrested him again, on a charge I had up my sleeve, waiting for an emergency like this. He was not living at home as he reported.

The commissioner was fit to be tied and ordered the man's release again. I sprang him, followed him to the subway, and arrested him with my ace in the hole—the charge that he was subsisting in part on the proceeds of his wife's prostitution.

The commissioner, choking with rage, read my report and had no alternative but to send the parolee back to Sing Sing.

He kept him there twenty-eight days, then reparoled him. And in twenty-eight days more the parolee was arrested for murder. He hung himself in his cell.

After that incident the commissioner told my immediate superior, "Hide that bastard Dressler somewhere. Bury him. Keep him out of my sight. I don't care what you do with him, but I never want to see the sonofabitch!"

So by the time a new commissioner came on the job I was a very disgusted young man. I felt put upon. I trusted no public official and was making plans to get out, come June and a Ph.D.

I didn't bother to drop in on the new commissioner, although protocol prescribed a handshake. Yet he and Jimmy Hines were directly responsible for my decision not to quit.

It happened this way. I had authorized an officer to put a parolee in the Tombs. Shortly thereafter, in lumbered a man with the gait of a Gargantua and a face to match. Why, he demanded to know, was his pal in the can? I refused to give him any information unless he properly identified himself and established his *bona fides*. Whereupon, following the classical style of address to public workers, he reminded me that he was a taxpayer, that my salary came right out of his pocket, and that he could cost me my job. I suggested he make a complaint to my supervisor.

"Nah!" he spat out. "I go to de top! I'll see Jimmy Hines! He'll call your commissioner!"

Hines, a major politician of national influence, was rumored to have been very close to the previous commissioner.

As soon as my visitor departed I dashed off a long memorandum to the new commissioner, reciting all the details. I prefaced the report with the statement that I wanted him, in fairness to me, to get my side of the story before he drew any conclusions after Jimmy Hines phoned.

An hour later I was summoned to the commissioner's office.

Adjusting a chip precariously situated on my shoulder and assuming a cocky expression, I entered the boss's room.

The commissioner, who was slightly exophthalmic, stared at me fishily. "Dressler," he said, "I read your memorandum."

"Yes?"

"Yes. And I didn't like it."

"Oh, no? May I ask what you didn't like about it?"

"I didn't like the fact you thought it necessary to defend yourself. That means you think I'm a ward heeler, and I don't like that!"

"I didn't mean to imply that," I said, still reserved.

"No, you didn't mean to *imply* it—you meant it! I'm not going to defend myself. There's only one way to convince a pup like you."

He called in his secretary. "Has Hines called today?" he asked her.

"No, sir."

"Has he ever called since I'm in office?"

"No, sir."

"If he calls today, I want you, without any explanation, to switch the call to Mr. Dressler."

"Yes, sir."

He dismissed her, stood up, and glowered at me. He poked a finger at me and growled, "When you get that call, I order you, I *order* you, to say exactly what I tell you. I want you to pick up that receiver and say, 'Mr. Hines, I have a message for you from Commissioner Canavan. Go spit in your hat!' "

That's how I happened to stay in Civil Service as long as I

did. Jimmy Hines never called, and possibly he had never heard of the gentleman who had called upon me, but I was convinced we had a new deal.

In fairly rapid succession I was promoted, by competitive examination, to case supervisor in 1934, district supervisor later that year, chief parole officer in 1936, and finally executive director in 1939, a post I held until 1948. Until 1939 my headquarters were in New York; after that, in Albany. During this same period the Division of Parole expanded. In 1931 there were sixty staff members throughout the state, in 1935 there were about a hundred and fifty, and by 1947, about three hundred. The budget grew from $60,000 in 1931, to about $600,-000 in 1940, and in 1948 was about $1,500,000.

Had a mug not invoked the name of Jimmy Hines, I wouldn't have been around for the exciting years.

CHAPTER VI

The Exciting Years of Parole

During these years, which began with only a good law and good intentions, we built a parole system the State of New York would be proud of for years to come. As I came to assume more responsibility and authority in the organization, I was privileged to be in the thick of this development.

We had to arrive at a point of view, a philosophy, that would be realistic and would produce results. Undoubtedly the man who did most in this direction was Commissioner Joseph J. Canavan. He was head of the New York Office part of the time I was "coming up," and he gave me encouragement, sound counsel, and personal support. It was he who had told me to tell Hines off, thus keeping me on in parole work.

Joe Canavan had been night city editor on two New York newspapers. It was not surprising, therefore, that he had a highly sensitized feeling for public relations. He knew what people would think before they started thinking. He was constantly concerned about the public relations of parole, and determined it must become a service citizens would be proud of. He sincerely believed in his work and was convinced that the best way to build solid good will was to have an organization deserving of good will.

When Joe began, the police were skeptical of us, to say the least. They remembered the old sloppy parole system and considered us a bunch of panty-waists who would sob over a parolee as he shot a policeman. We had to convince them otherwise.

Joe waited for the right moment to begin his campaign. Police Commissioner Lewis J. Valentine, a fine cop and an honest one, got up at a large public meeting to make a speech. Joe Canavan was in the audience, as were Dr. Joseph W. Moore, then chairman of the Parole Board, and I.

Valentine began reading his speech in a dull, fumbling voice. He was never an effective orator, but this time he seemed to be having more difficulty than usual. He muscled his way through one paragraph after another, but it was a stumbling performance at best. And as he proceeded his face expressed more and more puzzlement and surprise. He heard himself launch into an attack on parole generally, on the New York parole system, on the Parole Board—and here we were, right in the same room. Poor Valentine shook his head once or twice, as if to get the cobwebs out of his eyes. He tried to jump about a bit in his script, but each time he found a new paragraph it came out the same way—an attack on the sentimental, wishy-washy, incompetent New York Parole Board. At last the Police Commissioner tossed his leonine head defiantly, roared out the balance of his lines, and sat down, glaring belligerently at us. He'd said it, and, by God, now he was going to stick to it!

Up jumped Dr. Moore, his keen, intelligent face alight with fury. "For concentrated misinformation," he said, "I've never heard the like."

Now Joe Canavan arose—and he took my breath away by defending Valentine. The Police Commissioner, he said, spoke out of bitter experience. One could understand and sympathize with such a point of view. On some rare occasion a police officer is killed by a mad dog who happens to be on parole. Why wouldn't a police official remember that a long time with bitterness? But parole had changed in New York. There was a new deal on. And the present parole system would feel it had justified itself when a splendid public official, an uncompromising realist like Lewis J. Valentine, came out publicly in favor of what it was doing.

Valentine's nose fairly quivered in appreciation.

That evening Canavan, Valentine, and I sat in a cocktail lounge of a hotel, at a meeting arranged by Joe. The Police Commissioner was so contrite it was pitiful. Savagely he cursed the secretary who, instead of writing a special speech for the occasion, as requested, had given him an old one from the files.

"I didn't have time to read it before I got to the meeting. But when I started in this morning I realized it was a speech delivered years ago by a former commissioner!"

"I know," said Canavan. "I heard him give it."

Out of this incident developed an arrangement whereby I was to lecture regularly at the New York City Police Academy, to give all officers an understanding of the new deal in parole. And this, coupled with the fact that detectives and uniformed men were now coming in contact with a rather new breed of parole officer, did a lot of good. In time policemen all over the state developed a healthy respect for and a close camaraderie with parole officers.

At the Police Academy I tried to talk the policeman's language, to emphasize those features of parole work I thought the man on the beat would most want to hear about. I explained what sort of checks we kept on parolees, how we could help detectives by furnishing information regarding suspects, how willing we were to cooperate in any investigation of a parolee.

One day, during the question period, a uniformed man set me back on my heels.

"I've listened to you for an hour," he said, "and I don't hear anything to explain parole's reason for existence. Your work sounds just like ours—and we don't need two police forces. Don't you do *anything* to further a better social readjustment on the part of your parolees? Aren't you at all interested in rehabilitation of offenders?"

After that I changed my pitch. I realized I didn't have to talk down to these men.

If the police were initially suspicious of us, the newspapers were even more so. I don't believe there was a paper in the state that was for us in 1931. By 1935 I don't think there was one against us. This, too, was largely Joe Canavan's doing. What I did was merely a reflection of what I learned from him.

Before Commissioner Canavan came on the Parole Board it was customary to refuse newsmen any information—in fact, to refuse them admittance. As a result, they suspected the worst about any situation. Joe gave them information gladly, admitted mistakes, and relied on the press to give us the best of it when we were right. Suspicion waned.

I had contact with a large section of the New York City press in connection with the Redwood murder in 1937, in the investigation of which I played some part. The reporters found me aboveboard with them, and they reciprocated. They respected my wishes when I asked them not to publish certain information until the investigation was complete, lest they interfere with the administration of justice. Although the information I furnished the press was so sensational that it would

have been a banner headline scoop for any newspaper jump-
ing the gun, not a single reporter or paper broke faith with me.
I made a number of friends among the reporters in the course
of that investigation.

At its termination I suggested to one newspaper, the *New
York World-Telegram*, that it do a study of parole in New
York. I would give the writer *carte blanche*.

Floyd Taylor, a crack feature writer, was assigned. He asked
me where to begin. I told him, "Anywhere you want. See
what you want, do what you want, talk to whomever you
want."

"Where shall I sit?"

"Anywhere you want. There's a fairly quiet room down the
hall, with only three parole officers in it."

He appeared puzzled. Later, after he had written a highly
favorable series for the split page of his paper, he told me,
"You know, I came into this assignment very definitely skeptical of you and of parole. I first began to think you were on
the level when you let me sit in a room full of subordinates
—and Civil Service employees at that! A politician wouldn't
do that, because he knows that if there is any graft or skul-
duggery around, the Civil Service employee knows it and is
only too happy to blast the boss."

I am not suggesting that Commissioner Canavan and I carried the full responsibility of public relations, because we
didn't by a long shot. I am describing only those features with
which I had closest familiarity. In the New York Office we
were in a strategic spot, so far as public relations were concerned. It was only natural that a good deal of what was done
within the Division of Parole was handled through the New
York District.

Not only newspapers but magazines began to swing our way. Articles describing New York's parole system began coming out in top national journals, thus furthering progressive parole principles everywhere. Canavan was too astute to have any article written by a staff member. "When *we* praise parole," he said, "we're boasting. When *others* praise us, we're good."

A radio program, *Crime Doctor*, was originated by Max Marcin, and it did parole some good all over the country. Max asked us for help in establishing a pattern for the show. I worked with him (gratis, of course) for the next ten years. He had a central character, Dr. Ordway, who was chairman of a parole board. An inmate appeared before the board; the story flashed back to the events preceding his conviction; an audience jury voted to parole or deny parole. In the course of each show it was always possible to drop a few painless words about the meaning of parole. Parole officers were portrayed as decent characters, not clowns. The show was built for entertainment, but it was also one of the very few crime shows that managed to pass on a little information.

Here is a secret that has never been told—principally because nobody cares anyhow. I was the prototype of the Crime Doctor, that is, Dr. Ordway. Max built that character around his conception of me as a crime-busting, psychiatric-minded, two-fisted, never-bested, three-gun crime expert. He got that entirely inappropriate image of me while listening to some of my experiences over a bottle of really rare wine. I didn't mind the three-gun business, because while I carried only one at a time there was some reality in that part of the picture. But Ordway, I felt, was an insufferably suave, know-it-all psychiatrist. He must, however, have been convincing to the public.

The chairman of a parole board wrote him once, asking advice in a certain case. The Ordway on the air, of course, was simply an actor.

There were a couple of surprises for me in the history of *Crime Doctor*. One was that, in spite of periodic criticism from the public that parole was too lenient and released people too readily, the audience juries were embarrassing softies. Max was frantic, for he couldn't very well have the country listening to a story about a vicious, seemingly irredeemable rogue, only to have him "paroled" back into the society he had victimized. The ushers therefore picked the hardest-faced people in the audience—and they turned out to be made of the milk of human kindness. Max began to make his offenders worse and worse. "Parole 'em," the audience jury voted. In desperation he collected the ballots himself, took a quick look, and announced the vote that he thought was right. And it wasn't always the actual vote as indicated by the ballots.

The other surprise was this. At the beginning Max used strictly true stories, disguised, telescoped, altered only to make identification impossible. The public wouldn't believe them. "Fake," they said. They wrote in, jeering at any producer who thought a solid citizen would believe such things could ever happen. So Max began to invent stories—absolutely fantastic at times, but at any rate always completely fiction. The fan mail became immense. "We love your true stories." "What we like about *Crime Doctor* is that you tell nothing but the truth, none of this fantastic crime stuff."

I have since learned not to be surprised at this. Truth in the crime field is indeed much stranger than fiction, and time and again, in telling a harmless little story to some group, I have found it necessary to introduce a touch of sheer fiction merely to tone down the fact a bit so that the yarn would be believable. In this book, however, I have returned to the straight and narrow. There's not a line of fiction in it, and some of it will be hard to believe.

Another public relations program that helped parole was President Roosevelt's first National Parole Conference in 1939, which we spark-plugged and helped organize. At the President's request a group of penologists and social workers gathered in Washington to consider solutions to the many problems still unsolved in parole.

The President was still preoccupied with problems of economic recovery and regulation of business and industry. Nevertheless he took time to speak on parole over the radio. A number of us were present at the White House when he made his address.

He reviewed what his administration had done to combat crime and rehabilitate offenders. At one point his script called for his saying, "All of these direct attacks on crime which we have made . . ." In reading it, the President made a significant slip, revealing where his mind was at the moment. He said, "All of these direct attacks on privilege which we have made . . ." Realizing what he had just sent over the air, he stopped, looked at us, and began to chuckle silently. His body shook, his head swayed from side to side in characteristic gesture. Then he calmly corrected himself and went on with his speech. For all I know, President Roosevelt's slip of the tongue is to this day preserved on some wax recording.

By the time of the National Parole Conference, New York's system was flourishing. Its budget and staff were growing, its standards steadily improving. We would have got nowhere at all had we not had a completely united front at that time. Every member of the board, every administrator within the Division, was imbued with the same philosophy. It was a philosophy that had to be built slowly, for it was shocking to many of the sentimentalists who still people this field.

Bear in mind that up to then parole had been criticized as too lenient, sloppy, incompetent. Improperly financed, earlier parole systems operated with poorly equipped staff. Employees tended to be all cop or all sop.

We announced our premise, which later was to become pretty much accepted by every parole system in the country. Parole, we said, had a twofold function. It must *first* protect society against the parolee who is about to revert to crime; *second*, help those parolees who want to become and remain law-abiding. Society's welfare came first. We saw no real conflict here, for ideally we should be able to help a man change so that he no longer *wanted* to commit crime, in which case both society and the parolee would benefit.

What a howl went up, at first, among our fellow penologists! We were just a bunch of cops, they said. But we went ahead. We insisted that parole officers visit parolees' homes and jobs regularly. We had our men in the field every night, at all hours, hitting the dives, hangouts. We tailed suspicious parolees, made our own arrests. Jokes sprang up in the underworld. One went: "Be careful what you throw in that garbage can. There may be a parole officer in there."

Parole officers sometimes were credited with being more severe than policemen concerning certain behavior. Once two detectives walked in on a parolee suspected of burglary. He was in bed with a girl. The detectives, without identifying themselves, searched the premises to no avail, then flashed their shields. The parolee, according to the detectives' later story, heaved a sigh of relief.

"Jeezus!" he cried. "I t'ought yez was parole officers! Is dat all yez had, boiglary? I t'ought yez had me because of de goil. Yez won't tell de parole officer, will yez?"

Another time the twist was the other way. We walked in on a parolee wanted for burglary. There were detectives and parole officers in our group, but the parolee took us all for cops. We waited for the arrival of the parolee's roommate and accomplice. During our stay the parolee gave us a most edifying lecture on parole.

It started with his saying that he hoped, when he had cleared himself of the burglary suspicion, we would give him a clean bill of health with the Parole Board.

"Parole?" I asked. "You on parole?"

"Yeah, goddam it!"

"What's the matter?" one of my associates inquired. "You don't like parole? I thought it was pretty easy."

"Easy!" flashed the parolee. "Listen to this. On a Monday I quit my job. Tuesday morning the parole officer is at my house —he already knows, he ain't takin' no excuses, and he says I should be out lookin' for work every day. Wednesday, *eight o'clock in the morning*, the sonofabitch is at the house and he says, 'Well, why ain't you out lookin' for work?' Eight o'clock, this is! Why, the crazy bastard, I don't have to tell him, *he tells me* when I last went to the toilet!"

I don't want to create the impression that we were indeed only a sort of detective force. We concentrated every bit as much on helping those men and women who needed it and were safe risks. I will discuss this phase of our work later on.

Here I am trying to emphasize how we created a new point of view concerning one aspect of a parole officer's duties. We were banging away at the proposition that parole had to protect the public as well as help the individual parolee.

Most members of our staff accepted this premise enthusiastically. Some did not, because it meant a lot of night work, or because they couldn't adapt themselves to the law-enforcement function.

But here is an interesting fact. As we increased the intensiveness of our supervision, the rate of return of parole violators naturally rose, because we were identifying and eliminating our poor risks before they committed new crimes. And as the curve for technical parole violation went up, the line for crimes committed by parolees went steadily down, even in years when the state and federal crime index was on the rise.

And another interesting fact: The penologists of the sentimental school, who had tsk! tsked! about our "twofold function" concept, became progressively more mute. And one or two, in public speeches, even made such statements as, "We do not deny that one function of parole is the protection of society against the potential malefactor, . . . *but*."

In spite of the but, that was quite a concession.

CHAPTER VII

Parolees Are People

I believe there are two types of public servants. They can be distinguished by one criterion: how they regard people. To one kind of public employee, whether he issues fishing licenses or administers relief, people are paper. They are subsection IV of paragraph 298 of the Building Code; or page 92, paragraph 11, of the Manual of Procedure. Civil servants who feel this way don't see people at all in the work they do. They know the law and the rules, they do as they are told, avoid as much harassment as possible, and don't care a hang about the feelings, hopes, and fears of John Citizen. They see a shaky elevator but not the rider. They see an application for a hunting permit but not the hunter.

The other type of worker is just as assiduous in requiring adherence to law. But he constantly *sees* the person for, by, and because of whom laws were written. This employee, in a very real sense, considers himself a servant of the public. He has an obstinate faith in the proposition that in the long run the people are always right, getting what they want and deserving what they get. He never loses interest in his work because he is working for and with human beings and is constantly intrigued and attracted by the infinite varieties within the species Homo sapiens.

On our staff almost every officer saw parolees as people—

and not only as people but as individuals. Parolees were of all kinds, shapes, personalities, and characters.

It is impossible to generalize about criminals or offenders such as parolees. They don't fall into a mold. They are devils in some relations, angels in others. Some are suave, some rugged. They look like Wallace Beery or Alan Ladd or Robert Taylor. They are human like you and me.

But their conditioning has developed in some certain characteristics that can, cautiously, be said to be marks of the person from the underworld. That is as reasonable to expect as the fact that our conditioning makes us stand out in other ways —we are perhaps more ethical, more sensitive, and ever so much more pleased with ourselves.

In the early years I constantly compared parolees with clients of social agencies in which I had worked. There were many similarities. But one difference seemed to be, so far as one dares generalize, that parolees are more self-reliant than, say, relief clients. They can do for themselves. They need help here and there, but they like to feel independent. Compared to many people who come to social agencies for service, they rely less on outside help in settling domestic difficulties, health problems, and the like.

They are much more self-centered than the average normal citizen. They tend to see only their ways of doing and thinking. They consider themselves first. A hired gunman will shoot down a man he never met before, without any thought as to how the victim feels or what happens to his family. He is not beset by remorse. Rather, he grouses because he injured his pinkie in the imbroglio.

I knew an embezzler who had swindled over a hundred wid-

ows and elderly men out of their life savings, to the tune of
hundreds of thousands of dollars. At least one suicide was the
direct result of his piracy. During my interview with him in
prison, I asked him whether he intended making any restitution upon his release. He regarded me as if I were a fugitive
from a strait jacket. Instead of answering, he began to whine
about his treatment. The warden had failed to recognize his
superior qualities, had assigned him to laundry work. He was
much too capable a person to be doing such menial labor.

I inquired whether he had a list of the people and amounts
he had swindled. He replied in the negative and launched into
a tirade against the judge because that gentleman had, at the
time of sentence, characterized the defendant as "a human vul-
ture." What sort of business was that, for a judge to insult a
man as learned as the inmate?

I finally narrowed his attention down to me and insistently
demanded to know whether he planned restitution.

"Why should I?" he snarled. "Look how they've made me
suffer!"

This supreme egocentrism accounts in part, too, for the fact
that many offenders are sticklers for logic of a kind—the kind
that works in their favor. They generally resent an arrest not
based on the logic of the situation.

A parolee, Tim, was arrested on a robbery charge. The
police had heard someone call for help. As they arrived on the
scene they saw Tim sprinting down the street, while his victim
screamed he had been robbed. The officers gave chase. Tim
dived around a corner and threw his gun away. He peeled off
a leather jacket and ran on, dressed in a sweater. He threw
away his hat and took a cap out of his pocket.

By this time one detective was close enough to nab him. He brought Tim back to the victim, who promptly identified him. Tim was placed in the Tombs.

I came to get his story. He was very angry about the whole thing.

"Them cops had no right to arrest me! The guy that got stuck up says the fellow who done it was wearin' a hat. I had on a cap. He says he wore a leather jacket. I didn't have none on. I didn't have no gun when they grabbed me neither!"

"Did you rob the man?"

"Sure! But where did he get off, identifyin' me like that? He knows damn well I was dressed different! Do you call that square?"

In the same way a felon will seize on some one feature of an arrest to destroy the logic of a case against him—he thinks.

Tony had just completed a robbery and was dashing down the street. A cop who took up the pursuit ordered him to halt, simultaneously making a flying tackle that catapulted Tony through a plate-glass window. In the hospital the parolee growled, "He ain't got nothin' on me! I got it on him! How did he know I wouldn't stop when he ordered me to? He tackled me before I had a chance to stop. He ain't got a t'ing on me! I got him on assault!"

A more devious logician was Jeremiah Sullivan, henchman of gangster Owney Madden. Jerry hated me. When I became chief parole officer I told the man supervising Jerry that he was to allow the one-time big shot no special privileges. He was to drive no car, frequent no cabarets, and stay away from the race tracks. That last particularly rankled, for Jerry had long been accustomed to going to Florida for the season, along with a party of other gentlemen of whom I took a dim view.

Came the next racing season. Jerry appealed to me for permission to go to Florida. I refused.

He saw the commissioner. He refused.

At that time there happened to be some publicity in the papers about my doctor's thesis. It was called, demurely enough, "Burlesque as a Cultural Phenomenon." It would have escaped mention except that Mayor La Guardia had just closed the burlesque shows of the city. The papers played my thesis up with headlines such as "1001 Nights in Burlesque Earns Parole Chief Doctor's Degree."

Shortly thereafter Sullivan tried to appeal to the Governor through intermediaries who, Governor Lehman reported with a chuckle, pointed out that Jerry really shouldn't be restricted in his wholesome interests by a person of such low moral character as to spend 1001 nights in burlesque shows.

Sullivan later worked another *tour de force* of logic when convicted on a new charge and sentenced to the county penitentiary. As long as conviction was inevitable, he preferred a definite sentence of a year to an indeterminate term, which is what he received. The term was for anything from a day to three years, and Jerry had a hunch, with his record, he would get the book.

He appealed on the contention that he had been illegally sentenced to the penitentiary. By law, he pointed out, indeterminate penitentiary sentences were to be meted out only to prisoners capable of being substantially benefited by the "correctional or reformatory" purposes of the institution. If he is incapable of so benefiting, his maximum sentence must be one year of imprisonment.

Now, urged Sullivan, look at his criminal record. By no stretch of the imagination could it be averred he was anything but an incorrigible criminal. He was entitled to the one-year sentence!

Another noticeable characteristic, among some parolees, is persuasiveness of a very high type. Probably, however, this trait appears no more frequently among ex-offenders than in the general population. Its manifestations are often remarkable. All confidence men and some forgers, I would say, have pretty much a corner on the market in suave plausibility among underworld characters.

There was Count Marcel de Passey, a gentleman I met when I was senior parole officer. The Count was an international confidence man, with a criminal record that took several sheets to record. He was no Count (a pun is not intended). The closest he ever got to the upper classes of Germany (from which country he seems to have sprung) was when he swindled the aristocracy of enough money to lead to his imprisonment and subsequent banishment from the country. In the United States he was indiscreet enough to rate several sentences, and when I met him he was on parole from the last jolt.

A short, stocky man with a heavy guttural accent, he was possessed of the fiercest Kaiser Wilhelm mustachios it has ever been my privilege to behold. The occasion of our meeting was a little embarrassing to the Count. I had asked his parole officer to bring him in for questioning. It seems he had embarked on a vast project to improve the mechanisms of warfare and had collected considerable sums from people who believed he was building a new type of battleship, one far and away superior to anything that had ever taken to the waves before. He actually had what purported to be its framework resting in the harbor. Also, he had a letter, allegedly from the Navy Department, certainly on its letterhead, expressing great interest in the craft and asking how soon a few assorted admirals might witness a tryout—the sooner the better.

I questioned de Passey, but he was such a gifted double-talker that half the time I was talking to myself. Investigation proved the Navy Department letter was a forgery. The hulk in the harbor was just a hunk of junk. We locked de Passey up, pending further investigation. Meantime we notified all known investors of the developments and warned against further commitment of monies.

In spite of our evidence de Passey didn't lose his persuasive powers. He asked several of his victims to visit him in the Tombs, and he made with the hocus-pocus some more. As a result two attorneys, a state official, and the district attorney of a nearby county came in to plead with me that de Passey be released to complete his dreamboat so that the investors might collect their profits.

Gentry like these are in the minority. The majority of pa-rolees are accustomed to gaining their ends by rougher means. Certainly a characteristic of many offenders is toughness, born of hard living, deprivation, and the brutalizing influence of the rough and tumble of underworld life.

Probably ninety-five per cent of ex-felons feel bitter toward anyone with a badge. They hate, fear, and have contempt for "the law." One of the most difficult hurdles to get over in parole work is that barrier set up in the minds and emotions of offenders. It is in no small measure a commentary and a result of law enforcement's treatment of the underworld and even the non-criminal elements of a great city.

Kids in slum areas all too often grow up fearing the cop rather than respecting him. They discover he can be brutal, unfair, even corrupt. The adolescent takes a boot in the pants from a frustrated policeman unable to get a confession to stealing a tomato, and the citizen of tomorrow has received his first lesson in the way of the law.

By no means is such treatment universal. Every large city has some intelligent, understanding policemen who do a lot to impress youngsters with the dignity and essential fairness of the law. But by the time a young man has been arrested a few times; kicked around during interrogations; incarcerated in foul detention cells; befuddled and irritated by courtroom mumbo-jumbo; and incarcerated in prison, supervised by the none-too-occasional brutal guard, he has his opinion of the badge-wearer well formed.

That estimate, true or false, also bolsters his ego by explaining to his satisfaction why he got hooked and someone else didn't. Most parolees with whom I have talked seem to be truly convinced that "there ain't no justice." The rich get away with it. So do those with influence. "Look at Capone. I ain't nowheres near the hoodlum he is. Does he get a rap?" This from a parolee. (Was it Shaw who said if you steal a loaf of bread you go to prison while if you steal a railroad you go to Parliament?)

In short, the majority of parolees believe the law is venal. They cite chapter and verse. A policeman is indicted for a dishonest act, and that proves the entire force is corrupt. Mrs. Jones got fined time and again for keeping garbage pails on the sidewalk. Why? She didn't pay off. One man told me, "I had to take the rap because the insurance company protecting that safe I knocked off paid off to the cops to prosecute me to the limit."

This belief in the venality of the public official goes beyond individual parolees. Their families are equally convinced. And the law-enforcement officer is not the only alleged bribe taker. Any public official, from the president down, is considered, by some, "on the take."

In my experience I found some cultural differences in respect to this phenomenon. Undoubtedly this is due to the early experiences in each group. Offspring of United States-born parents are least susceptible to the legend. The better educated the man, the less likely he is to indict all public officials.

Certain Old World families, I found, took it as a matter of course that a parole officer should be—uh—tipped. It didn't necessarily mean that the donor expected an immediate and special favor. He was only buying immunity against "misunderstandings." Just as a European-born mother, as a matter of course and good nature, may tip the garbage collector at Christmas, so she may send love offerings to her son's parole officer. No insult is intended. In fact, most families were shocked when I suggested a gratuity implied that. At Christmas I had to refuse cigars, money, and bottles of wine from perhaps half the parolees on my case load who came from Old World families. When a parolee got into trouble, some member of the family often came to the front with an offer of a few dollars to "buy a cigar."

The Harlem Negroes with whom I had contact also were given to some attempt at bribery. Not as much as other culture groups, though, for those Negroes I knew couldn't afford the luxury. They were too poor. But when they did offer something it was more directly a bribe than a gesture of good feeling. Whatever produced it, they felt they had to pay off.

Shortly after I entered the Division an old, wrinkled woman laboriously walked into my office. I was making a preparole investigation on her grandson, an inmate of Sing Sing. That is, I was investigating his personal and family background and writing a report for the board's use in deciding whether to parole him or not.

This lady, in a soft, mournful voice, spoke lovingly of her grandson, her sole remaining relative. He had been wild, she said, but now he would do better. She needed him. As she spoke, she kept her right hand closed in a tight fist.

I told her that my function was only to submit a report. I made no recommendations. It would be entirely up to the board to make the final decision. They were the body who had to be convinced.

She put her right fist on the desk and extended the gnarled fingers. Onto my desk fell two crumpled dollar bills. "Will this help some with the board?" she asked.

A case like this makes me very angry—at society. What have we done, what are we doing, to our people, inadvertently or otherwise, to make the underprivileged feel they can have justice only if they buy it?

CHAPTER VIII

They're Not All Cold-Blooded

No, not all parolees are tough through and through. Very few are without some redeeming features.

Certain high-type, one-shot offenders can scarcely be called criminal. They are not by conditioned inclination more anti-social than social. We do not condone their crimes, yet must recognize that these offenders are essentially social beings. During the depression, for instance, many a respected and successful man committed an act proscribed by law, for the first time, in desperation. He did not thereby become a mad dog overnight.

In all eras there have been those who committed crimes of passion. A man kills his wife found in adultery. His crime is unforgivable; but after that moment of blind, hysterical passion, he may be, and often is, a decent, sensitive, reliable person of real integrity.

This must be understood if the public is to allow parole officers to act intelligently by differentiating between one offender and another. Some parolees need intensive, unremitting supervision. Others need sympathetic understanding and considerable help. Still others need nothing. They can stand on their own feet, be trusted; they will not revert to crime.

It may appear to be an indication of favoritism when parolee Pete Smith is allowed to travel while John Jones isn't. Or when

55

Pete is permitted to operate a car while John is denied the
privilege. But, properly administered, a good parole system
takes cognizance of individual differences and acts accordingly,
in the best interests of the parolee as well as of society.

For example, do you believe Dominick should have been
treated as a desperate criminal whose every move must be
checked? In seventeen years of law-enforcement work, I have
never come across a case that proved so conclusively what long
imprisonment can do to a man.

Dominick was a harmless little laborer in Brooklyn. A hard
worker, a gentle soul, he had never been arrested in his life.
He lived by routine, did a day's work, stopped for one beer
on the way home, arrived exactly on time for supper every
night. He and his wife rarely quarreled. Childless, they lived
a simple life, but Dominick didn't ask for more.

His wife apparently did. One day her husband finished a
job at midday. There was no more work that day, so Dominick
stopped for his one beer, arrived home at one-thirty P.M.—
and found his wife in bed with a man.

Dominick didn't blame the man. "He didn't know me," he
told me later, "so he didn't owe me anything." But his wife
did know him. Dominick went berserk. He picked up an ax
handle and brained her.

He was sentenced to death. Before the date of execution his
sentence was commuted by the Governor to a life term. Dominick began serving it in Sing Sing.

This was some years before World War I. Sing Sing was
being electrified, a form of illumination still pretty new at the
time. Dominick was put to work at this job. He liked it, proved
to have a natural bent for electrical work. He became an expert.

He also became a model prisoner. The guards liked him and respected him. Inmates often came to him for advice. Sing Sing became home to him. A simple man, he was relatively happy in his prison routine. When hanging ceased to be the mode of execution in the state, Dominick was the man who wired the electric chair. He saw no irony in the fact that he, who had barely escaped execution himself, was setting up the instrument that would snuff out the lives of others less fortunate than he.

For about a quarter of a century Dominick plodded away in prison. Then the Governor pardoned him out. The guards chipped in and bought him a set of tools so he could follow the electrical trade on the outside.

He was, of course, to report as soon as possible after release. A parole officer had been assigned to him.

He left prison in the morning. It takes an hour to get from Ossining to New York. By three o'clock Dominick hadn't reported. Technically that was a parole violation. Experience had demonstrated in the past that a man who failed to make his arrival report did so for one of two reasons. He never had intended to report, would have absconded from supervision immediately. Or he had stopped off for a few drinks and would next be heard from in some jail. Procedure required us to issue a warrant at once where a parolee failed to make his arrival report.

Dominick's failure puzzled me. Everything about him belied the parole absconder. He had never been a heavy drinker. He had left Sing Sing with high hopes. He had nothing to run away from. Where was Dominick?

I issued a warrant, but I instructed two parole officers assigned to the case to use it only if necessary. "Retrace his steps,"

I said. "Go to Sing Sing and work your way back by train. See if you can find him."

They didn't have to go beyond Grand Central Station. There, on the corner of Forty-second Street and Vanderbilt Avenue, they espied the parolee. He was standing on the curb, sweat pouring from him. From a pocket peeped a pet squirrel. In one hand he carried his tool kit. In the other he held a canary in a cage. Someone had told him the subway to the office was across the street. For hours he had stood there, terrified by the teeming traffic, unable to work up the courage to cross the street.

The officers brought him to me. He explained that when he went to prison he had rarely seen an automobile. A speed of ten miles an hour was fast. Radio was undreamed of. "Uptown" was Fourteenth Street. He had never seen a movie. Traffic lights were entirely unknown to him. What he saw on Forty-second Street was too much for him. He had entered prison a middle-aged man of the gaslight era. He had come out, an old man, in a world beyond his comprehension.

We set him up in a furnished room. For several weeks we had to deliver groceries to him, for he was too frightened to go out. Gradually he accustomed himself somewhat to the new world of speed and noise, but never quite enough to be able to take a job. He modernized himself to the extent of having a little radio. That was about all.

I visited him once. It was to be my last sight of him, for he died soon afterward. I remember he was as kindly as ever, as courteous and considerate. But when I told him he ought to go out once in a while, to accustom himself to liberty, he looked about him at his little room, shrugged, and sighed, "So this is freedom!"

It would have been sheer stupidity to treat that man, while on parole, as we might a gunman with a robbery record.

Other parolees have had qualities which the public, or some part of it, recognized and appreciated more than we in parole did. Jimmy Hines for example. A power in national politics, he was sent to prison when Dewey was blasting his way to fame and political fortune. The story that came out in court was not pretty, yet thousands of New Yorkers saw in Hines a lovable person.

During the trial I could look out of my window to the building where the Hines case was in progress. The streets in front of the courthouse were lined daily with the curious, the morbid, and the sightseers. Hines' emergence from the building brought applause, cheers, cries of "We're with you, Jimmy!" When Dewey appeared he was booed.

When citizens were told Hines had used his power to pervert justice and protect criminals, this was denied. Or the answer was, "Whatever he did, he was a good man. Didn't he give out food baskets every Thanksgiving and run a picnic for the poor people?"

Hines went to Sing Sing. When he was up for parole consideration the reporters jammed into my office to get word of the board's decision. Whatever the attitude of his paper, the individual newsman seemed, for the most part, sympathetic to "Jimmy" and hopeful of his release. When the board denied him parole, at least one paper lambasted us.

I certainly hold no brief for Hines. I mention the case only as illustration of the fact that some parolees have qualities that charm. Being human, they possess human characteristics. Many, for instance, appreciate a "fair shake" and want to reciprocate.

While still a parole officer I supervised a young man named

Bunny. He had considerable charm but little innate intelligence. An orphan, he had been raised by a tyrannical grandmother whose discipline drove the boy onto the street when he was still in rompers. From being a truant he became a petty thief, finally an armed robber. Paroled from a reformatory, he was assigned to me for care.

I discovered, on my first check, that he had quit his job for no reason at all. His grandmother reported he stayed out till all hours, sometimes didn't come home for days. I could have arrested Bunny for this, but I considered that I couldn't expect a twenty-year-old who had spent eighteen years in misery and two years in jail to change overnight. I located him and gave him another chance.

Within a week he had quit the job I got him, again left home. When I caught up with him I found he had been sleeping in hallways, panhandling for a living. I restored him to supervision.

Bunny disappeared.

Sometime later I had reason to suspect he was back in business as a holdup man. Victims gave descriptions of a powerfully built, red-headed, freckle-faced youngster with an angelic face and a big revolver. That answered Bunny's description.

One day his grandmother telephoned to say Bunny had visited her, left some laundry and asked her to wash it, saying he would return for it the next morning. The lady advised me to "pick him up now, before he kills somebody."

At five the next morning I was in her home, waiting. By noon Bunny hadn't appeared. I prepared to leave. As I was descending the tenement stairs I heard the outer door slam and quick, heavy steps run through the hallway. I stopped. The footsteps stopped. I waited. No sound. I made a dash down the stairs and into the hallway. There stood Bunny, his hands raised, waiting for me. I frisked him and found a gun. I put handcuffs on him and loaded him into a cab.

On the way to the office he mused, "Well, that's that. I was hoping this year I could stay out till summer. You know, I ain't been out long enough to go to the beach for almost three years. I was hoping I'd make it this year."

"I'm sorry it wound up this way, Bunny," I said. "But you asked for it. You had more than a fair chance."

"Oh, I ain't blamin' you. You done what you should. I can't complain."

Then he looked at me quizzically, talking almost to himself. "I don't know why I didn't plug you. The minute I come in and heard you on the steps I knew what was up. You *had* to come down sometime. I could have waited and plugged you."

"Why do you suppose you didn't?"

"I'm damned if I know," he confessed. "I thought to myself, this guy's been on the level with me. He gave me a fair shake. I ain't gonna hurt him. But, hell! That ain't no reason, is it?"

CHAPTER IX

Parolees Are Lovely Lovers

There is one characteristic of parolees I have no hesitancy in advancing as a proven phenomenon. Parolees are highly successful lovers. This is particularly true of the tough guy. He fascinates and holds his women. Time after time I have wondered at some gorgeous hussy who attached herself willingly and passionately to a crude, rude facsimile of Humphrey Bogart. My first year on the job I learned a lot about human nature in this regard, a lot I hadn't read about in books.

There was Hot Lips Harrington. He got the nickname by virtue of his trumpet playing. Hot Lips had a temper to match his jazz, and when he carved up a fellow musician in a Harlem speakeasy they sent him to Sing Sing. Paroled, he hot-footed it right back to the speak and rang the bell, determined to have it out with the proprietor who had turned him in. Someone opened the peephole and cried, "You ain't comin' in heah!"

Hot Lips sat down on the stoop, took out a razor, put it on his knee, and growled, "Is I ain't comin' in, ain't *no*body comin' out!"

Somehow they patched up their quarrel, and Hot Lips began reporting to the parole office. He seemed to be doing pretty well for several weeks. Then he landed in the Tombs, charged with assault. Seems he cut up one Celestine Harvey. We filed a parole violation warrant, which estopped bail.

I thought that was that, but suddenly the charge was withdrawn and Hot Lips was languishing in jail on our warrant alone.

That was the situation when Celestine Harvey marched into the office and sat down at my desk. She was a tall, handsome, buxom but shapely girl, given to dramatic gestures and pungent phrases. She demanded to know why Hot Lips was still in stir.

"Why, Miss Harvey," I ventured, "isn't it a fact that you and Hot Lips were—er—sort of living together?"

She smiled to indicate she knew I would understand, and answered, "Sure! A girl's got to socialize *sometime*, ain't she?"

"Maybe. But didn't he carve you up a bit?"

"Sure! From heah to heah!" She indicated a cut still plainly visible. "But there were nothin' to that!"

"Nothing to it! A man carves you almost from ear to ear and you call that nothing? How did it happen?"

"Oh, we was just havin' a sociable game of cahds."

"Well, maybe so. And now you've withdrawn your complaint. That means Hot Lips won't get a new sentence. But he's violated his parole and I'm going to recommend he be sent back to prison as a violator."

Celestine stood up indignantly. "Wheah's the boss?" she demanded, glaring balefully. "I wanna talk to the boss!"

The boss at that time was a man I'll call Major Bailey. His door was always open to staff and public alike. He would sit at his desk, a Between the Acts Little Cigar hanging by some magnetic attraction to his lower lip. When he became excited the Major stuttered and the cigar did a lively jig, yet never let go its hold on that lip.

I escorted Miss Harvey to Bailey's office, preceding her through the open doorway. "Major," I said, "this is—"

She didn't wait for introductions. She framed herself in the doorway, took a stance like a prima donna about to deliver a high C, and announced in perfect cadence, "Majuh, I'se Celestine Harvey. I come heah to talk to you about Robert Harrington. *He's* mah man, *ahm* his woman, I *needs* my lovin', *tu'n* him loose, Majuh! *Tu'n* him loose!" And she waved an arm in a majestic sweeping motion with each "Tu'n him loose!"

The Major gasped. His eyes darted from me to Celestine and back again. Then, with the same dramatic gesture that Celestine had used so effectively, he cried, the cigar bouncing wildly, "S-s-send him b-back, Dressler! S-s-send him back!"

But I was to learn that while an ever-loving woman stuck to her parolee boy friend through poverty and punches, it is sometimes hard to define what constitutes reasonable mayhem and what is not acceptable in the best underworld circles. Values become distorted in a society conditioned to rebellion against custom.

I had a young lad on parole to me from a reformatory. He was no bargain, having been a petty thief, burglar, and armed robber in quick succession. Now on parole, he was living with his young wife and seemed to be working hard and trying to straighten himself out. When I visited his home his wife, Mrs. Carlucci, timidly reported that Tony was a fine husband. He gave her his pay every Saturday. He never stayed out late. Everything was fine.

Then one day she came to the office accompanied by her mother, who more than made up for Mrs. Carlucci's timorousness. Tony's wife sat there, letting her mother act as advocate.

"You gotta send him back! He's-a no good! A bum! No good!" shouted the mother.

I calmed her sufficiently to be able to get the story from Tony's wife.

Carlucci, it seemed, hadn't been the paragon of virtue his wife had made him out to be. "He began running around," she breathed shyly.

"I see. And now you want him sent back."

"Well, I didn't mind *too* much when he began going with a certain girl. . . . I didn't even mind when he brought the girl home and had me fix dinner for the three of us. I didn't raise no fuss when he said the girl left home and would sleep on the couch in our place."

"Oh! You want her out?"

"Finally, he told *me* to sleep on the couch and the girl would —would use the bed."

"I see! That was too much!"

"No, not that. But"—and she slapped a hand down on the desk—"last night he socked me. I want him sent back!"

The kinds of women who considered parolees dashing romantics were positively amazing. I have seen several gorgeous showgirls tie themselves up to robbers and burglars, and not because they were gold-diggers, for the men in question had little in the way of assets, except, perhaps, a ready gun or skeleton key. I know a beautiful, talented, and highly educated concert pianist who stuck to her man through thick and thin, even when it was apparent he was robbing her blind. Several well-to-do matrons, to my knowledge, left their comfortable homes, and even children, to live in relative squalor with some denizen of the dives.

Perhaps, on second thought, it is not so incredible that women find the tough mug attractive. He is virile, manly in appearance if not in act. He suggests the cave man. He sets up in women's minds the conception of maleness double-distilled. And he plays up to that conception, consciously. Like most males, the criminal has a massive bump of vanity. But his idea of what makes him attractive is different from the notion held by the elegible bachelor squiring a Junior Leaguer. The side-of-the-mouth-speaking character, when I knew him, habitually wore a pearl gray hat perched high and precariously on his head. He affected camel's hair coats, slicked down hair, and leather heels that clicked as he walked. His clothes were tight, cut in close to the waist. He pretended indifference to his appearance, but it was a studied indifference.

As my knowledge of parolees' psychology increased, I developed the technique known to those detectives who read as "*cherchez la femme*." To discover what a suspect was doing, I would play on the jealousy of a girl friend. To inspire a man to settle down to a law-abiding existence, I encouraged marriage to a reasonably good woman. Sometimes the technique worked, sometimes not. But I learned never to underestimate the power of a parolee to bring out the best in a woman.

Tom was a case in point. He suspected his wife of playing around with the bartender on the corner. His duty was clear. He beat hell out of the barkeep, then rushed home, fire in his eye. He ripped off all his wife's clothes, gave her an unmerciful shellacking, threw an overcoat around her shoulders, and kicked her down the stairs.

"He could have thrown me out naked," she told the police, "only he wouldn't do that to a lady. Tom's a gentleman!"

CHAPTER X

More Deadly than the Male

All through my years in parole I heard people talk about "criminal types." Presumably a burglar looks, feels, thinks, and acts differently from a forger. A murderer is somehow constituted along different lines from a confidence man.

Actually, I found, after a little experience on the job, that there is no such thing as a criminal type, except within very circumscribed limits. Put a burglar, a sex offender, a robber, a murderer, and a kidnaper in the same room, talk to them at length, and you still couldn't pick one type of offender from another. Put them among a crowd of law-abiding citizens, and you couldn't differentiate one group from the other. Criminals look, and in most ways act, just like you and me. Researchers once mixed together some photographs of felons and police officers and asked subjects to separate criminals from law men. About fifty per cent of the time upholders of law and order were picked as criminals.

There are only two absolutely distinct types of offenders, so far as I can see. They are male and female. And I'd rather handle a hundred of the world's worst male thugs than one woman parolee.

There used to be a time when you could depend upon a woman criminal to be a lady. She might kill a husband or two, but she always took her arrest with dignity. She accepted her male captor as the superior animal, never talked back, and wouldn't struggle, lest that disarrange her skirts.

Stack that kind of lady up against the one I was sent to help arrest when I was still a beginner. She had absconded from her female officer. We subsequently located her in the flat she shared with a lover, also a parolee. That lover was meek as a lamb when we walked in. He was a gentleman. But Mary was no lady. She called me names I hadn't ever heard before and can't define even now. She went into hysterics, screaming she was being murdered. She refused to allow her room to be searched. She spat in my face. She dared me to arrest her. When I tried to, she scratched my face and kicked me in the groin. When finally I subdued her and decided to handcuff *this* one, she bit my hand. And when at last I had her wrist manacled to mine, she demanded to go to the toilet! Topping everything, when she appeared before the Parole Board a month later, she said I had tried to seduce her.

That incident convinced me that styles in crime change, like manners, morals and hats, at least in so far as women are concerned.

Moreover, the terrifying fact is that not only are women offenders worse harridans than they were before, but there are more of them. In 1933 some 22,948 females were arrested for major crimes. By 1949 this number had more than tripled—to 78,585. Prior to the 1920's women accounted for perhaps one per cent of all arrests for major crimes. In 1949 they accounted for almost ten per cent.

Celia Cooney, in my experience, signalized the beginning of the new era, when women parolees ceased being the weaker sex and took the gun to the stronger one. In the early twenties she went into partnership with her husband; their business:

robbery with a gun. For her day this was so shocking, so un-
heard of, that she made headlines over the entire world as the
notorious Bobbed Hair Bandit. Whoever heard of a girl doing
such an unfeminine thing! Celia was news because she was so
novel a phenomenon.

Yet even she was still enough of the older generation to be
comparatively a lady. On parole she gave some trouble, but
did so with restraint. She squandered some savings foolishly,
against her parole officer's instructions, but when censured for
this she didn't assault that estimable lady. She merely cried, as
a proper female should.

The newer crop of female parolees kept our staff in a state
of perpetual frustration. They used their feminine wiles not
only to commit crime but to outtalk, outcry, out-logic, and
outlast practically any woman parole officer.

They were a hard breed. They no longer got headlines for
their crimes unless they had pretty faces and shapely legs.
Women offenders were no longer news—they were nuisances,
and they were as predatory as any man. On top of that, they
had a diabolical way of denying it. In my years of service it
was my misfortune to deal with women gangsters, burglars,
robbers, pickpockets, shoplifters, blackmailers—everything
except rapesters. And I know some of them were guilty of
rape, although it was the man who was convicted each time.
I had such an unholy dread of the female on parole that as soon
as I assumed charge of the New York District I made it a rule
that no male parole officer should ever be asked to supervise a
female parolee. When I became executive director, this rule
was applied to the entire state.

Of course, I was aware that our culture had changed rapidly
in the twenty-five years following World War I. By the end

of that war women had become independent wage-earners and achieved greater personal freedom. And as they emerged from their protected status, styles in recreation began to change. The hand went off the cradle and the foot went onto the brass rail. Unescorted women could appear in public dancing places. There was more and more free mingling of sexes, more opportunity to meet men on their own terms, more temptation to act with men in crime.

When women wore bustles, they *couldn't* climb a fire escape to commit a burglary. By the time I was in parole, they either wore slacks or didn't care *how* they looked on the climb upward.

I became convinced that in some criminal operations women were more capable than men, better equipped, and infinitely more happy about it all. Take blackmail. There was a time when men, bent on this enterprise, hired a girl to act as lure in the badger game. She was an employee, that was all. She enticed the victim into a compromising position; the thugs walked in and set the price. Nowadays women have eliminated the middleman. They do the entire job themselves.

There was Fifi, for instance. She was, even by the time I knew her, after she'd served a prison term, a beautifully built, passionate-faced Latin type. We thought we'd have trouble with her on parole because we couldn't see how a breath-taking hussy like that would be satisfied with a humdrum existence and menial toil. When she came in to make her first report I had the officer bring her to see me.

I resolutely fixed my gaze on the ceiling and informed her that we would give her the strictest sort of supervision. We would lock her up at the first sign of drinking or frequenting places where rich and willing men might be found. I told her she'd have to take a job, hold on to it, and be satisfied with a modest income.

In a rich, husky voice that sent shivers up and down my spine, she said that was exactly what she intended doing. She'd had enough of prison. "I was young and foolish. Men turned my head." Now she was more mature. She would know how to behave.

And behold! Fifi took a job as maid with a wealthy suburban family. The lady of the household knew Fifi had a record and took pleasure in the fact that she was giving the girl a fresh start. She encouraged Fifi to consider herself part of the family. She made Fifi's brother welcome when he chose to call. Our parole officer visited the home once and chanced to meet the brother, Charles, a young man with fiery red hair and a Greek-god physique. Charles told the officer that Fifi had really settled down. "I even asked her to come out and have a birthday drink with me, and she wouldn't. She sure *has* changed!"

This happy state of affairs went on until, a year later, the man of the house came to see me. A portly, dignified gentleman, his hand trembled slightly as he placed his derby on the desk. His face showed worry. Stumblingly he came out with his story—and a plea that I, as discreetly as possible, remove Fifi from the household and tell her to keep her mouth shut.

Seems, Mr. —— said, he had seduced Fifi. He'd gone mad about her. But, of course, marriage was out of the question. Wouldn't do to get a divorce and all that, you know, only to marry a—uh—you know. When he'd explained this to Fifi, that simple-minded child just wouldn't understand. She had demanded money, and he'd given her some. From then on it was more and more money. He'd paid out over twenty thousand dollars. He'd have gone on paying, except now Fifi was demanding a cool twenty-five thousand as the price of silence. She was going to have a baby. And she was going to have it in a hospital nearby. And she was going to list the father's name unless . . .

We had to argue the gentleman into making complaint to the police. He did so only when it became evident that disgrace was coming, one way or another. Fifi was convicted of extortion. In the course of the trial it came out that the red-headed Charles was not her brother but her lover.

Fifi gave birth to a baby. It had fiery red hair.

Blackmail is not the only role in which women excel. They are natural guntoters too. Mobsters' molls have become common phenomena. They comfort their men, carry the rods so that a cop's frisk won't reveal anything incriminating on the male suspect. I knew a girl, Texas Mary, let's call her, who was the paramour of a mob leader, head of a gang of robbers. She would accompany him and an accomplice to the scene of a holdup and wait outside while the men went in to pull the job. That completed, the robbers would come out, pass her the gun and loot, which she would put into her bag. As they ran off in one direction, she would saunter away in the opposite direction. If police came on the scene, they would chase the men, who were "clean," not the nice-looking girl, who had the evidence.

On occasion women have even formed their own criminal aggregations. In New York prisons I interviewed a half-dozen ladies, part of a larger gang organized for systematic fur thefts. Each woman was in her late fifties, had a long, unsavory criminal record, was hardened, cold, and as calculatingly professional as any male criminal. After starting in Chicago, the mob

moved from city to city, stealing expensive furs from swank
stores. They worked their way to New York, started back
again, were caught halfway along the charted route.

Picking pockets has become a female enterprise too. Once
our Parole Board interviewed a veteran dip at Bedford Prison.
Her record was so bad that the commissioner interviewing her
told her at once she would not be paroled. She was burly, tall,
and almost feeble-minded. The commissioner, usually a kindly
man, this time somehow found it possible to comment, "You
don't look to me like the type who *could* pick a pocket. It
takes some brains to pick a pocket. But I guess the record
speaks for you."

The lady bristled, highly offended at this slur on her professional competence. But she said nothing and flounced out of
the room. As the Parole Board was having lunch in the prison
later that day, the woman returned and with a triumphant glint
in her eye gave the commissioner back his watch and chain.

Among the most troublesome of our parolees were the shoplifters. They were inveterate; they just wouldn't work legiti-
mately; and they invariably went into hysterics when we interviewed them as suspects. Today there are more women than
men operating at this trade.

Women are also going into crime requiring some amount of
physical prowess, even rough stuff. In 1949 there were 820
females arrested for criminal homicide; 965 for robbery; 6195
for assault. There were 541 arrests for carrying or possessing
dangerous weapons. Where a generation ago a girl like Celia
Cooney was a sensation, today her imitators are commonplace.
Ma Barker, cigar-smoking, gun-toting leader of a desperate
mob, was a product of her age. Kathryn Kelly, the wife of

George "Machine Gun" Kelly, not only used a gun but blue-printed her husband's jobs and instilled in the cowardly George enough courage to carry out the plans.

A sample of the female desperado is Vera, a woman I knew briefly when she was a parolee. Her career began when her husband taught her to steal from doctors' offices while the medico was giving him an examination. She progressed to shop-lifting. When her husband deserted her, Vera was on her own. She tied up with a bank robber, became his mistress, then went out on jobs with him, as a full partner in crime. Captured and convicted after a series of spectacular bank robberies, she broke jail. Recaptured, she broke out of prison twice. When I last heard, she was in a federal penitentiary and hadn't managed to steal the key yet.

But my horror of the woman offender is based less on her crimes than on her parole behavior. Not that she reverts to crime more often than men on parole. The reverse is true. The majority of female parolees do stabilize themselves. But when they go sour they're vinegar.

I used to have parole officers bring before me, when I was in charge of the New York District, certain parolees suspected of violations of a serious nature. That gave the parolee a chance to be heard before a warrant was issued for his or her arrest. A man would be surly at times, or he might cringe and wheedle, but he'd talk sense and admit the logic of a situation at least part of the time. A woman wouldn't. She would double-talk, go off on tangents, and, failing to accomplish her purpose, go into hysterics.

Maybe that's the natural consequence of being a woman. But I shudder for the parole officer of the next generation. For there will be more, not fewer, women on parole.

Beginning with World War II women have jumped the rates for crimes of personal disorganization. War work and the absence of their menfolk were contributing factors. One war year some 5417 were arrested nationally for prostitution and commercialized vice—at least so the record shows. Actually FBI records, whence comes this figure, are very incomplete. Undoubtedly there were ten times that many arrests, unreported. For other sex offenses, 2783 were reported arrested. And 483 were apprehended for drugs, 6438 for disorderly conduct, 16,272 for intoxication, 8067 for vagrancy.

And since the war the rate is not diminishing to prewar levels. Naturally a woman who becomes habituated to drink in wartime isn't necessarily going to break the habit when her husband returns from the front. A woman who became promiscuous may remain promiscuous. Of women arrested in 1949, nearly half had prior fingerprint records.

There is little likelihood that the crime rate among women will decline. We have too many regulars, too many newcomers every year who will become regulars.

CHAPTER XI

Crime: Amateur and Professional

Outside of classifying offenders as male or female, I know of only one other practical breakdown. They are either amateurs or professionals.

If a man ever stuck a gun in your ribs and demanded your money, chances are your assailant was an amateur criminal. If your pocket was picked, you were victim of a professional "cannon." When someone, in a melodramatic whisper, offered to sell you a suit of clothes below wholesale price, something he hinted was a little "hot," you were dealing with a professional criminal too. The suit wasn't stolen and the salesman was a "slum hustler," a type of confidence man.

The difference between an amateur and a professional isn't widely understood. Result: We treat both alike in court—except that the professional gets the lesser sentence.

I have known thousands of both amateurs and professionals, and they are as unalike as college professors and stripteasers.

A common misconception is that the number of crimes committed by an individual determines whether he belongs in one category or another. It is believed that because a man committed twenty burglaries he must be a professional. This is not necessarily so. In fact, most burglars are rank amateurs.

Some amateurs are criminal by accident. A man who runs

someone down while driving recklessly is guilty of man-slaughter.

Some are criminal by inner compulsion. Something inside a man makes him rape, kill, or assault. Like William Heirens, who murdered a woman, then scrawled on the wall, "For heaven's sake, catch me before I kill again. I cannot control myself."

Most amateurs are persons who, needing money, think the only way to get it is by crime. They hope to pull one job, then quit. They may have extensive criminal records, but they don't expect to remain criminals for life. And they know their acts are wrong.

The professional is different. He gets into crime deliberately because he prefers it to any other mode of life. He doesn't ever intend to quit. He doesn't care whether crime is right or wrong. He has contempt for amateurs and is proud of being a professional. His inveterate nature is illustrated by the pickpocket I had on parole to me while I was a field man. He had recently emerged from prison, been at liberty some two months, then one fine May day was arrested for picking pockets at Coney Island.

Disgusted, I visited him in jail. "Well," I said cynically, "I suppose you're going to tell me you're innocent?"

"Innocent? Hell, no!" he responded. "But what gets me is they had to go and catch me right at the beginning of my season!"

Professionalism is no dream of the romantic fiction writer. It is a fact. The underworld itself recognizes it and makes a clean-cut social and business distinction between criminals who belong in the profession and amateurs who don't.

Like the doctor or lawyer, the career criminal meets certain

criteria common to all members of a profession. He selects his
vocation carefully and intends to devote his life to it. He then
gets an education in it, as systematically and thoroughly as does
the medical student studying biology. He puts himself through
school. There are many such unchartered educational centers.
The faculty may be fairly large or may consist of only one
professor of crime. The student must meet such entrance requirements as will demonstrate his innate ability and integrity.

Graduated *cum laude*, the criminal wants a just return for
his training and skill. He feels he is entitled to recompense for
his years of arduous preparation. He doesn't think he ought to
work for peanuts.

In New York, until recently, there was a great safe blower.
He was one of the last of the "soup men," who crack safes by
blowing them open. After long years in this honorable profession hoary with tradition, he retired to the cloistered halls of
a tenement flat, where he took on students. They came from
far away to study under the master. In the senior year he would
lay out a job, supervise the preparations, and send his pupils
out to practice and bring him part of the proceeds. Police knew,
by examining the remains of a safe, when they were dealing
with the professor's interns, so characteristic was the technique.
The headmaster died, honored in his profession, not alone for
his skill but for the success of his pedagogical methods.

Like lawyers or social workers, the criminal often belongs
to a professional protective organization that gives him moral
support, upholds standards in the profession, and fights for his
rights. It is a rather fluid affair, moving its headquarters frequently and changing its officers when jails demand the attend-
ance of incumbents. It supplies information on likely victims,
what areas to avoid, which cops are tough. It eliminates unfair

competition. Territories are cut up among members. Persons wishing to become professionals are given the brushoff if they don't seem to have the stuff.

Occasionally an organization affords itself the luxury of a professional magazine, to further research, disseminate new techniques, and keep members in touch with one another. In tone these periodicals tend to be a cross between the *American Journal of Psychiatry* and *Variety*. For understandable reasons they are short-lived. But I once received (in the U.S. mails!) several consecutive issues of a paper, now defunct, whose articles included: "How to Beat a Rap," "How to Stand Up under the D.A.'s Questions," "The Easy Way to Do Time." There were also social notes, like "Big Jake is wintering in Joliet. Dropped in Chi."

An organization, when it exists, may represent the profession of crime in general or one specialty of it. For there is a hierarchy among professionals. Some difference of opinion exists as to just where each specialty belongs, but all agree that the confidence man is top of the heap. Men like Yellow Kid Weil, the greatest con man of all time, and Dapper Don Collins, a close contender for top honors, are royalty.

Safe crackers are usually considered next.

Then come counterfeiters. Lesser fry regard with awe the man who studies chemistry and printing and engraving in order to put out a phony bill. And they bow down in worship before the genius, perhaps apocryphal, who issued such a perfect hundred-dollar bill that even the United States Treasury couldn't weed out the bad from the good and had to withdraw the entire legal series from circulation.

After the counterfeiter comes the forger. That doesn't mean petty larceny amateurs, who aren't considered even second cousins. The career man is someone like Eddy Romford. He forged instruments to the value of $560,000 before he entered San Quentin. He was so good that when he came out interested parties prevailed upon him to accept a liberal pension in return for his promise to retire.

Shakedown artists are a step lower. They operate blackmail schemes, subtle or otherwise.

Pennyweighters follow. They steal gems from jewelers in broad daylight. One of our parolees worked this classical scheme: Elegantly dressed, he entered one of the swank Fifth Avenue jewelry shops. He was, he said, acting for President Roosevelt. He was to pick out a fine piece to be given by the Chief Executive to some visiting royal person. Naturally the salesman brought out the very best in stock. The gentleman selected a truly distinctive and expensive item. Would he take it with him, the clerk asked? Oh, no! He was only the errand boy, as it were. Would the store kindly deliver the article to the Roosevelts' New York home? Of course!

Whereupon our parolee left, hied him to the vicinity of the Roosevelt house, and from a vantage point observed the messenger deliver the package to a maid. He then dashed to a telephone and called the Roosevelt residence.

"This is ——, jewelers," he announced. "Did our man just deliver a package to your address? Yes? We're terribly sorry. An awful mistake! It was meant for another patron. We will send a man right out to pick it up. We'll be ever so grateful if you will give him the package. He will give you a receipt, of course. So sorry to have troubled you."

The thief called for the package and was gone.

Professional robbery and burglary are rare today. But there

are the "heels" and "boosters," the shoplifters. Heels walk in, secrete something, and walk out. Boosters do the same, but engage the salesman in conversation, distract his attention, then grab.

At the bottom of the scale, by general agreement, are pickpockets.

Gangsters are seldom considered part of the hierarchy. Most professionals dislike criminals who use force. It's bad for business. It turns on the heat. And gangsters are often lone wolves who don't adhere to an accepted, traditional procedure.

This procedure involves a code which is a common bond among all members of the truly professional underworld. To be sure, like any other putative or real code of the underworld, it is followed only within reason, only so long as it pays the follower. But its very existence signalizes the incorrigibility of the careerist.

The code insists that thieves should never steal for thrill or revenge, only for gain. I once had a professional jewel thief picked up and brought to me for questioning. Incredible as it seems, he had been identified from a Rogues' Gallery picture as the man who had sexually assaulted a young woman. As soon as my line of questioning revealed to him what our suspicion was, he stiffened, sniffed haughtily, and informed me, "When I'm working, I'm a thief. Stealing is a business. I never mix business with pleasure!" (He was subsequently entirely cleared of suspicion of rape.)

This same feeling is evident when amateur and professional get together, which is usually only when they are forced to share a jail cell. The careerist will be courteous but distant with an amateur arrested for rape, assault, or even theft. He figures

there is something wrong with a man who has so little control
as to assault someone. As to the amateur thief, he's a bungler,
likely to get a nearby professional into trouble.

The code further provides that when a professional thief
learns another is in danger, he must do all he can to tip him
off, even if he doesn't know him. A shoplifter was once working a New York department store. He had moved into position to purloin what he was after when he spotted a man filch-
ing an article from a nearby counter. He didn't know him
personally but recognized him as a professional. He also knew
that he himself was being tailed by a woman who might be a
store operative. He figured that if *he* could spot the other's
thievery, in no time at all the detective would too. He brushed
against the other thief, muttered "Nix!" and that was enough.

One professional will avoid doing anything that might en-
danger another professional. When two shoplifters meet in a
store they do not speak. Each figures he may be known to the
store detective, and his talking to the other thief will cast suspicion on that gentleman too.

A man must help a brother professional even if he hates
him. Criminologist Edwin Sutherland tells of a booster, Little
Eddie, who disliked Jake, another booster. Jake got locked up
in Chicago. Eddie heard about it and approached a fixer to ask
how much it would cost to spring Jake. The price was a hundred and fifty dollars, and Eddie put it up, saying, "I hate the
no-good bastard, but I can't let him lay in the can for a hundred and fifty dollars."

Loyalty, of a sort and within limits, goes further. "In on
the good, in on the bad," runs the maxim. If a member of the
mob goes to jail, the others tax themselves to pay for the lawyer,
send the brother in crime some goodies, perhaps support his

woman. Many mobs have a central fund, a sort of community chest, called "fall dough." A percentage of each man's gross goes into the kitty. When a member gets in trouble, fall dough is put up to help him. It is a sort of underworld social service.

There is a saying, "Take a phony fall to help a pal." A parolee of ours was arrested and charged with a theft of which he happened to be innocent. He found he could buy his way out in the state where he happened to be. It would only cost him a C note. He paid the money. As he explained to me, after he was finished with parole, in this manner he freed himself without much trouble and at the same time kept suspicion from being directed at the guilty man. But protocol called for repayment of the hundred dollars by the thief who had pulled the job. The parolee went into the local underworld, discovered the identity of the man, and presented his bill.

Among shoplifters there is a saying, "Don't grift on the way out." It means, don't steal some furs, say, then stop on the way out for some handkerchiefs. Not only is that dangerous because you're not clean of the first haul, but there may be someone else working the handkerchief counter. You got your score. Let him have his.

Every one of these precepts indicates that the professional regards his work as a lifetime career. He is our inveterate criminal, the true incorrigible. The outlook for his ultimate reform is dismal. Dealing as I have with offenders in both the amateur and professional categories, I can testify that one can easily distinguish between the two types. The professional is matter-of-fact about his trade; he plainly considers it a career. Appeals to his better self fall on deaf ears. He is quite cynical about this. He plans to quit only when forced to do so.

I sat as a substitute member of the Parole Board in an insti-

tution where we were interviewing a pickpocket with over
a hundred arrests to his discredit. He kept whining and pleading for another chance. He was, he swore, all through with
crime. He was so obviously a career man that I expressed some
skepticism that he would ever turn over a new leaf. He looked
at me, aggrieved, held up a gnarled, twisted hand, and cried,
"Mister, I *gotta* retire! Since I come in here I got arthritis.
Them fingers ain't what they used to be! I can't work no more!
I *gotta* quit!"

The irony of our system of criminal justice is that the professional takes fewer chances than the amateur, as a rule, and
suffers milder penalties. He is clever, hence frequently escapes
arrest. This is not as true of pickpockets and shoplifters as it
is of other professional operators.

The penalty for a professional's crime is usually less than
that for an amateur's, because of the kinds of crime undertaken
by the former, to the exclusion of certain other offenses that are
almost always the work of amateurs. A robber who steals fifty
dollars may get a maximum sentence of ten or twenty years
in some states. The confidence man rarely draws over two or
three years. Pickpockets may get ninety days at a time. A
pennyweighter told me, "I always study the cost of a crime in
a state. For a take of a hundred thousand before I'm caught,
I'm willing to take a chance on a year in the can. Those are
good odds in any game."

I have long pondered the problem of the professional thief.
It seems insoluble, but at least we should be realistic and stop
treating careerists the same as amateurs. Probation (suspended
sentence under supervision) should rarely be offered the professional. In prison, where there is usually a shortage of trade
training classes, the existing facilities should be reserved for

the amateurs first. The careerist rarely wants to substitute a trade for a profession.

Most prisons are limited in psychiatric service. Let it be used for the amateur. Many an amateur does feel there is something wrong with him. The professional is certain he's all right.

Nevertheless, prison officials always want to accept the possibility that a given professional, for one reason or another, sincerely wants to turn honest. Such a rare specimen should be identified as early as possible and treated accordingly. A well-run institution can determine who are the fakers intent on "conning the warden," and which men really believe they are through with crime.

On parole, the professional must always be considered a dubious risk. He is entitled to decent treatment and a fair chance to demonstrate whether he intends to be law-abiding. But he requires constant and intensive supervision, for if he decides to go back into the racket he will be shrewd about it. It will take good police work to detect it.

And if we are ever to discover what makes the professional thief tick, we must get down to some basic research. Criminologists know very little about the crime careerist. They have concentrated their research on amateurs, as the most numerous and fruitful material. But scientific study of the professional would yield some results for society. We would know better how to treat him, and perhaps how to change him.

By study and by statute, our aim must be to force professional thieves to the conclusion of the anonymous reformed "bunco man" who wrote his autobiography in collaboration with Will Irwin in 1909. He reformed, he says, because "an honest dollar is the only dollar that don't do stunts on your pillow at night."

Later in this volume I shall have more to say about the causes of crime, both amateur and professional, with individual cases that may help to bear out my contentions. But first it seems important to get on with the actual operation of parole—and this entails a digression into the steps that lead up to it.

CHAPTER XII

Incarceration: Forerunner of Parole

Every parolee was once an inmate of a penal institution. He served part of a sentence there, then was paroled. Hence every parolee has been deeply influenced by an incarceration experience, which will affect his parole period.

What is a prison, or reformatory, like?

It's a place of abnormality, of degradation, of hopelessness, and often of perversity. Country-wide, our prison systems are pretty miserable failures. Here and there will be found one penal institution which serves as an exception: it is the exception that proves the rule.

We're hypocrites about our prisons. We've been saying for years that we no longer send men to institutions as punishment. Oh, no! We send them away for safe custody until they no longer are menaces. But while we've got them, we treat them —that's what we sent them away for, treatment. We want to treat them, not punish them, so they'll come out better, not worse; so they'll be less willing to victimize society. What does it profit us to punish a man if that serves only to harden and embitter him, to make him more vicious, more of a menace to all of us? No, we will treat him, turn him out social rather than antisocial.

That's what we say we're doing. That's what our annual

reports say. And it's practically all on paper, for theory and practice are far apart.

To treat inmates we must have some kind of classification and segregation, some separation of types of prisoners so that social contagion doesn't set in, one inmate learning from another, being infected by him. But in most of our penal institutions youngsters mingle with oldsters, first offenders with ten-time offenders, burglars with robbers, rapesters, forgers, murderers, sex offenders, and wife deserters. They all work together, play together, eat together, and sleep together. Young men learn from the old-timers, look up to the tough guys. And finally, at public expense, we graduate them with a liberal education in crime. At public expense we have given them new techniques and devices.

If a prison is to be a place of treatment, it must have a program of vocational and educational training that means something, that will teach inmates skills by which they can make a decent living on the outside. Most of them came in unprepared for and untrained in any skilled operation. Here, where they have almost nothing *except* time, is an opportunity to give them a way of making a satisfying, honest living.

Most prison programs, the machinery involved and the teaching methods, are antiquated, obsolete.

If a prison is to be a place of treatment, it needs to have a guidance program, through which an inmate may receive help in solving his personal problems. Many enter prison in a state of shock. They have been suddenly cut off from all that is familiar to them. They wonder what happened to them, why it happened, what is going to happen. They worry about families, their own state of mind and emotions. Many want help.

In most prisons the guidance staff is insufficient to treat any appreciable proportion of the inmate population. In fact, in the majority of prisons there is no guidance staff at all. Psychiatry and social work are relatively unknown.

There are some exceptions, but these are rare. Until we are prepared to overhaul our prison systems, whole hog and without mercy, we will be turning out men worse than they were when they entered penal institutions. That is indeed a gigantic irony—that we spend millions of dollars a year to teach men crime and depravity.

Here is what I mean when I say our prisons fail. This is the story of Eddie the Eel. I knew him throughout his career.

"Eddie," the Juvenile Court judge said, "you've been on probation for stealing bicycles. Now you take a car for a joy ride and smash it up."

Eddie hung his head.

"But," the judge continued, "you're not a bad kid. You're only fifteen. You can still get a grip on yourself."

The youngster looked up expectantly.

"I'm going to send you to a reformatory. Know what that is?"

Eddie gulped. "Yes, sir. A jail."

"No." The judge shook his head. "It's a place where you can reform. You'll be treated kindly. You will be taught a good trade, how to behave. It's up to you. Good luck!"

The first day in the reformatory Eddie felt pretty good. His cell wasn't much smaller than the tenement room he had shared with two brothers. The food wasn't like hot dogs and hamburgers, but it would do. Maybe he *would* learn better!

Then his education began.

"Hey, you!" called an inmate in the play yard.

"Yeah?"

"Whatcha in for?"

"Stealin' a car."

The older boy chuckled. "You'll learn! You're a punk! Know what that is?"

"No. But I don't like it!"

"Don't blow your top, kid!" said the seasoned informant, grinning. "A punk is a small potato. Don't be one. When you steal, steal big! Come on, I'll show you the ropes. Relax, kid!"

As Eddie and his self-appointed mentor, Timmy, circled the yard, the older inmate told the newcomer how to "keep your nose clean."

"You follow the rules when the screws are around. If you see a guy cheatin', you dummy up. You work when they watch and you loaf when they don't. That's all."

But Eddie wasn't having any. He wanted to learn that trade, behave himself, and come out to make good.

When a guard was rough because Eddie got in the wrong line, the boy took a shoving around and kept quiet. When he failed to police his cell according to Hoyle, and the keeper spat tobacco juice on the floor and ordered him to clean it up, he did.

Eddie thought he'd like to learn to be a machinist's helper. So he went into the prison shop and worked hard for a while. Then he asked the shop instructor, "Will I be able to get a job working this machine on the outside?"

"Hell, no, kid!" said the teacher, laughing. "These machines went out of date ten years ago."

So he got transferred to masonry and soon was laying as good a brick as the next man. But they didn't pace him fast enough to entitle him to get a union card on the outside.

He entered the farm class. They put him to milking cows. And that's all they ever let him learn.

Then the assistant superintendent sent for him.

"Say, what's the matter with you, kid? Why all the transfers? Aren't you satisfied with nothing? From now on you're pushing a mop!"

And the boy was a hall porter from then on.

When he began to cut corners, they gave him bad conduct reports. When he snapped back at a guard, he was put in solitary for insolence. When he emerged, bitter and sullen, cursing the disciplinarian under his breath, he was told to do the bends—to squat on the balls of his feet for an hour—until the pain was so excruciating he stood up—and went to solitary for "resisting an officer."

From that day on he did his time the way Timmy had taught him. He shirked when he could, worked when he had to. He listened to the boys' exploits and thought, "Maybe *I'm* wrong."

He was released in two years. It cost the taxpayers $695 a year to maintain a person in the reformatory, so the bill for that bit of rehabilitation came to $1390. They gave him a suit of clothes, and five dollars too.

When he returned home, his old man was drunk, as usual. So Eddie went to live in a furnished room with Timmy, who had also been released. He got a job in a machine shop, but they fired him because he didn't know the work.

So when Timmy urged him, he shrugged—and helped cut lead pipes out of an empty apartment. They got caught.

"Eddie," the judge said, "you're not an incorrigible criminal. I sentence you to a term of one to three years in the county penitentiary."

Eddie didn't know it, but a penitentiary is a place where you are supposed to become penitent. But how?

There was no classification of prisoners to segregate the worst from the best. Eddie rubbed shoulders with petty thieves and gunmen, drug addicts and burglars, pickpockets and pimps. His cellmate was a veteran criminal, as Eddie soon found out. Homosexuality was also rife in the institution.

The cells stank because slop buckets served as toilets. The food was terrible and the guards worse. They were political appointees and ran the institution accordingly. If you had money you could buy your own food and cook it in your cell. One inmate even hired another as chef and valet. Favoritism was the rule. If you were "in," you lived; if you weren't, you suffered.

There wasn't much work, and Eddie was idle most of the time. He hated that, for idleness, he knew, makes you stir crazy.

Eddie had plenty of time to chew the fat with the others. He listened open-mouthed to stories of the big hauls in crime. He became ashamed of himself, and when asked, "What did you get dropped for?" mumbled something about "larceny." It sounded better than "petty theft." He looked up to the old-timers and learned many a new technique. He determined that next time he would steal big.

No one advised otherwise, for there was no psychiatrist or social worker to try to change his attitude, and the warden didn't have time to see prisoners.

When Eddie was released at the end of eighteen months, he was out for the big time. Meanwhile that term cost the tax-payers $731.25. And, oh, yes, Eddie got a suit of clothes and fifty cents to start him off in good style on the right road.

He was bitter. Even in jails, he reflected, the rich get the gravy; if you pull strings you get ahead. There was no justice in justice.

Yet he still harbored the flickering hope that he could make the big haul and turn honest. He rode the rods to another state. He specialized in flat burglaries. Then he got arrested again. While he was ransacking an apartment a woman awoke and screamed, "Catch that man!" He had wiggled out of trouble so often he'd won the nickname of the Eel, but this time he didn't get away from the law.

"Eddie," the judge intoned, "you are on the road to becoming a desperate criminal. You were on probation and failed. You had the opportunity to reform in a reformatory and deliberately chose the path of crime. Penitentiary didn't change you. I'm going to sentence you to five to ten years in state prison."

Eddie was in the big time. They sent him to a prison that cost the taxpayers eight million dollars.

"Well," he smirked, looking up at the big house, "if this place don't cure me, nothin' will!"

"Okay," growled the reception clerk, "you're jugged. Go get mugged and bugged."

"Huh?"

"What are you, a wise guy? Mugged: you get your picture took. Bugged: the psycho doc studies your brain. Got it?"

"At least," thought Eddie, "in a classy heap like this, you get a chance to tell the doc what bothers you."

The psychiatrist was as patient as possible, but he had forty-two other arrivals to see. He asked all about Eddie's childhood. Were his parents good to him? Did he wet the bed? Was anything bothering him?

Eddie told him he had never had a chance. The going was too tough. He never had any money. Not even in jails was he taught how to make an honest living. Prisons had given him a raw deal. They made him mad, desperate. Nobody cared about him. "What's wrong with me, doc? Am I nuts?"

The doctor smiled reassuringly. "You'll get along in here. I like your attitude."

Eddie's ice-water blood warmed a little. "Am I gonna see you again, doc?" The psychiatrist grew apologetic. "I'm afraid not, Eddie. I'm the only psychiatrist here, and all I can do is examine new admissions and—er—those who become insane."

In the yard it was the old story. The same motley mob. The same talk about the big time. Only now there were more genuine big-timers strutting among the lesser fry.

Some fellows were learning trades. But there was shop room for only forty per cent of the inmates. Eddie was given a mop.

He seethed. He resented being watched at every step. Was no one ever going to trust him? What about a little honor system?

"Ho!" laughed a pickpocket. "Brother, you're lookin' for what they call a minimum security prison, one of them things without walls. We ain't got one in this state. Why, this wall alone cost a million bucks!"

So Eddie did time, six years of it, and it cost $550 a year. That put the taxpayers out $3300.

Paroled, he wrote Timmy to come on. They hijacked trucks. They shot it out with the cops in a payroll robbery before surrendering.

"Eddie," the judge pontificated, "you are a desperate, perverted, incorrigible criminal. You have victimized the society that nurtured you. I shall make an example of you to warn all desperadoes of your ilk to stay out of this state. Ten to twenty years in the prison for incorrigibles!"

So it started again. Same routine, same monotony, same degradation. Only now the small fry looked up to him with awe. And he was teacher to the punks.

Those fourteen years he did cost the taxpayers, at $625 a year, $8750. It cost Eddie whatever remained of his decency.

He came out a maniac. He organized a gang and roamed the country, shooting, bludgeoning, plundering. He served two more terms, costing the people $6000 more. And finally he was captured in a gun battle in which a policeman was slain.

Thus ends the saga of Eddie the Eel, a $20,171.25 story illustrating why prisons fail.

They fail because *we* have failed miserably, shamefully, to run them properly. Ninety-nine per cent of all inmates must come out sometime. Only one per cent will die or be executed while in custody. We have not run our prisons to reform the ninety-nine per cent. Instead, inmates are embittered, hardened, stultified.

There are exceptions. A few, very few, prisons are run along progressive penological lines. A few, very few, teach a man a trade, treat him decently, help him change his attitude, give him psychiatric care, personal guidance.

Eddie was one of society's failures because society had failed him. Do you hope he finally gets into a modern, progressive prison, where his warped mind might conceivably be straightened out?

That, unfortunately, will never be. Eddie was executed.

CHAPTER XIII

First Step Toward Parole

Chewing furiously on a wad of gum, the inmate faced the Board of Parole. He was about twenty-eight. His hair stood straight up in a startling shock. He swayed nervously in his chair throughout the proceedings which were to determine whether he should be paroled or not.

"What is your name?" I asked.

"How's that, Jackson?" he spat back.

I let it go. The record told us who he was.

"You've only been arrested the one time, I see," I began again.

"Okay, Jackson, okay!" he barked.

Because of the gum in his mouth I wasn't certain I'd heard correctly. I tried a different approach.

"If we consider paroling you, you understand you must have a home and job to go to."

"Okay, Jackson, okay!"

"And this report says you haven't got either."

"Okay, Jackson!"

"You haven't?"

"Okay, Jackson!"

"Do you know of someone who will offer you a home or job?"

"Okay, Jackson, okay!"

If you were a member of a parole board, how would you decide a case like this? Would you parole the inmate or not? Was he insane? Impertinent? A jokester?

A parole board member is expected to be a judge, a Solomon, almost a god. He has power over people's lives, their liberties, their future. He must decide, on the basis of inexact criteria, who is and who is not fit to be released. This is a fearful responsibility, one that would make any capable board member deeply humble.

The young man I have described above wasn't insane. He was simply very tense. Like so many others, he had entered prison counting his minimum sentence by years. Later he began figuring it in months. As his parole eligibility date came closer and closer he calculated the passage of time by days, then by hours, finally by minutes. By the time he stepped into that hearing room he was unable to think or talk. All that came out was a comedy line he had heard the night before on the Jack Benny program.

Other inmates demonstrate tenseness in other ways. They weep, lose their tempers, or remain mute. It is difficult to evaluate a prisoner fairly on the basis of the one, hurried interview a parole board affords him, but that is the object of the hearing. The board seeks to select fit material for parole.

I have sat on many New York State Parole Board hearings, by special commission of the Governor, because of the absence of one of the regular commissioners. I have participated, by a conservative estimate, in at least a hundred thousand interviews with inmates seeking parole, and I still don't know how to select infallibly only those individuals who will never again revert to crime. I don't know, no board member knows, and nobody on earth knows.

The best we could do was study an inmate's background as some sort of prognostication of the immediate future. We did this through the preparole investigation that was furnished us on each inmate. And, in spite of many handicaps, we gained something from the face-to-face talk with the prisoner.

The three members of the Parole Board met in each prison of the state once a month. They sat behind a long table, the inmate on the other side, facing the board. A hearing stenographer recorded all that was said. Usually a prison guard was also present, dating from the time when, in quick succession, at Sing Sing, one prisoner tried and failed to bounce a chair off Commissioner Fagin's head; and another tried and succeeded in bouncing an inkwell off his eye. The resulting mouse was a beaut. It was deemed wise to have some sort of protection in hearing rooms thereafter.

Many inmates came in with beautifully rehearsed stories. They were coached by other prisoners supposedly wise in the game. Usually we could detect the rehearsed act, which tended to fall into one of several categories.

There was the man who denied any guilt whatever. "They got the wrong guy" were famous last words. Also, "I had a bad lawyer. He advised me to cop a plea [plead guilty], so I done it. But I'm innocent."

There was the prisoner who admitted guilt, but "I recognize I done wrong; it was the fault of bad company. Gentlemen, you give me just this one chance, and you'll never regret it!"

There was the masochistic type. "Gentlemen, I'm glad I got this term. The way I was goin', I was bound for the hot seat, for sure. This rap sobered me. It taught me a lot. Now if you

gentlemen give me just this one chance, you'll never regret
it."

There was the more astute student of dramatics who picked
up some special line. Once we were given, in identical words,
the same argument by three men in the one prison: "Gentlemen, it's true I departed from the straight and narrow, but
please bear this in mind. I am a victim of circumstances, the
product of an underprivileged environment. Now if you gentlemen will just give me this one chance . . ." This bit of
mumbo-jumbo undoubtedly came from a "stir lawyer," a curious breed of man found in every penal institution. For money
or for free, he advises inmates how to behave before the Parole Board, how to explain infractions of prison rules, on what
contentions to take out writs protesting improper sentence.
Stir lawyers are great ones for devious logic—and they love
their work.

It was they who advised inmates on another story for the
Parole Board. The commissioners, for some reason, kept asking for several years where inmates got the guns with which
they committed their crimes. The inmates, for some reason,
kept giving the same answers until, discouraged, the board
gave up. It seems guns are secured by criminals in only one of
two ways, judging from the stories we got. "I found it in a
garbage can" is one. "I found it in a vacant lot," is the other.
Our garbage cans, I would estimate, are repositories for guns
in the ratio of about one per two cans. And treasure hunters
need do no diving for sea treasure. There are hundreds of
thousands of dollars' worth of pistols waiting to be retrieved
in vacant lots.

The most intelligent inmates needed the least coaching and

came in with the more original approaches—and the most meaningful because they were genuine, whether genuinely good or bad.

Board members reacted according to their own personalities to the various inmates, of course. We have had, on the New York State Parole Board, those who were sadistic, sympathetic, oversympathetic, objectively scientific and detached, pontifical, clowning. We have had those who thought themselves God, others who considered themselves public servants working in the interest of the people, and still others who deemed themselves so unimportant to the proceedings that they fell asleep during hearings.

Any board meeting was an amazing proceeding. It held, within the confines of a few hours and one room, great tragedy, comedy, drama, pathos, and bathos. It was not alone the serious offenders and the "famous" personalities who supplied the most color and interest. Human interest was to be found everywhere.

The confidence men always intrigued me. They were so inveterate, so clever and ruthless. Usually they felt superior to the board members and took few pains to hide the fact.

Once, during World War II, one of these arch swindlers appeared before us at Sing Sing. He was the object of some special interest because he was a German national, and we were at war with Germany. His parents were both German, although he had been born in Paris while the family was traveling.

Dr. Joseph W. Moore, then chairman of the Parole Board, conducted most of the interview. He was a psychiatrist, a brilliant wit who pulled off his *bon mots* with a poker face.

"I see," he said, "you are a German."

The inmate drew himself up and remarked, with emphasis, "I was *born* in Paris."

"But you are German?'

"I was *born* in Paris," the bunco man repeated haughtily.

"Your parents were German?" Moore persisted.

"I was *born* in Paris!"

"Huh!" the doctor snorted. "If a cat had kittens in an oven I suppose you'd call them biscuits!"

The most frustrating cases were the prisoners who entered into no discussion; they only wept. And those who argued, but also whined, pleaded, cajoled for the chance to go free.

Fritz Kuhn, the onetime Bund leader, was this sort of prisoner. Outside, he had been a strutting bantam rooster, a bully. When he entered Sing Sing for stealing Bund monies, he remained cocky. Then, transferred to Dannemora, he learned in double-quick time that he was no special grade of inmate. They gave him the tools and told him to go shovel manure.

By the time he appeared before the Parole Board he had his act well in mind. The board expected a *Heil, Hitler*, but Kuhn bowed obsequiously when he entered. He listened courteously and intently to every word spoken by a commissioner, then launched into his spiel. In piteous tone he swore he had been framed—he was absolutely innocent. Had he been un-American? Good heavens, no! Had he run the Bund? Why, he was a mere cog in the vast machinery of the German-American Bund, a little fellow who joined what he thought was a club for outdoor exercise! Was he a menace to the United States in wartime? That really broke him down. He a *menace!* Why, he loved this country, never had plotted against it, never would.

The whole thing, gentlemen, was this: His associates had stolen the money under such circumstances as to make it appear Kuhn was responsible. They wanted him out of the way so they could take over. That's what it was all about. (Why a mere cog had to be got out of the way he didn't make entirely clear.)

Kuhn pleaded for his liberty shamelessly, tearfully, without a scintilla of self-respect.

He was denied parole.

In contrast to the Kuhn type was the person who neither cajoled nor blustered, who maintained his self-respect throughout.

Richard Whitney impressed me that way. He had been imprisoned for a tremendous larceny committed while he was president of the New York Stock Exchange (although the thefts, as I recall, were not perpetrated on the Exchange itself.) Because of his background and the friends he still had, he might have tried to throw his weight around, been arrogant. Or he might have played it as Kuhn did, claiming complete innocence.

He didn't. He acted not at all. He put on no show. He was courteous but not servile. He didn't fawn and he wasn't aggressive. He admitted his guilt, but he didn't flagellate himself in penance. He answered questions directly and simply. He didn't plead for parole, nor did he say he deserved not to be paroled, as some inmates do, hoping the board will therefore parole them.

We paroled Whitney.

At the time a newspaper attacked us, saying we paroled Whitney because he was an aristocrat, held Kuhn because he wasn't.

As a matter of fact there was some slight difference of opinion on the board itself regarding these paroles. I was due to substitute for a particular commissioner who would be away on vacation. He spoke to me, trying to sway my judgment. He said were he on the board that month he would refuse to parole Whitney because (1) he was a well-to-do person who had had every privilege and should have comported himself better than some thug who had a shabbier rearing; and (2) the public would be offended by his release. Listening to the commissioner, I was inclined to agree with the first point, as a general proposition.

About Kuhn the board member had no strong negative feelings. He would not object to parole although he realized that, particularly in wartime, this might be ill advised. Hence he would vote either way.

I told the commissioner I would make up my mind after I had studied the record and seen the inmates. I would commit myself in no way.

I could have held up the parole of Whitney (as the man for whom I substituted would have), for it took a unanimous vote to bring about the release of an inmate. Any one commissioner held the veto power.

I voted to release him—and not because he was "upper class." He had committed a dastardly act, but it had victimized a few men of wealth, not hundreds of little people to whom a thousand-dollar loss might mean the eradication of their life savings. It seemed to me that the major question was how Whitney would behave when he got out. As a menace or a decent citizen? I felt from his demeanor and his record that the odds were all in favor of his being a respectable citizen. On that proposition I voted his parole.

About Kuhn I felt differently—that he was a danger to any society, would remain a menace, was basically and by preference a criminal, a thug, and a dangerous psychopath.

I didn't, personally, have a chance to vote against the parole of Kuhn, much as I should have considered it an honor and a privilege. The commissioner I replaced came back in time for that hearing. But I freely confess that I did my level best to keep the other board members steamed up against the possible parole of the Bund leader.

Some of the persons who appeared before us testify to the fact that truth is often stranger than fiction.

There was the man and wife serving terms for torturing their own eight-year-old girl. They whipped her, chained her to a bedpost for days at a time, put a red-hot poker to her tongue and legs, and once ran a hot wire directly through her tongue. One bitter cold day, when over a foot of snow had fallen, they divested her of most of her clothes and pushed her out of the house.

What impressed me most, as I talked to these subhuman parents, was the stoicism with which they discussed their acts. They had no noticeable remorse; seemed puzzled that we should consider them sadistic monsters; and remarked, each separately, that they were only punishing the child for her own good.

I remember, too, meeting an incredible person, one of the men involved in the attempted murder of Durable Mulloy. As I recall the facts, a mob made the acquaintance of certain unfortunate derelicts, fed them, housed them, and gave them plenty of liquor. Their lives were insured, with mobsters as the beneficiaries. It was planned to kill each poor bum in such a way as to make death seem accidental.

For Mulloy death by pneumonia was chosen. The mob got him thoroughly drunk, then shoved him into a snowbank, fully expecting him to wind up on a slab in the morgue, the inference being that, while intoxicated, he had fallen into the snow and failed to extricate himself. But Mulloy, perhaps through complete absorption in and by alcohol, had apparently built up a terrific resistance to the elements. Whatever saved him, the fact is he showed up again among his supposed cronies just as they were congratulating themselves on a job well done.

Next time they had a taxi driver run the intoxicated Mulloy over, back up over his body, and run forward over it again. In spite of this cavalier treatment, Mulloy lived to tell the tale and to gain for himself the sobriquet Durable Mulloy, a nickname he had full well earned.

The inmate involved in this plot, like the sadists, was obtuse about the suffering of anyone but himself. He showed not the least remorse. This is something I have noticed in a great many cases involving murder and near-murder. Perhaps the absence of human sensibilities which makes it possible to commit an assault or homicide in the first place explains the inability to feel guilty or unhappy about it later.

Jimmy Hines seemed to me deficient in guilt feeling, too. When he appeared before us at a Parole Board hearing at Sing Sing he showed no contrition. He was evasive and denied having committed any offense whatever. The inference he tried to create was that he had been framed by Dewey to further Dewey's political ambitions. And when the board denied him parole, he sued out a writ, contesting the authority of the parole commissioners. He lost the action. When he next appeared before the board for reconsideration he had turned somewhat sweeter. He shrugged off the writ as a regrettable action, something his lawyer had insisted upon.

Most pitiful of the cases that came before us were the prisoners who didn't want parole. A sad lot, thoroughly defeated, sometimes near-senile, senile, or feeble-minded, they preferred to remain in prison. The prospect of facing the outside world, where they had been so unsuccessful, was too much for them. The necessity of earning a living terrorized them. They were, for the most part, men who had spent many years in prisons and were now too old to begin a new pattern.

There was an old Negro man known in the institution as Pork Chop, because that was what he loved above everything else in the world. A harmless, sweet-tempered man of perhaps seventy-five, he had built up a record of over a hundred arrests for petty offenses.

Smiling warmly, he said to us, "If it's all right with you gen'mens, I'd ruther stay right heah."

"Don't you want to go out?" he was asked.

"Naw, sir!" he said, chuckling. "I got all the comfort I needs right heah. Got no one left on the outside. What I wanna go out for? Got all my friends right heah."

Those friends were the guards, who had given him the butt concession. He was allowed to clean the corridors, appropriating to his own use all the cigarette butts he could find. Usually his pockets were stuffed with them, a not inconsiderable fortune for a prisoner without money. Pork Chop also shined shoes for the guards, in return for which they chipped in now and then and presented him with a pork chop. What more did he need in life? He had cigarettes, friends, a bed, and pork chops.

Another man who didn't seem to care much whether he went out or not very likely thought life in prison was considerably easier than what he would find if he returned to his family in the deep South. There he had a wife and so many children that he'd run out of names. The last two were officially baptized Coca-Cola and Pepsi-Cola. "Couldn't think of no more," he explained.

I was not only perpetually fascinated by inmates, intrigued by the varying techniques and antics of board members, but also very much interested in the institutional personnel. With some of it we had little contact. But directly or indirectly we were influenced in some of our judgments by wardens and psychiatrists.

Lewis Lawes had a tremendous reputation as a great humanitarian and warden. Certainly in the years I knew him his work was slipshod and his institution shot through with favoritism and lax administration.

In my opinion, Warden Bill Hunt, considerably less publicized, ran the best-administered prison in the state at Attica. Discipline was strict yet easy, in the sense that inmates knew just what the rules were; by following them they stayed out of trouble; by infracting them they received immediate punishment. There was no favoritism whatever. A man who did his job got along. A man of great influence outside was exactly as privileged—no more and no less—as the day laborer. I never knew Hunt to ask the Parole Board for special consideration for any inmate. And each of his parole recommendations, pro and con, was carefully considered and taken at face value by the board.

Dr. Walter Wallack of Wallkill Prison was—and probably is—the most imaginative, truly and sensibly humane warden in the state. Except among penologists, his name isn't known—certainly not nearly as well as Lawes'. Wallack runs a medium

security prison, an institution without walls. Someday someone will do him and his prison full justice by telling his remarkable story.

The psychiatrists, where there were such, were also all kinds,
all flavors. There was Dr. Ralph Banay of Sing Sing, who
furnished excellent reports to the board. Dr. Ralph Brancale,
at Attica Prison, was extremely practical and helpful. One
could read his reports and understand them. Not only that,
they made sense. Some psychiatrists rode hobby horses to
death, and, so far as the board was concerned, their reports
were a total loss.

One man was a Freudian who out-Freuded Freud. He once
asked a young lad what work he wanted to do when he left
the institution. The kid said he wanted a job as plumber's
helper.

Aha! The psychiatrist jumped on Freud's back and dashed
madly off into a psychoanalytic nightmare. Plumbing, he reported, of course brings to mind pipes—pipes filled with water.
Pipes filled with water, hmmm? Well, what does that make
you think of? A penis, of course! The boy was jealous of his
father's role with the mother. The lad had "penis envy." He
wanted to be a plumber's helper because it would symbolically
mean he was replacing his father as a man and husband.

Personally, I thought the inmate wanted to be a plumber's
helper because he couldn't be released without a job, the easiest
person to get a job from was his father, and pop was a plumber
who would offer the boy a job.

CHAPTER XIV

The Pumpkin Pie Kid

Of the thousands of cases I observed in prisons and reformatories as a substitute member of the Parole Board, none got such unanimous sympathy and understanding as the Pumpkin Pie Kid. He touched all our hearts. I sat on the board throughout the successive months of the action to be related here and witnessed the developments from beginning to end.

It began with a good-natured argument between myself and Commissioner Joe Canavan. I had read a book—that's really the beginning of it. The book dealt with "short-contact therapy," describing how one could help, influence, change the outlook of a person in one or two brief interviews.

I remarked at this particular board meeting, in suitably academic and pontifical terminology, that I believed it possible, in spite of the tensions of a board meeting, occasionally to influence an inmate by the very manner in which he was spoken to. Short-contact therapy, I said eruditely, was possible and should be attempted by us.

"Who dat?" Joe Canavan asked. He liked to tease me. Now he began to take me for a ride. After each hearing conducted by him he would turn to me and ask, with great respect in his voice, "Dr. Dressler, was that a therapeutic interview?"

Then there came into the hearing room a red-headed, freckle-faced boy of about twenty-three. He was distinctly underage for the norm in that prison, which meant he had seriously misbehaved in Elmira Reformatory and had been transferred as a discipline problem.

By the rotation system we used, it was my turn to open the interview.

"Patrick," I said, "we'd like to consider paroling you. We've got to know something about you and your family, but you won't furnish such information."

"Why don't you go take a flying leap and —— yourself, you —— sonofabitch," Patrick replied.

All three of us sat up, electrified.

"What's the use your askin' me questions?" Patrick went on, his voice rising higher and higher. "You bunch of —— know you ain't gonna parole me anyhow, so go —— yourself, you bastard!" And he got up and started to leave.

The guard took him by the shoulder and spun him back into his chair. Patrick snarled, his choleric face alight with fury.

"If he doesn't want to talk to us, let him go," I told the guard. Patrick gave me a baleful glare and marched out, slamming the door behind him.

Incredulous, we consulted the record again. Pat had been transferred from Elmira because he had incited to riot, stalled in the shop, manufactured a knife, attempted an escape, assaulted a guard, and—the final act leading to transfer—stolen an egg.

Since arriving in prison he had refused to work, resisted an officer, smoked after hours, and falsely claimed to be of a certain religion in order to get an extra breakfast periodically furnished by one of the chaplains. He had last been punished the very morning of the hearing, and he was convinced there wasn't a chance in the world he would be paroled. The hearing must have seemed a mockery to him.

The guard told us he'd see to it Pat received another punishment for his behavior before the board. I asked that he not even report the incident. At my request, word was sent to Pat that he would still be given a hearing should he choose to come in while we were sitting.

Shortly before we were to leave he asked to be heard. He presented himself and in a low tone of voice said, "Gentlemen, I'm sorry for the way I talked. I was nervous. I came in just to apologize. After the way I talked, I'm not askin' to be paroled. I don't deserve parole. I just came in to apologize."

Each board member leaned forward interestedly, ready to consider the boy's parole. But Pat, since his original arrest, had refused to say who he was, where his parents lived, who might be in position to help him. He was practically anonymous. And he had refused to give parole any information sufficient to investigate his background or set up a home or job for him.

I now approached this delicate subject. "You see," I said soothingly, "we're not trying to pry into your personal business. We're not going to force you to go to any home or relative you don't like. We're only trying to understand you so we may help you get on your feet. We've got to know something about you to be able to send you out of here into something that won't start you off with two strikes against you. Will you try to understand that?"

Pat's head was down. He mumbled, "I think I understand. I figured you men was all right when you let me walk out of here without a pinch. I guess I been too suspicious. I guess you do wanna help me."

"You bet we do!" I said.

Joe broke in, "So why don't you give us the name and address of your father and mother, or some brother or sister, who will help you?"

Pat thought it over. When he looked up his face was wet with tears. "Thank you, gentlemen," he said chokingly. "You're treatin' me better than I deserve. But—but it's a hard thing to tell you, after all these years. I'll have to think it over." He couldn't give up his anonymity that easily.

"All right, think it over," Canavan said. "We'll see you next month and talk about it some more."

Pat nodded and left.

"You know," Canavan said, his face serious, "if it can ever be said we influenced a man right at a hearing, I do believe this is the man. I think you really helped the guy in this one talk, Dave."

I shrugged modestly.

Next month the boy appeared again. His prison conduct had improved. He was tense but not surly. After some discussion he gave us names and addresses of his parents and relatives in Brooklyn. He listed schools he had attended and the one job he had held. We said we would see him next month, after investigating his story.

There wasn't the slightest truth in any of Pat's allegations. The school hadn't heard of him; the employer never employed him; the parents and relatives were nonexistent.

When we met him in the prison again, I reproached Pat. Why had he sent us on a wild goose chase? Didn't he want us to help him?

He told us to go to hell, to go take a flying leap, etc., and he slammed his way out of the room.

Even with the noblest of motives, that ordinarily would have been enough for us. There was no earthly reason why we should plead with a man to allow us to parole him. But we were challenged. Here was this lad with the mercurial ups and downs. Here was this business of short-contact therapy. Maybe . . . We sent word we'd see him again if he wished.

He came in, chastened and contrite, apologizing humbly. Joe talked with him this time. He emphasized over and over that we couldn't help the inmate unless he cooperated. We wanted to help, but he wouldn't let us.

At last Pat came out with some new information. He had no idea as to the whereabouts of his parents, he admitted. And if he did know, he wouldn't live with them. He disliked them. He had no use for his several brothers and sisters—except one, a brother in New Jersey, a farmer.

"I don't know if he still lives there, or if he would take me in, but he was all right. Only he got mad at me at the end. He might not take me back."

"Why," Joe asked, "did he get mad?"

"Guess I was a no-good kid, that's all. I haven't seen him since I'm eight, but I still remember—oh, boy!—those pumpkin pies his wife used to make. Mmmhh!"

Now there was nothing Joe Canavan loved more than fresh pumpkin pie. He beamed at the kid. "And you think you'd like living and working on a farm?"

"With pumpkin pie like that, I'd work anywhere!" Pat radiated ecstasy.

After the inmate had left Joe snorted at me, "*You* talk about short-contact therapy! Pumpkin pie, a farm, a brother—and

I save a boy from the chair." He was half-kidding, but half-serious too.

From then on we spoke of Pat as the Pumpkin Pie Kid.

A parole officer visited the farm in New Jersey. The brother still owned it. He scarcely remembered Pat, he said, he hadn't seen him in so many years. He would take a chance, give him a home, put him to work, but "if he don't behave, you'll have to take him right back, I'm warnin' you! I won't stand for no nonsense around here. I got kids of my own to look out for."

So we looked forward with pleasure to our next interview with Pat. He was all aglow as he walked in, grinning from ear to ear. His hair looked redder, his freckles bigger, and his eyes brighter.

We told him we were approving the home and job. He thanked us profusely.

"Now work hard," Canavan admonished. "Convince your brother you mean business."

"Yes, *sir!*" Pat cried happily.

"And we inquired," Joe said slyly. "Your brother's wife still makes pumpkin pies!"

We wished Pat the best of luck, approved his parole, and felt very good about it. We had, we were certain, done some constructive work here.

Two weeks later I led a group of men in a raid on a Riverside Drive apartment where we expected to find two robbers and an arsenal. We did. We also found the Pumpkin Pie Kid, stretched stark naked across a bed, getting over a marijuana jag.

The trio were holding up summer resort hotels in New Jersey. Headquarters was the farm of John, Patrick's brother. Only John wasn't Patrick's brother. He was the gang leader.

He had posed as Pat's brother simply to be able to recruit a good man.

We—all of us on the board—had been very neatly "conned" by our overeagerness to perform a short-contact miracle.

Wherever Patrick is at the present time—and it is in some prison, judging by the sentence he received—I hope he has some pumpkin pie occasionally.

CHAPTER XV

They Can Make Good

Joe McGurk, to coin a name, sat before us at a Parole Board hearing. His face was frigid, his eyes shot fire. His was the cruelest physiognomy I have ever met up with inside a prison.

His unwholesome features were but the mirror of his soul. Of his thirty-five years, Joe had devoted twenty-one to juvenile delinquency and crime. Of his forty-four arrests, forty-one were for assaults, schlammings (near deadly assaults), stabbings, shootings, and other forms of mayhem. For nine years before he entered prison he had terrorized an upstate New York city as leader of a gang of hoodlums who worked at bootlegging, "protection" rackets, and a bit of compulsory prostitution. Every member of his gang was an expert marksman and knife-thrower, and each demonstrated his prowess on numerous and sundry, not to say perfectly law-abiding, civilians and police officers. Big Irish, as McGurk was affectionately called by his henchmen, was himself supposed to have been responsible for the untimely death of at least three persons, one a woman who was about to testify against him. Yet the law dealt gently with him until a new and uncompromising district attorney went out himself, collected the evidence, and put McGurk in jail. From there it was a mere step to court and a five-year prison term—the longest sentence Big Irish had ever received.

Now he was before us, not for parole consideration, but to be told the board regretted it couldn't hold him any longer. He was a "definite sentence man" who, under a law then in force, had rated a "flat" term. Off his five years he automatically earned ten days a month for what was termed, ludicrously enough, "good behavior and work willingly performed." When his sentence, less "good time," was served, it was mandatory he be released. But the difference between time served and the maximum sentence, about a year, would have to be spent under parole supervision.

The commissioner addressing the inmate made it amply clear that the board had no faith in him. If it had a choice it wouldn't release him. Since he had to come out, he'd better watch his step, for he could be returned as a parole violator even though the board had nothing to do with releasing him. (A curious quirk in the then law.)

As I listened, I agreed with every word the commissioner said. I was ready to bet dollars to fruit lozenges Big Irish would be back in the clink within a month. Either that or on a mighty rampage of crime.

McGurk went down to New York—to get away from his old haunts and associates, he said. He took a job in a meat-packing house—a hard, dirty job. He had a tough, unsympathetic parole officer who didn't even try to influence McGurk, considered it would be futile.

We checked Big Irish day and night. We tailed him, frisked him, gave his flat the once over more than once. We never found a thing wrong with McGurk.

He married a winsome slip of a girl half his size and one-quarter his weight, and she became boss lady in the house.

He finished parole satisfactorily. And when I last heard

about him, more than four years after release, he was a hard-working, happily married man.

This story points up two facts. Many men do make good on parole. And sometimes no one on earth can hazard a guess why.

Parole officers are charged with the duty of trying to help parolees so that they readjust satisfactorily into the community. They are supposed to influence men and women to lead better, more satisfying and satisfactory lives, to the end that they no longer want to commit crime.

And if parole officers can't and don't do this at all, then parole has no purpose. The fact is, they do influence some parolees.

But while there are those who change for the better because of a parole officer, there are others who seem to do so in spite of a parole officer. And there are many who, like McGurk, just become law-abiding under circumstances that lead to the belief parole neither harmed nor helped them materially. Big Irish had an officer so convinced the ex-felon would revert to crime that no effort whatever was made to influence him.

For one reason or another, the majority of parolees will not resort to crime again. Women revert less frequently than men; adult males less than adolescents; feeble-minded parolees least of all. I advance no hypothesis on why this should be so.

Many factors contribute to the eventual outcome of a parolee's career. Sometimes an all-absorbing talent or hobby will do it. Joe, a young man under my supervision when I was a parole officer, came out of Elmira Reformatory with a newly discovered skill—he had become interested in painting. The institution didn't have enough work or training courses at the

time to keep all inmates busy, and so the officials were happy
to allow Joe to spend his time at this innocuous pleasure.

When the boy, aged twenty, came out on parole, he was
completely wrapped up in art, wanted nothing else. He held a
job, but his interest was in painting. His spare time was spent
at it. My belief is he didn't have time to think of robberies or
hanging out or girls or much beside his great passion.

He was no genius. You will find him hung in no gallery.
But neither has he been hung anywhere else. Correction: He
hangs in many a kitchen and office. He does calendar art: not
the girlie-girlie sort, just locomotives and bears and trees and
flowers. But, so far as I know, for seventeen years now he has
kept out of trouble with the law.

There was more innate ability, apparently, in another of my
parolees, a flamboyant chap with a fantastically adventurous
background. He had tried his hand at blackmail, grand larceny,
and a slight touch of forgery. Although he thought he had
great dramatic talent he got little enough encouragement from
me. I urged him to get a job of work, stay away from the
flashy stuff. While, to make me happy, he labored behind a
soda counter, deep in his breast he nurtured a secret desire. He
had but a short parole period, and when that was up he figur-
atively thumbed his nose at me and entrained for Hollywood,
where he got a job as technical adviser—on prison pictures.

Occasionally it has been my good fortune to discover a
talent for a parolee. When I was parole officer I had under my
supervision a great big hulk of a boy who was, by examination,
a low-grade moron, close to being *very* feeble-minded. Paul
was built tall, broad, and sturdy. When he shook hands with
me his fingers wrapped themselves almost twice around mine.
His face usually bore an expression of bewilderment; actually

it was because he had to concentrate hard to understand what went on about him. And when he did comprehend, his face lit up in a sweet, childlike smile of gratification.

Paul didn't have a bad record as records go. One pinch for stealing a pair of roller skates; on for striking a streetcar motorman; one for bashing the principal of a continuation school on the nose. Then he went to Elmira, aged eighteen and looking twenty-five, for assault—a real good one. He was walking down the street with his girl, minding his own business, when he heard someone make an ugly noise and an uglier comment about the young lady. Paul couldn't quite make out what the comment meant, but the noise was familiar to him and he took offense. He looked back and saw four fellows standing at the corner. He couldn't figure which of them had insulted the girl, so he strode back and beat them all up. He wound up by throwing one of them through a plate-glass window.

On parole Paul was sweet, docile, very friendly, and anxious to please. The first evening he reported he brought me a box of cigars. I refused it and explained that we didn't accept gifts and he didn't need to offer them. He'd get a fair shake anyhow.

He listened intently, puzzled, then hurt. "You don't want 'em? Dey ain't your brand?" he asked in his strangely soft voice.

"It's not that," I answered. "We aren't allowed to take gifts. But thanks anyhow."

"Me mudder said to ax you, if you don't like dese, would you come to de house for a bottle of wine?"

"We can't take gifts, Paul. Thanks a lot."

"You mad at me?" he asked, his face registering pain. "I done somethin' wrong?"

"Here!" I cried in desperation. "Give me one of those cigars, will you? You keep the rest."

I lit mine, helped him with his. His face relaxed into a broad, happy smile.

"I'm glad you ain't mad," he said softly.

That was the way it went.

But Paul's hands kept getting him into trouble. He couldn't keep them off people. He got into several scrapes, but we straightened them out, on the theory that there was no point in returning Paul as a violator. He was a baby mentally. Unless he really became dangerous, why incarcerate him? I cautioned him, scolded him, and he looked at me, pained and puzzled. Once he agreed, "Yeah. I gotta loin to keep me hands in me pockets. I'm sorry you're mad at me, Mr. Dressler. It won't happen no more."

But it did. One day Paul left for work at daybreak, as usual. (He helped a man who owned a garbage-collection truck.) Somehow (he couldn't explain it later) he felt insulted by a passer-by, hauled off and socked him; the man fell to the pavement—out cold. The cops arrested Paul. Turned out he had knocked out a professional fighter who held some sort of championship.

When the fighter came to, he refused to press charges, on advice of his manager. Humanitarianism had nothing to do with it. It would be very bad publicity to have to get up on the stand and admit that he, a professional, had been knocked out by an amateur in one blow.

So Paul went free, and I got the commissioner to restore him to parole, because I had an idea.

"Paul," I asked him, "how much do you make on the job?"

"Gee, I don't know, Mr. Dressler. I didn't ax him."

"What do you mean? Don't you see what he pays you?"

"Gee, no, Mr. Dressler. He gives it to me mudder."

I found out from her that he earned two dollars and fifty cents a week. (This was during the depression.) His mother didn't mind that he earned so little. She wanted only that he be kept busy and out of mischief.

I asked Paul, "Did you ever box?"

"Who, me?"

"Yes, you!"

"Gee, no. Yeah, now I just remember. In de El [Elmira Reformatory] they used ta let me box in de gym."

"Would you like to try for professional boxing?"

"Could I do it? I t'ought you ain't supposed to fight on parole."

"What do you think you've been doing since you're out? So now fight for money."

I should have known better, of course. He wasn't bright enough to become a clever boxer. He thought of ducking when it was way too late. But my advice changed the course of his life, nevertheless. Paul became a sparring partner for cheap and beginning fighters. He was good enough for that. What gave him steady work was that he at last learned to keep his hands in his pockets. He didn't want to hurt a fellow. He couldn't defend himself effectually. So he invariably wound up on the canvas, with a terrific thud. The fighters loved that.

Paul didn't make a fortune, but he earned more than he would have on the garbage truck. I don't know whether he's still at it. But at least five years after he had knocked out that professional boxer, Paul hadn't been arrested again and was in good standing on parole. I know this because at that time I asked his parole officer to bring Paul in so I could give him his parole discharge papers. The parolee beamed when I explained this meant he didn't have to report any more.

I asked if he had won any fights. His smile vanished, his head dropped. "Gee, no, Mr. Dressler," he mumbled. "You ain't mad, are you?"

I don't know whether I had a special affinity for the feeble-minded or whether it was mere coincidence, but I had another case in which a far from brilliant lad made good, in a manner of speaking. But this was through no newly discovered talent. It was due, no doubt, partly to chance, partly to good fortune, and partly to a passion for gambling.

Johnny was almost, but not quite, as low-grade intellectually as Paul. I had one devil of a time with him. He would disappear for weeks. He would lose his pay gambling on the horses. And, worst of all, I suspected he was working for a bookie. I couldn't prove this, although I tried hard. When I asked Johnny he would grin impudently at me and answer, "Who, me?"

He managed to complete his parole period, largely through my generosity. We had a sort of joshing relationship by then. When he came in for the last time he announced that he had struck it rich, had won several hundred dollars on a horse.

"I knew I couldn't lose. I got the tip from the smartest guy in Brooklyn."

"Who's that?"

"Little Auggie Pisano." (A notorious racketeer of the era.)

Now, Johnny said, tongue stuck deep in cheek, he was really going to go legit.

"Johnny," I asked wearily, "a year from today, will you still be out of jail and legit?"

"You wanna bet?" he asked quickly.

"Sure! I'll bet a dollar."

"I'm entitled to odds, but I'll take it." He grinned. "A year from today I'll be out of jail. That's a bet."

A year to the day, Johnny was in the office.

"So you're out of jail and legit," I remarked.

Johny winked. "The bet was only I'd be out of jail."

Every year, for something like seven successive times, Johnny arrived, we went through the same ritual and he collected his dollar. Then he stopped coming in. I don't know why. I claim him as a "success" case because I haven't heard he's in jail. But between us, five will get you ten, he's not really been legit since he first left the Elmira Reformatory.

If I had a chance to bet on what single factor led most men to settle down to a law-abiding existence, I'd gamble on the love of a good woman. I'd even gamble on the love of just a reasonably good woman. Time after time I have seen a young man, unstable, wild, and irresponsible, fall in love with a wholesome girl and shed his wayward habits. True, I've also known parolees to tie up with the wrong woman—and results were very bad indeed. But on the whole I would say men known to the Division of Parole seemed to be about as successful in selecting satisfactory mates as, say, a random list of just-graduated college men.

Parolees do become good husbands and family men. They do learn to love children. They get into the habit of working for family. Many a parolee can honestly say, "A good woman made a man out of me."

And I can even cite an implausible but absolutely true case of a bad woman who made a man out of her husband.

It wasn't clearly established whether Leo was dull-witted or merely so undereducated and overilliterate as to create that impression. Sometimes he acted quite shrewdly. Like the day he kissed his wife, left home for work, sneaked back a couple of hours later, and found his spouse in bed with his brother Marty. Leo didn't like that. His wife already had one child by Marty. Leo had forgiven Mae that. After all, women are weak. But now! He turned right around, went out, and got blind drunk. Then he smashed a window and grabbed some bottles of whisky. When the police came he smashed the bottles over the officers' heads. All in all, he got himself a nice little sentence —five to ten years, and lucky at that. You don't go around smashing cops on the head in New York.

When he was paroled Leo was advised by his parole officer not to go anywhere near Mae or Marty. He agreed, for, as he said, "No time have I ever looked for trouble. It always come to me."

But it seems that he became restless and unhappy. He felt life wasn't worth living without a family. So, unbeknownst to his parole officer, he went to see Mae, who greeted him with a smile. Leo forgave her everything.

Two months later he came into the office, grinning from ear to ear, to make confession. He was back with his wife, had been for eight weeks now, was no longer restless. There would be no further urge to crime. He was very happy. "I found I'm still a man. I been living with my Mae for two months and we ain't lost *no* time. Last night I became a father!"

I wish I could say he named the baby Marty, but he didn't. It was a girl.

CHAPTER XVI

A Most Unbelievable Character

Sometimes it is the good fortune of a parole officer to influence a parolee constructively by the mere twist of a wrist, by manipulating the environment a bit.

Larry isn't *the* most unbelievable character I've ever met by a long shot, but his story is unusual enough for it to seem advisable to emphasize that Larry did, and I hope does, live.

I met Larry when I was a parole officer. According to the record he was at that time twenty-five years old, intellectually brilliant, a high school graduate, and the recipient of eight arrests prior to this, his first conviction. He had been sentenced to Elmira for grand larceny in the first degree. He had been pretty close to the big time, working with a mob of jewel thieves. His job was to get into swank bars, restaurants, and private parties, to "finger" jobs for the mob. He would inform the boys which ladies had valuable gems and where and when they could be most conveniently purloined. The jobs were burglaries (breaking and entering), not robbery (attacking a living victim). This meant that Larry had to have the suavity and charm to hobnob with potential victims. He had to be able to make friends and influence people sufficiently well to discover, arrange, or surmise when and where a bedizened lady would go to sleep and where she characteristically stached her jewels before retiring. This, you can readily imagine, required a man of considerable talent.

The mob would follow Larry's blueprint and burglarize the lady's jewel case while she slept. For certain reasons, she sometimes wouldn't even make complaint to the police.

Larry was bright and adept enough so that he could have risen to the rank of at least second in command, but he preferred his particular specialty and was quite satisfied with a lesser cut and incidental divertissement. He was extremely important to the boys, who knew a good property when they watched it operate, and realized it would be impossible to find, in their narrow circle, a man as capable of holding his own in the best society.

Then occurred the inevitable phenomenon any statistician could have warned the boys against—the operation of the law of averages: pull the same type of crime often enough and you will be caught.

Larry had fingered a rather plain-looking dowager. Perhaps his heart wasn't in his work. At any rate, when she found her jewels missing one morning she suspected the ingratiating and charming young man whom she had met in a swank night club two evenings before. And by some chance she knew what name and address appeared on his driver's license. She was no fool, this one. And she didn't mind complaining to the police. Larry was apprehended. He didn't have the jewelry, for he himself hadn't pulled the job. He didn't rat on his pals. But when a criminal receiver was caught with some of the gems, he turned in the mob leader and several confederates.

When the criminal aggregation was broken up there remained some unfinished business that would need settlement

at a later date. Only about ten per cent of the loot had passed
to the receiver. Somebody else had ninety per cent. Larry insisted he had never seen the stuff except on milady. Tony, the
gang leader, swore he had passed it on to Hal, his lieutenant.
Hal swore, equally vehemently, he had given it to Larry to
hide somewhere. There the matter rested when the trio, plus
some associates, found themselves in stir.

Hal was convicted but died while awaiting sentence. Tony
was found not guilty—one of those little twists of fate that
make a detective's hair stand on end. Larry received a brief
reformatory sentence.

Upon his parole he came under my supervision.

I instantly suspected him of almost anything. I liked neither
his record nor his looks. He was well dressed, personable, affable, and too damned smooth. But what riled me above all
else was that he ostentatiously carried under his arm, title up
and out toward me, a copy of Will Durant's *Story of Philosophy*. I thought: This is a smart boy, *very* smart. And I wasn't
thinking of intelligence.

Larry was downright smug about me. Invariably courteous,
he nevertheless seemed to be saying to himself, "I must be
considerate of this chap. I'll have to limit myself to simple
language and only the broader facial expressions."

He was sickeningly sanctimonious too, constantly mouth-
ing saccharine aphorisms and mottoes. Opening his eyes wide,
he would remark, for instance, "You can depend on me, Mr.
Dressler. I'll never again offend against society. I've given my
parents enough heartache. I intend to spend the rest of my life
making it up to them. My trouble was that I used to find it
easy to get by on charm. But I realize now that handsome is as
handsome does."

I almost choked him, but hesitated, and the wave of revulsion passed, along with the opportunity. He who hesitates is lost, he might have told me.

I put Larry down for a thief, a thief worth watching.

I had to change my mind a bit within the next two months. Every time I checked I found Larry working—in a factory, at that.

I visited his home. His Old World parents were self-respecting, deeply religious people, comfortably situated. Highly emotional, they spoke rapturously of Larry's behavior. It was obvious they adored their only son. Both the father and mother said they wanted to help keep Larry straight. At any indication of backsliding they would notify me, for they preferred to see their son back in the reformatory as a parole violator than in prison on a new sentence.

When I visited the home at midnight Larry was in bed.

He reported regularly, discussed literature and philosophy with me until my teeth were on edge. He smiled at the skepticism I must have inadvertently displayed, and once he remarked, "Well, that's part of your business, being suspicious. It's part of my business to prove I'm all right. To each his appointed task, you know."

Irritated beyond control, I flew in the face of existing evidence and tailed him on general principles one night. I saw him leave home after dinner, proceed to a coffee pot on Gunhill Road, palaver there with some men, after which all of them went upstairs to a pool parlor. About eleven o'clock Larry left and returned home.

Investigation disclosed that the pool room was owned by Tony, former leader of the jewel ring.

When Larry next reported I swallowed my canary and

asked, "What do you do with yourself after work? You can't stay home every night."

"Oh, I go to a show now and then, that's about all."

"No hangouts?"

"No! I told you! I've caused my people enough heartache. No more of that."

"See any of your old pals?"

"Look! If I see one a block away I duck for the nearest hallway. I'm going to make this parole!"

I said nothing.

A week later his mother asked me to visit. I did. She cried as she revealed that Larry was running around again, becoming evasive. She feared . . .

I tailed him again. Same result. Same hangout.

Next report night I figured I would get Larry to lie again, then crack down.

He came in smiling, as if *he* were the cat that ate the canary. He opened up at once. "You know, if you want to know what I do nights, just ask me. Why go to the trouble to tail me? You have a right to some family life evenings."

He had spotted me, and he now admitted that he had lied about his activities. He insisted, though, that his motives were honest. His old gang, he explained, was trying to locate the jewels stolen in the last job. Larry suspected Tony had them. Tony suspected Larry. Tony insisted Larry must either turn back the gems or go to work for the gang again.

Of course, Larry told me, he had no jewels. He had no intention of starting with the mob again. So he palavered with them as a method of stalling them off. He didn't want them to become rough. He'd been afraid to tell me all this before, he said. "You know, a burned child dreads the fire."

He promised to stay away from the gang entirely. "Next time you tail me, I'll be as clean as an Ionic column."

Then one day he walked in, unscheduled, smiled, and said, "Oh, I see I got here ahead of the cops."

"Huh?"

"Aren't they on the way? I was sure they'd want to question me this morning, so I dropped in."

"Why?"

Just then the phone rang. A detective wanted to know where he could lay hands on Larry. I told him he could come right down to the office.

Larry explained. Last night he had visited a friend in Long Island. An hour after he left, the friend was found in a lot, beaten up and unconscious. This, the parolee said, was the work of the mob. It had a double purpose. It might force Larry back into the gang by indicating what they could do to him, next time. Failing that, Tony would throw suspicion on Larry as the last visitor to the home of the injured man. This, Larry said, proved he was trying to shake the mob.

Whatever it did prove, it didn't establish that Larry had been the perpetrator of the crime, and the police didn't hold him.

I decided the time for action had come. On the whole, I was now ready to believe that the parolee was on the level. I hated his patronizing airs, his kindly concealment of the fact he considered me a moron, but—I had to accept the evidence—he seemed on the legit.

This feeling was confirmed when Larry was shot at in front of his house the same day he had been in the office.

Yes, the time for action had come. I thought I had better hold Larry in the Tombs, get the police to round up Tony and his men, and try to get to the bottom of this thing.

I sent for Larry. He came in, a copy of Spengler's *Decline of the West* under his arm. We chatted aimlessly a minute, then my phone rang. A voice said, "Hello! Dressler? Stacy of the Eighteenth. Is Larry there?"

"Yes."

"You weren't planning to arrest him, were you?"

"Well—" I couldn't talk in front of the parolee.

"Well, listen. The sonofabitch is plenty hot. But the captain asks you turn him loose. We'll tail the bastard right out of the building. We've got him dead to rights. We'll nail him on a new crime. All *you* have is a parole violation. Okay?"

"Okay." I replaced the receiver.

Larry was smiling sagely. "That a detective?" he purred.

"Why?"

"Well, I'll tell *you*. That was *not* a detective. I was tailed here by the mob. They figured they would get me off somewhere where it's quiet and give me the business. Now they think maybe you're sending me back. So they claim to be copper, ask you to turn me loose. I'll leave here and walk right into a bullet in the Bronx!"

"Aren't you being a little fantastic, Larry?"

"You think so? I'm asking you to hold me here. Search the ground floor. You'll spot a guy with a gun. That'll convince you. Then lock me up. I want to go back to the El! I've tried to go straight and they won't let me. I need protection!"

This time there was no mistaking Larry's earnestness. We searched the ground floor, found a fellow in a phone booth, gun in pocket.

I placed Larry in the Tombs and telephoned his parents. They came in and hysterically begged me to send the boy to Elmira for his own protection.

That, of course, was no sensible answer to the problem. I was now convinced Larry had been trying to break away from the gang. Why send him to jail for trying to be law-abiding? I got from the parents the name of a well-to-do uncle of the parolee in a Southern city. The parole authority there investigated him for us. He indicated he would gladly put Larry to work in his business, let him live in his home. The parole authority there would supervise him, furnish us reports.

We sent Larry off. At the train he said, "You know, one of my greatest liabilities is I've got a smooth tongue and I'm no dope. It makes people like you think I'm *too* smooth. You never believed in me, but that was a mistake. You think you're taking a gamble now, and I'll show you I won't let you down." He was carrying under his arm Volume II of Beard's *Rise of American Civilization*.

The change of environment was apparently all he needed. He settled down, married the daughter of an influential politician, and when I last heard from him he was a successful businessman and civic leader.

A stitch in time saves nine, they say.

CHAPTER XVII

A Woman Rediscovers Herself

Ellen was helped by parole to some extent, but mostly it was her own ability to control her destiny that accounts for her story.

Her parents died when she was an infant, and she was raised by a grandmother in a small Pennsylvania village. When she was nine years old she was seriously injured in an accident. A local medico administered a narcotic to relieve pain. From then on, and with gradually increasing intensity, according to the girl, she began to want, then need, the drug. By adolescence she was a confirmed addict. Her grandmother was too aged and enfeebled to realize what was happening.

Ellen would do anything to procure a deck of heroin. She seduced the town physician, then blackmailed him into supplying her with prescriptions. When that unfortunate man died suddenly, Ellen was cut off from her source of supply. In desperation she left home without any explanation, wandered about until she met a taxi driver with "connections." Ellen was his mistress as long as he supplied her with drugs. When he could no longer do so, she pushed off again.

She was was by now a handsome young woman, tall, brunette, of very slim build. Men found her attractive. Yet, at this point in her life, she donned men's garb, cut her hair short, and began to act and feel like a man. Talking about this much later, she speculated that while under the influence of drugs she must have been initiated into this form of sex deviation.

Despite her inclinations, she could change to feminine clothes, become an attractive female, and exercise womanly blandishments in order to interest men and get them to furnish her with heroin.

She traveled aimlessly from city to city, a lost soul, unscrupulous, as all confirmed addicts are. She blackmailed and stole to get heroin. And at last, overcome by craving and unable to procure narcotics otherwise, she entered a drugstore in a New York community, dressed as a man and armed with a gun. She demanded heroin. The pharmacist put up a fight and Ellen shot him. A police car cruising past at the moment quickly seized the girl.

The druggist lived and testified against Ellen, who was sentenced to prison for robbery and assault. She received what was, for a woman, a very stiff sentence. But she was fortunate the crime hadn't been that of murder.

Years later she was released, with something like eleven years of parole before her. She was then thirty-six years old. Her hair was white; otherwise she was youthful in appearance. Away from drugs, she had put on weight, filled out, and no longer had the attenuated figure that had made it possible for her to pose as a man. She was womanly in appearance and asserted she was now a woman by feeling and preference.

Now if Ellen could go on for the rest of her life cured of the hunger for drugs and restored to normal sexuality, it would indeed represent a pretty remarkable feat of self-treatment on her part. There is a general opinion among psychiatrists, I believe, that drug addiction is a neurosis; that an addict rarely

cures herself; that the neurosis must be treated, which means
professional help. Ellen had no such aid. Moreover, passing out
of a confirmed lesbian phase into normal sex life is not easy,
and it is rarely accomplished without outside psychiatric help.
Here again, the girl had to fight the battle alone. Her prognosis
on parole, therefore, was not very favorable.

She reported to a woman parole officer, who recorded that
Ellen was "immaculately neat, pert, and still quite good looking." She was carefully courteous during the interview but
somewhat cold and reserved. She emphatically stated she was
through with drugs. She intended to stay away from her old
haunts and associates, she said, lest she be tempted. She wanted
to go to another part of the state entirely. "I've lived and died
one life. I want to begin again."

She was permitted to move to another city. The parole
officer in that area found a job for her as a kitchen hand in a
restaurant. Ellen took it, even though she was intellectually
superior to that sort of work. She enrolled in night school and
studied stenography. She became interested in some local clubs,
where she acted the perfect lady and was extremely popular.
When the parole officer asked Ellen if she still had any desire
for drugs, she answered frankly, "Yes, at times. But if I don't
drink or run around, if I keep busy, I'm able to fight it."

She had been out about a year and doing well, having risen to
the post of hostess of the restaurant, when she called and in a
tense voice asked the parole officer to come to see her.

Ellen was in tears, almost hysterical, when the officer arrived. She had received an Easter card from a former inmate
with whom she had been intimate, years before, on the outside.
The two had had narcotics jags together. The card read:
"Darling. Remember us? I found out where you are, you

know little me. Now write me and tell me all about things. I'll be out very soon and I'll come see you. Hannah."

The card had been "kited" (smuggled) out of the institution. Ellen very obviously was not at all tempted to resume a relationship with Hannah. She had status in her community, she was happy, and on the way to carving out a new life for herself.

The officer advised the girl to write Hannah that she was all through with the kind of life she once had led. This the parolee did, making it clear she didn't want to hear from the inmate again.

She also changed addresses, moving to another part of the city. She completed school and got a job as stenographer to the head of a dental laboratory.

About four years after her release on parole she came into the office, upset and crying. On the job she had met an elderly man who fell in love with her. She was herself no longer young. She thought she loved the man, a retired engineer. Should she marry him? Should she reveal her past to him?

She was advised to talk this over with her pastor. So far as parole regulations were concerned, she need only tell the man she was on parole. As to the details, she could get the advice of her spiritual adviser.

She married the man, telling him she had gone away for an assault on a beastly employer. What scared her was his remark, "As long as you weren't a murderess, or a drug addict, or something like that, ha! ha!"

The couple moved to another city. To her new officer Ellen often exclaimed, with tears in her eyes, that she was happier than she had a right to be; she had a wonderful man and was going to make him happy.

She became a leading civic worker, and women of the community looked up to her. Her contacts with the parole officer were carefully arranged so that Ellen's record would not become known.

Suddenly Hannah popped up, along with a pal Grace, also a drug addict. They located Ellen, visited her when she was alone, demanded money for drugs, or else they would tell her husband all the dirt about her. Frightened, Ellen gave them what she had and didn't tell her parole officer.

They came back again and again, and the distraught woman began to fake her household budget to get more money. Finally, realizing she had a bear by the tail, she telephoned her parole officer, apprised her of developments, and said she wasn't going to "dishonor the man who made a new life for me." She was going to commit suicide and wanted the officer to explain to her husband what it had all been about.

The officer argued desperately, then said she was coming right out. When she arrived she told Ellen she would have the police track down Hannah and Grace. Surely they would have drugs on or in them, and could be arrested without involving Ellen. The parolee, though, wouldn't consent to getting the women into trouble through her own efforts. She said she would wait for their next move.

The next move was that the local sheriff got an anonymous call to the effect that Ellen's home was a drop for a narcotics ring. Hannah, denied further money, obviously hoped an investigation on any pretext would bring Ellen's record to light.

The sheriff apologetically entered the house and explained to the woman and her husband about the tip. Ellen's husband was furious. Ellen turned to stone. She told the man he was free to search.

Then her husband shouted, "If there's a grain of dope in this house, it's mine!"

That got Ellen. She became hysterical and screamed that she was innocent of any wrongdoing now, but that she had been deceiving her husband about her past. She told the whole, true story.

Her husband broke down and sobbed. "I've failed you, Ellen. You never felt you could tell me this before!" He said he didn't give a damn what she had been, she was the whole world to him now, and that's the way it was going to continue.

We were able to lay hands on Hannah and a taxi driver who had been her confederate in the blackmail. Grace was never apprehended, to my knowledge. But Ellen and her husband were not troubled thereafter.

When she was widowed, a year or so later, Ellen opened an office supply shop and did reasonably well at it. She outlived her husband but a few years.

There are three features of her story that have always interested me. One is that Ellen really licked the drug habit entirely on her own. The second is that she was able to return, quite contentedly, to a normal sex and married life, without the slightest professional help. The third is that, after her confession in front of the sheriff, the latter kept Ellen's background entirely to himself. One careless word would have been catastrophic. The community never found out.

The next time someone makes the usual ridiculing comment about the rural constabulary, I hope you will remember the sheriff in Ellen's case. A local law-enforcement officer often can ruin a reputation in one sentence. It is very difficult, in a small community, to keep the goings on about town confidential. Yet many a small-town police officer carries inviolate the secrets that could wreck careers and lives.

Parole may have helped Ellen a bit. She helped herself much more. But a sheriff made it possible for her to live out the balance of her reconstructed life in the home she had learned to love.

CHAPTER XVIII

Medal of Merit

The "success story" of which I, personally, am most proud, is one that brought me one of my dearest friends—Roy. He was young, not a confirmed offender but well on his way. I did much less for him than he did for himself. That's always the case. The ex-offender himself has to do the work.

Roy was a kid against whom the cards were really stacked. He lived in a ramshackle Brooklyn tenement, son of an alcoholic father and a mother who spent her later years in a mental hospital. Roy's brother was a robber, married to a shoplifter. Two other brothers were burglars. A sister was a petty thief.

The old man was rough on the kids, and Roy spent most of his time out of the house. He took to sampling his father's liquor at eight, playing truant at nine, thieving a ten. At seventeen he was in a reformatory with eleven arrests on his record. He was paroled at the age of eighteen.

That was when I met him, as his parole officer.

He was a handsome lad, of rough-hewn features and slovenly dress. He slouched in his chair, growled answers to my questions, and made it obvious by his surly manner he wasn't having any part of a man with a shield.

I thought, This is a boy I'd better watch.

Next day I visited his home. He wasn't living there. I checked his job. He had been fired for punching the foreman in the nose.

When he reported to me again I asked, "Living at home?"

"Yeah."

"Working at the same job?"

"Yeah."

"You're not telling the truth. I've checked and I know."

He snarled. "Okay! So I lied! I ain't gonna live wid dem bums and I ain't gonna work for no slave drivers. So send me back to de can! I'm gonna wind up in d'electric chair, anyhow, someday!"

Technically Roy was a parole violator. Yet I couldn't really blame the kid for not wanting to live with *that* family. My job was to protect society against the malefactor, but I was also charged with helping men get back on their feet so that they no longer wanted to victimize others.

I decided to try. I arranged lodgings for Roy in a boys' club. I was lucky enough, in those depression days, to know of a job he could fill. He ambled out of the office without so much as a "Thanks."

When he reported the following week he told me, of his own accord this time, that he had quit the job. "De boss got smart, so I punched him."

As for the room, "De beds have bugs and de guys got bats in de belfry." He had been sleeping in parks, and if I didn't like it, "You can send me back! If you don't, I'll wind up in d' electric chair someday, see?"

He was asking for it—and he almost got it. Then I happened to glance down at his wrist. On it was a tattooed a date.

"What's that?" I asked, curious.

His braggadocio subsided. He murmured, "Dat's de date I

went to de ref. I wanna remember dat date as long as I live."

That gave me my first inkling that his toughness was part pose.

"How do you eat?" I inquired.

"I don't, unless I meet a pal."

"You're not involved in any—?"

He sneered. "If I pull a job, you'll hear about it."

"Are you going to pull a job?"

"Not today." He grinned maliciously.

Roy's case could have been handled in one of several ways. He could have been locked up. I could have ordered him into a home and job whether he liked them or not. And I could let him suffer the natural consequences of his actions until he got burned often enough to want to do better because that hurt less. I though the third choice was worth a whirl.

I told him that if he were arrested for sleeping in parks he'd have to take his medicine; but when he was ready to live in decent quarters I'd be there to help him. He stared impudently.

I instructed him to come to our employment bureau every morning and to see me before reporting there. There was method in that last stipulation. I thought that in a relaxed atmosphere I might get under that tough skin. When Roy arrived each morning I would announce, "I haven't had my coffee. Come on out and we'll talk while I eat."

I would offer him breakfast and he would refuse. But gradually he relaxed. One morning he accepted a glass of milk. He chatted a bit.

I discovered that he was incredibly naïve in spite of his tough-guy attitude—which was good. An immature lad is easier to help stabilize than an older man already fully patterned in conduct. Some of Roy's notions were astonishingly childish.

It doesn't seem possible, but once, when at breakfast I asked him why he didn't drink coffee, he snorted, "It gets you syphilis."

"What!"

"Yeah. You drink coffee and you get noivous. Coffee leads to smoking; smoking leads to drinking; drinking leads to goils; and goils give you syphilis. No coffee fer me!"

Of me he was frankly suspicious. "You ain't paid to be nice to us guys. You're supposed to grab us, not feed us."

"Is that how you feel about the law?"

"How else?" he shrugged. "I been kicked around by flat-foots since I was a kid."

Came the day when Roy announced he was ready to sleep in a house. I had found an aunt whom he hadn't seen in years. A fine, comfortably fixed woman, she agreed to take Roy in. He remained a week. She favored her own children over him, he grumbled.

Then we got the boy a summer job in a beach hotel.

He came home suntanned, neat and clean for the first time. And for the first time he shook hands. He took out a notebook and showed me he had recorded every nickel I had spent on him. He put the money on the desk. I took it. His self-respect deserved that.

Roy's attitude changed. He held jobs a little longer. He punched foremen in the nose only every other week. He took a dismal ten-dollar-a-week flat and demonstrated a knack for business. He bought two army cots, knocked together some furniture out of boxes, and rented out one room at ten dollars a month. He cooked for himself and his roomer, charging the latter five dollars a week. He figured he was in clover.

His change in fortune made him feel better about the world.

For once he had a home, a job, some money—the honest way. Maybe he even had a friend. He began to treat me almost as if I were his equal.

On his birthday I sent him a card. He came in, tears in his eyes. "Nobody in my whole life ever done a thing like that," he said.

Somehow he found out my birthdate and came in with some cigars and a necktie. Proudly he said, "I bet when you buy a cigar you pay maybe a dime apiece for them. And a dollar for a tie. Because you don't know how to bargain, see? Know what I paid for them things? The cigars was three for a nickel and the tie a quarter, off a pushcart in Delancey Street!"

The cigar almost killed me, but I figured it was healthy for Roy to experience giving of his own free will. What was my health against his?

I tried to develop in him a taste for a better standard of living. But he wasn't interested in curtains, water closets, electricity, or radios. His home was good enough.

When he became unemployed again I decided to try something most unorthodox. I hired him to clean several thousand books in my home. He would earn some money, I thought, and at the same time see another way of life.

I discovered then he wasn't tough so much as self-conscious. When my wife admitted him he mumbled his name, grabbed a rag, and went to work. Invited to lunch, he sat at the table, eyes lowered, saying not a word except "Yes, ma'am" or "No, ma'am."

Preparing to leave, he loosened up. "I been lookin' this place over. You ain't got no protection against boiglars. Look at them locks! A boiglar could sneeze his way in!" He outlined a plan for security.

"If we get new locks, will that keep burglars out?" my wife asked.

He grinned. "Not a good one like me! You lock your door against the honest man. A good thief can always get in."

We took to inviting Roy for dinner. His self-consciousness diminished. At times he was almost gay. But his progress was uneven. When things got a little tough he would brood, become irascible. Doubts assailed him.

Late one night, during one of his periods of unemployment, Roy showed up at my home, walked into our unlighted living-room without a word, and sat down. I knew something was on his mind. I didn't urge him to talk. I waited for him to be ready to explain why he had come.

For an hour we sat there in utter silence. Then, "My brother's after me to go on a h'ist job," he offered.

"What will you tell him?"

"I don't know. When my luck goes bad, I'm afraid."

"I don't think you're going on a h'ist. If you were, you wouldn't be telling me about it."

"I'm afraid," he repeated thoughtfully.

Then the dam burst. Painfully, through the darkness, he sent across the room all the blackness and doubt and despair that were in him. He discussed his childhood privations, his past crimes, his reformatory experience, his fear that he couldn't make good. For three hours he poured out his heart, alternately upbraiding and defending himself. He examined himself as if he were a doctor looking at a germ through a microscope.

When he had talked himself out I said, "Roy, you've got the guts to face the future or you wouldn't have had the courage to face the past like that. You don't need to fear."

Dawn was coming through the window. The boy arose, his face serene. "Yeah," he uttered, as if in revelation. "I don't need h'ist jobs." He smiled. "So long, Pop! Thanks for listenin'!"

He had long called me Boss. Now it was Pop. And at that stage I was, to him, the father he needed and didn't have. Later I was to become a brother. And I knew the time would come when I could be, not Boss, or Pop, or even a brother, but only a good friend. That would be the final, essential step. It would mean Roy no longer needed to lean on me.

He got another job and kept it. He began to live better, moved into a nicer place, put up curtains. And he bought a radio—"like yours, only I didn't pay as much."

Still, there were times when he doubted himself. Once I asked him to let himself into my apartment and bring me a wallet I had forgotten. He looked at me curiously but went. When he returned he demanded, "Look in the wallet. See if it's all there!"

"I wouldn't know, Roy. I don't remember how much I had."

"What was that," he jeered, "a test? Wasn't you afraid I'd walk off with the joint?"

"No," I answered. "If you can trust yourself, I can trust you."

He grinned. "I ain't sure I trust myself. Look in the wallet!"

The brooding, the doubts, came less and less frequently. As time went on, Roy got better and better jobs. He learned the discipline of work, how to stick to it. He proved to have outstanding mechanical ability. And, of course, he was a natural at business. He made money out of money. On one job he got his regular pay, worked overtime for pay and a half twice a week, bought a little truck and served as bus driver transport-

ing workers to and from the factory; and in his spare time he
did odd jobs for other workers, such as getting their watches
repaired, shopping for birthday gifts, "anything honest for
pay," he explained.

During one period he was preparing to go around the world
as an ordinary seaman on a freighter. He loaded up on wristwatches, dozens of them.

"What in the world are you going to do with all those
watches?" I asked. "Wear them on your ankles?"

He winked. "All sailors are gamblers. I'm going to run a
raffle a week, for a watch. I pay two dollars for one. I collect
twenty-five on the raffle. What's more, I'm taking twenty-
five overcoats, to sell to the Arabs."

"Are you crazy? Who ever heard of Arabs wearing overcoats in the desert?"

"It gets plenty cold there. They'll wear them."

They did.

Wherever he worked, his zeal and steadiness were such that
he soon was promoted. He rose from factory hand to oiler,
finally to foreman in a large plant.

I received several promotions too. "Jeez!" Roy exclaimed
to my wife when she gave him news of my last step upward.
"Pop and I have gone a long way together, haven't we?"

He was right. He had traveled a long journey.

But on one subject he was adamant. He insisted he was of
and in the underworld and would never be a traitor to its code.

"The time will come," I told him, "when you'll decide you
belong in the world, not the underworld."

"Huh!" he snorted.

Yet in subtle ways he was already disassociating himself
from the underworld. He learned through the grapevine that

I was to lead a raid on a dangerous mob. He appeared at the rendezvous of my party and told me he didn't approve of my intentions, "locking up some poor bums." But he didn't want me to get shot, nevertheless. If we crashed the back way, he had discovered, we would be expected and be shot at. Now, if we went up that roof and down the fire escape . . .

And when later my squad emerged, Roy was on the street. A detective playfully made a lunge at me, and Roy, uncertain who he was, popped him on the jaw. Now I was no longer Pop, who could handle himself, but a brother who needed to be protected.

The turning point in Roy's career came shortly thereafter. Walking along the street, he heard a woman scream, saw a man with a gun dash out of a store. Before he realized what he was doing, Roy took after the robber. The man pegged a shot at him, but Roy made a flying tackle, brought the gunman down, and held him for the police.

And then he was aghast. He came into the office, clutching a newspaper with his picture on the front page.

"What did I do?" he moaned. "I was crazy! That wasn't my business! I'm on the other side!"

When the police asked him to testify before the grand jury he flatly refused. "I'm no rat!" he told me vehemently.

"Roy," I remarked, "there's a lot of difference between a rat and a citizen who does his duty to uphold law and order."

"I don't give a damn!" he shouted. "They can't make me testify! Will it be a violation of my parole if I don't, like the cop says?"

"No, it won't. Of course the D.A. can force you to appear, by subpoena. But the decision is up to you. You must decide to protect a robber or the public."

"Then I'm damned sure I won't testify!" And he stalked out.

He testified—without subpoena. And in doing so he cut the last cord that bound him to the underworld. He could walk alone now, unshackled and unashamed, among decent citizens, a member of their world.

That was fifteen years ago. I have been in close touch with Roy ever since. He is married now, has a fine job, owns a home and two cars. He has more money in the bank than I have. He's raising his three children so they won't have two strikes against them to begin with.

I'm no longer Pop or a brother. I'm just a good friend. At times, in fact, Roy treats me as his junior, particularly when I buy something without his advice and he figures—as he invariably does—that I could have got a better bargain. He and his family visit with mine. His children play with mine. Roy has grown up. He doesn't need to be dependent on me because he is sure of himself and has the love of his family.

Looking back, he says he certainly would have reverted to crime except, "All of a sudden a guy with a badge acts like he likes people. I didn't run out on you because there was nothing to run away from."

He's through with crime. Yet he got an unholy laugh out of something that happened when he was in the Army. Home with a chestful of decorations for heroism, he pointed to one citation and guffawed. "How d'ya like that! Me, Roy, the guy with eleven pinches, home with a Good Conduct ribbon!"

CHAPTER XIX

They Don't All Succeed

As I entered the saloon I sensed danger. Something about the crowd at the bar put me on my guard. This would be tough.

But there stood the man for whom I held a warrant. It was my duty to take him into custody.

I walked toward him, and as I did so, five or six men ranged themselves near him, silently challenging me to go farther. Several held stevedore hooks in their hands.

I pulled a gun. There was a rush toward me. I fired, again and again.

As the smoke cleared, the patrons were lined up against the wall, hands up. One lay on the ground, knocked out by a blow to the jaw. My prisoner was handcuffed to me. I replaced my gun and swung out of the place, the parolee docilely accompanying me.

No, it didn't happen like that at all. But that's how it was reported by a female reporter for a New York paper. "Dr. David Dressler, the youngest Chief Parole Officer in the country," she clarioned, was a hard-hitting, dashing, two-gun guy in a Stetson hat. Her story caused me so much chagrin that I had to write to friends and professional associates, explaining that the story had not come out of my mouth.

Actually what happened, and what the reporter's feature article was based on, was this: I walked into a saloon to arrest a man for parole violation. He *was* there with friends; he *did* have a stevedore hook; his friends *didn't* seem to like me.

I came up and said, "Pat, let's have the hook."

He gave it to me.

I said, "Let's go, Pat!"

He went.

But it is a fact that parole officers must take chances and are bound to get into dangerous spots at times. About fifteen per cent of parolees are convicted of new crimes while under supervision. Maybe a few more fall by the wayside after their parole terms are up, but probably less than another twenty per cent. That means some seventy per cent will behave pretty well. The fifteen per cent, though, can be dangerous.

There has been a lot of argument as to whether parole officers should make arrests, but I won't go into that here. I'll just say that I'm convinced a parole system that's worth its salt *has* to make its own arrests, with the cooperation of the police. It *has* to protect the public. Therefore a parole officer never knows when and where trouble will pop.

I had a young Elmira boy under my supervision. He lived in Long Island but constantly hung out in Harlem. I didn't like that, because it was through association with hoodlums there that he had committed the crime that brought him to the reformatory.

Although I warned him to stay out of Harlem, I received information that Otto was back in his old haunts. When he next reported I laid down the law. If I ever found him in Harlem, I would arrest him on sight.

A week later I discovered that Otto not only continued to frequent the forbidden territory but was associating with, and probably working for, a young thug, Roberto, leader of a gang of petty thieves.

I went into Harlem and, by rare chance, while walking along, spotted Otto, plus Roberto, plus four other evil-looking lads. They saw me too. At once they lined up across the sidewalk, forming a barrier. Otto took off and into a tenement. There was no point in pursuing him.

This was a situation that had to be faced. If I turned and walked away, I would never again be able to control a single Harlem parolee, for word gets around fast. If I piled into the men, I'd get my brains knocked out; I couldn't lick them all.

I decided to take a chance. I'd make the leader lose face. As the group stood glowering at me I walked swiftly up, grabbed Roberto by his shirt, and threw him against a stone wall. He landed with a thud. The other boys sauntered away as if they had just been passing by and were going to keep on passing by.

I heaved a sigh of relief as I observed a uniformed policeman round the corner. To attract his attention, I took hold of Roberto again and shook him back and forth. "You sonofabitch!" I said, emboldened by the success of my maneuver. "I'll punch you in the nose every time I see your ugly puss around here!"

By this time the cop was upon us. Manfully I threw Roberto against the wall once more, and as he bounced I reached into my pocket to get my shield, to identify myself.

Whacko! The officer's club hit me a vicious blow on the head. I reeled. The cop pulled a gun and rammed it into my belly.

"Reach for that gun again, you lousy bum, and I'll blow your brains out!"

My brains weren't down there, but right then I learned

never, but never, to reach for even a handkerchief when in the immediate environs of a policeman.

About Otto—I got him that night. He went back to the reformatory. Lucky at that. He beat a burglary rap, even though he was guilty.

The most terrifying moment of my life was handed me by a parolee known to the underworld, for excellent reasons, as Harry the Ape. He was one of the first cases I had to supervise. Harry had finished a prison term for robbery and assault. The latter offense had been so brutal that it had led to considerable publicity at the time. After relieving his victim of his wallet, Harry had pitched into him with bare fists and smashed the man's face into such a pulp that it didn't even faintly resemble a human being's. "The guy gave me some lip," Harry later explained to police.

I interviewed him the first day he was out of Sing Sing. He towered eight inches above me, weighed about two hundred and fifty pounds, and every ounce was iron muscle. His prognathous jaw was blue, his nose flattened, and his brow beetled. He chewed a cud of tobacco. His arms hung like a gorilla's. His hands were hams.

We were in my office, and his first words scared me out of six inches of growth and at least that many months of sleep. I had introduced myself, told him that I was his parole officer and that I would be calling at his home soon. He glowered at me through bushy eyebrows, his beady eyes showing no intelligence whatever. In slow, measured tones he growled, from deep down, "You try to get in my house, mister, and I'll break you in two." He said it quietly, without heat. I knew he was only making a statement of fact.

They Don't All Succeed

I was young and chipper in those days—and there were forty
other parole officers in the room. So, scared as I was, I squeaked
that I would, by God, visit his home, and if he refused to admit
me, I'd consider him a parole violator and bring him out—that's
what I said—bring him out "vertical or horizontal, whichever
you prefer!" My voice quavered a little and I hoped Harry
would construe this as anger.

He was kind enough not to laugh in my face. He merely
brushed me off. He looked at me, spat, grunted something, and
left. I told myself—and the forty other officers—that the grunt
signified Harry the Ape had given in to Dressler the Intrepid. I
would, I averred, visit his home the very next day, just to make
my moral victory decisive.

I made good my threat. With beating heart, I touched the
bell of his Bronx apartment. I pressed just once, waited exactly
one second, then started down the steps. But I stopped. If I left
now, I reflected, I'd never be back—I knew that. So I waited.
Happily no one answered even when I rang a second time.

My troubles seemed over. Harry the Ape never reported to
me again. He didn't live at home. He became a parole absconder
immediately, and a warrant was issued for his arrest. Theoreti-
cally I was supposed to keep searching for Harry, but I wasn't
overconscientious, feeling reasonably certain my missing ape
man would be arrested on a new charge sooner or later.

There followed a series of robberies in which each victim
described a behemoth of a man—or gorilla—who had shoul-
dered his way into a liquor store, gun in hand, just as the place
was closing. And each time the gunman, loot collected, had
beaten his victim into complete insensibility. Several of the
unfortunate men had been near death, hospitalized for weeks.

Meantime I was diligently supervising more tractable and

less hairy parolees, which carried me to every part of the city.

I was on the Lower East Side one afternoon, to visit a parolee in a dank, cold-water tenement flat. I entered the vestibule and mounted the stairs. It was dark, and I stumbled a bit. I reached the first landing and started along it toward the stairway leading to the upper flight. As I approached it, a door opened, and in the dimness I vaguely discerned a figure coming toward me. I paid no attention and moved forward—until the figure stopped, almost colliding with me. I stopped, focused my eyes in the darkness, and looked upward at the man standing two feet from me and towering almost a foot above me.

It was Harry the Ape.

He had his hand in his jacket pocket. He stared directly at me and grunted, "I got a gun in this pocket, mister." I heard a click as he spun the chamber.

By the grace of Providence I had my hand in my jacket pocket too. Cornered, I could only defend myself.

"I've got a gun in my pocket, too, Harry." And I let him hear a click. "We might kill each other, I might kill you, you might kill me. But *my* pistol has a hair trigger."

We looked at each other.

"Kill me," I went on, "and you get the chair. If I kill you, I'm in the clear. And . . . I . . . have . . . a . . . hair . . . trigger."

His lifeless, imbecile eyes stared at me, unblinking. His brow knit ever so slightly.

"Give me the gun, Harry," I urged quietly. "You'll get a Sullivan Law rap and save yourself the chair or the morgue."

It took about three seconds—the most terrifying I have ever spent. Slowly Harry lifted the gun out and handed it to me.

I placed it in my pocket, snapped handcuffs on my prisoner, and we started down the stairs.

I almost collapsed going down—this time from relief. Harry the Ape had had a gun in his pocket; in mine I had had a can of pipe tobacco. The click Harry heard was the lid snapping open.

.I wasn't an uncommon specimen in the Parole Division. Other officers encountered danger in various forms, proof that not every parolee "makes good." One man was viciously beaten over the head with a blackjack. Another was walking along Fourteenth Street one night when a figure came out of the shadows and knocked him cold. This was done on general principles by a parolee who just didn't like people who carried shields. Later this parolee achieved fame of a sort. He went to the electric chair—one of the Mad Dog Espositos.

Some years ago a man named Pechter was kidnaped and held for ransom. I received a call from a man who identified himself only as Morris, saying he wanted to negotiate the ransom and would do so only through me. I didn't know why I was elected, but I made arrangements to go to a certain house in Brooklyn to meet my mysterious caller. Naturally detectives were going to act as backstop, but they would have to remain a block away, lest they be spotted and the whole deal fail.

When I entered the house in question I found Morris to be an insane man who knew as much about Pechter as I know about baking rye bread. But Morris knew how to swing a hammer, and this he was prepared to do the very second I stepped in. Fortunately he started swinging just before I got the door closed. I zoomed through what was left of the opening and sizzled right down the street at a clip so fast I was half a block past the detectives before I could slow up.

Another time I was having trouble with a parolee whom I suspected of gang affiliation. He denied it, but my information was good. When I threatened Pasquale with arrest if he didn't desist from his criminal associations, he became surly and practically threatened *me*.

Then I received a telephone call. A subdued or muffled voice said, "Mr. Dressler, we wanna see you—about Pasquale."

"Who are you?" I demanded.

"We wanna see you," the voice persisted. "You better come see me. You'll be sorry if you don't." His tone was downright sinister.

I said, "Give me your address. Maybe I will come see you."

"Pasquale, he will bring you." And the voice now sounded like that of Orson Welles.

I hung up, determined to get an explanation of this from Pasquale.

Meanwhile I walked along the streets looking furtively over my shoulder, ready, in a split second, to dive down some sewer.

Pasquale, when I spoke to him, denied he had any idea who could have telephoned. "You can't make me take de rap on *dat!*" he grumped

I received another call, from the same person, I guessed. This time I agreed to come. Pasquale would call for me.

I arranged to be tailed by a group of parole officers and detectives. "Make note," I pleaded desperately, "of the exact minute I get into wherever it is I'm going. If precisely thirty minutes from then I haven't come out, or haven't pulled down the blind as a signal, you get up there and kick the door right in!"

The day in question, and Pasquale, arrived. He was grinning. His scowl was bad enough; a grin was positively unnerving.

"Now I know who called ya," he purred. "Before I didn't know. Now I know."

"Who was it?" I queried.

"Me uncle," he said, chuckling ghoulishly.

"Oh!" I sarcastically exclaimed. "Your uncle, eh?"

"Yeah!" Pasquale burst into a sardonic laugh. "Me uncle. He wantsa talk to ya about somp'n."

I let him see me strap a gun on. I saw to it he observed me sticking a blackjack into my pocket. Ostentatiously I slipped handcuffs into the other pocket.

"Come on!" I quavered.

We took a subway and rode interminably; got off and took a cab; left it to climb a stairway leading up a hill. We emerged on something called Pinehurst Avenue, in Washington Heights. I groaned at the realization that my colleagues would certainly not be able to tail us up this hill without being conspicuous. They might not be able to reach the top in time to observe what house we entered.

"In here," Pasquale said. As we walked into the rather respectable-looking apartment house I caught a flash of one of our men getting to the top of the hill. By the time we were mounting the steps, my colleague was right behind us, until he saw what apartment we were bound for, whereupon he went up an additional flight as if that were his destination. The apartment was number sixty-two. Pasquale rang.

Immediately the door was flung open. An arm shot out and grabbed me. It pumped my dank and flaccid hand, at the same time propelling me into the apartment. The door shut—hard.

My host was a roly-poly little man, about sixty years old, who could not have been above five foot nine in his shoes. His paunch made it seem most unlikely that he could do much garroting or even schlamming. And his face was positively angelic.

It was indeed Uncle Vito, a lovable old man with a delightful vein of humor and an accompanying cackle that made him sound like a hen that has just laid a basketful of eggs. Uncle Vito didn't exactly talk—he squeaked.

Briefly, he wanted to bribe me. He did so out of sheer naïveté. That, he earnestly believed, was the way to do the business at hand.

"You, Pasquale," he squeaked. "Getta the vino for the gentleman!" Pasquale hopped to obey the order.

Uncle Vito wanted to pay me money so that I would allow Pasquale to leave town. Why, I asked, did Pasquale want to leave town? Pasquale, it seemed, *didn't* want to leave town. Uncle Vito had decided Pasquale was *going* to leave town and had arranged with Uncle Fiori in Paducah, Kentucky, to take Pasquale and "make a man outta da loafer. He's-a gonna make him a-work in da factory. Make a man outta him."

I explained that if the proposition was *bona fide*, we would approve it without my receiving a bribe. If it wasn't on the up and up, a bribe wouldn't help. We'd look into it, investigate. How about Pasquale? Was he prepared to go?

"You, Pasquale!" Uncle Vito frowned fiercely at the parolee. "You wanna go see Uncle Fiori?"

Pasquale licked his lips. "Yeah, sure, Uncle Vito," he muttered.

The business of the day being settled, Uncle Vito called in the rest of the family. Had he been a gangster planning to ambush me, he would have been eminently successful, for he had the facilities, I discovered, for secreting an Army division. I would have sworn there was not a soul in the apartment besides us three. But now, out of nooks and crannies, came Mrs. Uncle Vito and an assortment of nieces, nephews, sons, daughters, and grandchildren—to a total of eleven.

Uncle Vito uncorked a bottle of red wine. He filled glasses, then handed me one. He lifted his and prepared to make a speech. The rest of the clan waited respectfully.

"I drinka to my friend, da parole officer, Mr. a-Dressler," Uncle Vito said. "He's a fine friend da whole family. He's a-gonna make a man outta dis loafer, Pasquale. I drinka to our friend . . ."

Crash! The door broke off its hinges and slapped against the wall. A second later two detectives vaulted into the room, guns drawn.

It had been exactly thirty minutes since I entered the apartment. I had forgotten to pull down the blind.

Unfortunately not all cases in the dubious category ended as happily as Pasquale's. Angelo's story is quite different.

He was an affable but not very bright boy. He was not feeble-minded, yet not what you'd call of average intelligence either, and he didn't do miraculously well in the parochial school he attended.

This made his mother most unhappy. (The father didn't count. He did what mama said.) She believed that everything one wanted in life could be gained by hard work and prayer. Angelo's school failures, therefore, must be due to laziness and insufficient time spent on his knees.

She whipped him out of his laziness and onto his knees. She read him moral lectures and led him in prayer. She promised him Paradise if he studied and Hell if he failed 4A.

He failed. He was so frightened he ran away from home.

When the family caught up with him, mama whaled him, prayed with him, then, being basically a good woman, promised him anything he wanted if he would work hard at school. Angelo picked something he had yearned for most of his life —a cornet. He got it, even though the family could ill afford it.

Thus, at age eleven, the boy became a musician. He was fairly good at the cornet, and he dedicated his life to it. He gave up his playmates for it. He also gave up studying.

His mother devised a fiendish punishment. For any bad reports from school, the cornet was taken away for a certain period of time. Angelo fumed and raged and suffered under this system until he attained the age of seventeen. He hadn't finished school yet, and it is doubtful if he had the capacity ever to finish. But his mother insisted, and Angelo reluctantly persisted. Then one day, as punishment, she not only took away the cornet but sold it.

Angelo left home. Soon he was arrested for petty theft. Next he stole a bicycle. Then he burglarized a store. He was arrested in a pawnshop, dickering for a cornet, and was sent to the Elmira Reformatory.

I was his parole officer when he came out. He was nineteen, dark, wiry, with a massive shock of black hair. He could be most genial, with a broad, endearing smile. Or his face could take on a diabolical expression when he was angry. Then he seemed murderous. That is how he looked, as a rule, when he mentioned his mother. He never called her "mother," incidentally. It was always "she" or "her." "She wants me home eight o'clock every night. . . . I ain't gonna give her a cent." He had been more or less forced to return to live with "her," since he would not have been paroled otherwise.

He went to work, paid his mother for room and board, and

put some money aside toward a cornet, which he eventually was able to purchase.

He came bouncing into the office one day, his face aflame with joy. Grinning mysteriously, he opened a bag and extracted the instrument.

"Look at it!" he gloated. "Ain't she a beaut?" He lifted it to his lips and let out a blast of martial notes that brought other officers scurrying. A few cadenzas and a couple of minutes later, Angelo put down his cornet and panted, "*She* ain't gonna lay hands on this one!"

During the immediately ensuing period my principal occupation seemed to be visiting the family, urging the mother to bear in mind that her son was grown up, that he could no longer be treated as a baby, and that he merited some respect and affection rather than punishment and rejection. She would agree in theory but add, "He's-a my boy. He no gonna grow up a bum! He's-a got ta go ta church, ta make confession, ta . . ."

Each time the mother upset Angelo, he would go into a veritable manic spell, raging and roaring at her. She would become hysterical, go on her knees and pray. I would be sent for on occasion, and I would try to restore the semblance of peace and extract a promise from each to behave.

Basically it was an unwholesome, untenable situation. Sooner or later, I knew that Angelo, erupting into one of his violent rages, would strike his mother. I tried to get her to agree to allow him to live elsewhere, but she would have none of that, although he very much liked the idea.

He became somewhat attached to me and would drop into the office when he was particularly blue or upset. Once he remarked, "My father, he don't do nobody no harm, but he don't do nothing for me, either. *Her*, you know what I think of *her!*" Then he grimaced to show he was only kidding and said, "I'll have to adopt you for my family."

In truth, it wasn't so much that he liked me as that he needed someone before whom he could blow off steam. His one real love was his music. When I once told him that he seemed not to want to give anyone much affection (meaning his parents), and that I believed he perhaps didn't feel the sentiment of love, he remarked, "I never had no practice at it when I was a kid." He was no doubt right.

The big blowup came when Angelo had lost his job, about the fourth in a row. His mother reproached him angrily, since he had been fired for laziness. He replied in kind. In a frenzy she grabbed the cornet, threw it to the floor, and jumped on it.

With a roar Angelo lunged at his mother, shoving her over so that she fell to the floor. Leaning down, he deliberately slapped her face and left the house.

He didn't report to me after that, and I had to issue a warrant for him. I didn't hear from or about him for months. Later I discovered that he had become a bandit, going on periodic forays. He would rob at the point of a gun, get himself a bit of a grubstake, then retire to play the cornet until his money gave out. He lived in a furnished room.

Curiously, now that religion wasn't forced on him, he became very much attached to a priest. Angelo visited him frequently and divulged, among other things, that he was a parole absconder. The priest urged the boy to surrender himself, but, the counsel falling on deaf ears, he dropped the subject. He suspected, he later told me, that Angelo was engaging in crime, but, without proof, he could hardly face him with it. He made the boy welcome and tried to help him.

Then Angelo fell upon unusually hard times. He pawned his gun, couldn't redeem it, and was unable to commit a stickup. He broke into the church poor box and stole a few dollars.

The priest suspected Angelo and said so, but the parolee denied the theft. The priest, however, telephoned me and told me where I could pick Angelo up.

I came upon him in his room. When he saw me his face hardened, his jaw tightened. He looked sinister. "The Father turned me in, did he?" he snarled.

Meanwhile the police had taken latent fingerprints off the poor box, which proved to be Angelo's. He was formally arrested on complaint of the good Father who had befriended him.

Angelo was taken to the Tombs to await trial. Next day he went berserk in his cell, shrieking and sobbing hysterically and tearing up his bedclothes. When a guard rushed him he tried to kill him. He refused to come out of his cell, and the personnel let him remain there, hoping he would quiet down. However, he announced that he proposed to tear the cell block down, and that he would come out quietly only if I came to see him.

I was sent for. When Angelo saw me he did calm down. His body trembled, his jaw quivered, his eyes were glassy. He recognized me, but he was completely mad. He let me put him into an ambulance, and they took him to Bellevue.

Grimly I went to break the news to his mother. She let out a shriek, fell to her knees before a picture of the Virgin Mary, and moaned, "It's-a da family, it's-a da family!"

When she was more composed she brought out a photograph album and related a story that made the shivers run up and down my spine.

Angelo had almost perfectly recapitulated the history of an uncle in Sicily. The album showed the latter as a dark, mustachioed man with a massive shock of black hair. He closely resembled the parolee.

This man, as a boy, had been somewhat lax in his religious obligations, and remiss in his school work. He too had cherished a musical instrument. His parents forbade him to play it. They considered other than church music sinful. He ran away, served time for petty crimes, came out of prison, and became a notorious bandit, a sort of Robin Hood character. A priest befriended him, either not knowing or pretending not to know the bandit's true identity. The padre often gave Angelo's uncle a bed for the night or a meal.

Then the priest came upon the bandit rifling the poor box. By moral suasion rather than force, he was able to bring the thief to the police. In jail the musician-bandit went mad and committed suicide.

Almost step by step Angelo had followed the life pattern of his uncle. He even attempted to commit suicide in the hospital. When last I heard about him, many years ago, he was enduring a living death, incurably insane.

Crime and Happenstance

There is some difference of opinion, in and out of the under-world, as to whether crime pays. There are several ways of regarding the matter, hence a number of possible answers, including yes, no, maybe, sometimes, and never.

No one can precisely figure the odds on arrest and conviction because all the best-laid plans of men in crime are subject to devastating disruption by at least one factor—coincidence.

To illustrate, here are some cases in which men officially became "parole failures" through happenstance. That is, they were detected by sheer chance.

As head of the New York District I instituted, at the request of Commissioner Canavan, a system for centralizing granting parolees permission to leave the city when necessary. Were it not for this system, five men would have escaped prison terms.

Parole officers were frequently found to be lax in investigating why a parolee wanted to take a trip out of town. Sometimes men were allowed to leave the district under most unsatisfactory conditions. One parolee asked to go to New Jersey to buy snake plants. He went across the river, with permission, and shot a rival racketeer. Certain notorious characters were allowed to travel about for their health, said health usually to be found at race tracks in season.

So we made it a rule that if a parole officer thought a parolee should be allowed to leave the immediate area, he must submit a memorandum and recommendation to me. Thus all such communications came to my desk.

Parole Officer Smythe had under his supervision a man named Ralph, a lazy, shiftless fellow who never held a job longer than a month at a time. He wasn't concerned over the fact that his family subsisted on relief most of the time.

Smythe ordered Ralph to report to the employment bureau daily.

"You want me to come in every day?" Ralph asked. "Then give me carfare."

"Walk in if you have to," Smythe roared, "or skate in on your backside!"

Faced by the horrifying possibility that he might find himself employed, Ralph asked for permission to visit an uncle in Riverhead, Long Island, a farmer named Jones. If he stayed the week end, Ralph said, he might wangle himself a job on the farm. "That's woik I like!" cried the Bronx-born and -bred parolee.

I read Smythe's memo recommending the trip and scribbled across it: "No. If this man wants to work, let him work in town." I put the note aside, to be reconsidered when I'd cooled off.

Several hours later I received two memos from, respectively, Officers Williams and Gates. The former requested permission for parolee Frank to visit a cousin named Jones in Riverhead. Gates asked that parolee Pete be permitted to spend the week end with his nephew Jones in Riverhead.

Obviously a plot of some sort was afoot for a rendezvous in Riverhead. The men concerned, each under the supervision of a different parole officer, hadn't expected central clearance of information.

We allowed the three to go. Then, in concert with State Police and a federal probation officer, we called on Mr. Jones. He did have a farm. He also owned and operated a counterfeit plant. This was the week end when the "green goods" was to be given to some smart lads for distribution. Five men went to prison because the parole office had centralized its procedures.

The fate of Mike hung on a different kind of accident. If he had invested a quarter and destroyed the evidence, Mike would have spared himself a rap and his pal might not have taken a trip up the river.

Detectives were working on the case of a mob suspected of bank robberies and other crimes. Under a court order, the police tapped the telephone of one Sam, who was supposed to be the leader. After months of wiretapping and surveillance of suspects, however, it became clear that Sam was not the leader. The identity of the latter could not be ascertained. The police had no address for him, did not know what his nickname might be, let alone his name, and had no description of him. There was but one possible clue: he usually got in touch with the mob through another person, a parolee, Mike. Mike never visited headquarters; he telephoned messages and instructions to Pinky, who usually answered the phone in the apartment where the mob hung out.

The time arrived when the police could wait no longer. It became imperative to crash the flat at once. The ringleader would not be there. But, after that raid, the police planned to dash to Mike's house, hoping to glean some evidence there that might lead to the boss.

On the appointed day police crashed the headquarters flat and arrested six men. They found a trunkload of money stolen from a bank and a veritable arsenal.

Then they dashed to Mike's home. I met them there, with the parole officer in charge of the case.

Mike received us calmly. There was, he knew, no direct evidence against him. In surly tones he denied any imputation of association with criminals. He denied having called the headquarters flat. He denied knowing whoever might be the boss of the outfit.

We searched the place thoroughly: nothing at all in the way of incriminating evidence was found. But, going through a drawer, I came upon a card handed out by sidewalk photographers to people whose pictures they allegedly (and sometimes) snap. Send in the card with a quarter and you get the picture. Mike hadn't done so.

We held him in jail on suspicion. I invested two bits. Back came a photograph showing Mike walking down the street, one arm about the shoulders of a man I immediately recognized as another parolee. He was the boss.

Another parolee, Jerry, was wanted for hijacking. When police and parole officers hit his house only his wife was home. We remained in the apartment all night, arresting man after man who came by. But no Jerry. He went on the lam, and efforts to locate him failed completely. We had the henchmen but not the leader.

Several months later, on a steaming hot day, two detectives were driving along the Lower East Side when they developed a flat tire. Cursing, they got out and jacked the car up. The usual crowd of gawkers gathered. As the sweating officers bent

over their labors a man detached himself from the crowd and
came over.

"Want a hand?" he politely asked.

They looked up. It was Jerry.

Had he been less courteous he would have spared himself
some years in prison.

It's that occasional break that restores one's good humor.

Even more fantastic was the coincidence in the Tresca case.
It produced happenstances that hit the front page of every
newspaper in New York City.

We had a parolee, named Carmine Galante, about whom
we were vaguely suspicious. There was nothing definite against
him, but on general principles we felt he should be tailed to
see what happened.

We also had a parole officer new at the business. As part of
his training we wanted to give him some surveillance work
and assigned him to tail Galante out of the office when the
latter next reported. An experienced officer was to accompany
and help the newer man. The plans were so laid, and I thereafter lost contact with the situation.

Several days later, coming to the officer on the subway. I
read in the paper about the sensational murder of Carlo Tresca,
philosophical anarchist and a man apparently respected and
admired by some highly respectable people, including Mayor
La Guardia. Tresca had once hurled a bomb at Mussolini.

Last night, it said in the paper, as Tresca walked along the
street, a car drove by, shots were fired, and the car swung
away, leaving the anarchist dead. A car, presumed to be the
murder vehicle, was found abandoned a few blocks down,
near a subway kiosk. The paper listed the license number.

I got to the office and plunged into the day's work. Toward noon I picked up a report furnished by the supervisor detailing how the new officer had tailed Galante. The parolee loped out of the office so fast, he said, it was impossible to follow him without becoming conspicuous. Galante ran to a car that stood in front of the new Tombs building, its motor running, the door open, and jumped in. The car speeded off. The officer could record only the license number and the time—seven-forty P.M.

Something about the report was vaguely disturbing, but I couldn't put my finger on it. I came back to the document several times, puzzled.

Then the solution was brought to me. Parole Officer Sydney Gross, the experienced man on the Galante operation, came in excitedly.

"The Tresca murder car, the one that was abandoned— the license number is the same as on the car Galante drove away in!"

At seven-forty that car had driven Galante and an unknown person away from the Tombs building. At about eight o'clock that car had carried the person who fired the fatal shots that killed Tresca.

I don't know why Tresca was murdered. There have been all sorts of theories. It remains a murder not quite solved. My guess is that Tresca was killed for political or other reasons by hired killers who themselves had no political affiliations. They simply murdered for a price.

Galante, arrested, was not convicted of the murder, and, last I knew, was freed after a parole-violation sentence. He refused to confess to any murder, naturally. As long as the driver of the car remains unapprehended, there is no inducement for anyone else who may have been in the car to talk. There is no chance of playing one man against the other. There is no proof or legal imputation that Galante was the triggerman or anywhere near the scene of the crime.

All I can say is that Galante was in a car carrying certain license plates. Twenty minutes later a car bearing those plates passed Tresca and someone from inside shot and killed him. Galante may have been in the car at the time. He may not.

But he wouldn't have become a suspect, been arrested, served a violation of parole term, except for the curious coincidence that he was tailed on general principle the very night the murder occurred. And Officer Gross remembered the license number when he read it in the paper.

CHAPTER XXI

One Side, Watson!

Everyone who knows that I have done law-enforcement work assumes I am fairly popping with experiences of brilliant deduction. Actually, detection rarely operates as it does in whodunits. Examination of cigar ash and analysis of dust found in pants cuffs play little part. Deduction is indeed necessary, and there is a peculiar fascination about it. But just as often as not, the direct, bull-in-the-china-shop technique winds up a case.

I did my most concentrated imitation of Arsène Lupin in the case of Giovani, who was parole public enemy number one for years. When he was being taken from the office to the Tombs as a parole violator, two men hopped out of a car and knocked the parole officer down. Giovani and his confederates sped off.

I was senior parole officer at the time. As a matter of staff morale it seemed important to organize a relentless search for the absconder.

It *was* relentless. And it continued for a decade. During that period there was scarcely a week when a posse wasn't out following a clue or a hunch. Working on the Giovani case became such a habit that whenever a parole officer wanted a night out he told his wife he was assigned to work on it, and she believed him implicitly. I think we did some fair detective work in the case.

An efficacious principle in police work is: Figure where a man is going to be. Get there first, and let the thief come to you.

We figured Giovani would come home for Thanksgiving or Christmas. We watched his parents' house. No luck. We kept a constant check on family doings. On the birthdays of members of the family, the house was under observation. On his mother's anniversary, Giovani drove up in a flashy Cadillac. We waited for him to re-emerge from the house. He left the back way.

Some years later a sister was getting married. Giovani, obviously emboldened by years of liberty, was to give the bride away. The church was loaded with officers when the ceremony began. The bride and family came down the aisle—but not Giovani. There had been a last-minute substitution.

We surrounded the hall where the wedding reception was to take place. Giovani, we learned later, went to the house instead, kissed the bride, and was off.

We heard he was running a gambling place in New Jersey. Every Friday he came over the George Washington Bridge with a bag of money to deposit in a New York bank. We knew his car, even its license number. We didn't dare ask for the help of the police in that particular New Jersey city, for they protected the joint, according to state troopers of that area and the FBI. So we planted our men on the New York side of the bridge, ready to grab Giovani if he came across. Later we discovered that an advance car preceded his. If it spotted us, Giovani took another route.

He became a numbers racketeer in New York. After much undercover work we located a flat in Harlem he visited once a week to negotiate business. We posted a car at every corner while some of us stationed ourselves in a warehouse, keeping the flat under observation by telescope. We saw Giovani inside, watched him prepare to depart. We signaled our men to be on the alert, to cut him off whichever way he went. Giovani got into his car and sped off. It turned out that just at that moment the parole officers in the particular car that should have prevented his escape considered it essential, en masse, to enter a restaurant to go to the men's room.

There were no further clues about Giovani for a long time. The trail became very cold. It began to seem as if we ought to drop the search. About half the staff had been replaced since the escape of the parolee. He was only a vague symbol to the newer men. Nevertheless we stuck it out.

By now only two brothers of the absconder were still of school age. We located the institution they attended and enlisted the cooperation of the physical instructor. Horsing around with the kids, he casually asked Giovani's brothers what various members of the family were doing.

"Whatever happened to Giovani?" he inquired. "He used to be one of our best softball players."

"He's in Florida," one of the boys said proudly.

"That so? Where?"

At this point the other brother said something quickly in Italian and both lads clammed up.

We practically ran over Florida with a fine tooth comb and discovered that a Giovani had bought a house in Miami and was operating an electrical appliance store there. We swooped down on him. He was a Giovani, but not ours. The very day our men closed in on the Miami suspect, the man we wanted was thrown out of a hotel in New York for having a woman in his room. This we discovered a week later.

None of these detective methods ever got us Giovani. All our deduction went for nought. What tripped Giovani up was having coffee in bad company.

One day he was in a cheap restaurant in New York when detectives came in, looking for a certain burglar. They didn't find their man but frisked all the customers, on general principles. They found a deck of heroin on Giovani.

But lest you believe that keen deduction never pays off, let me cite the case of Syd Gross and the Patrolman Casey murder.

Casey was walking along the street one evening, in mid-Manhattan, when a man came up to him, leveled a pistol, and shot him down. The killer dashed off, leaving his gray hat behind him.

Police went into high gear. The city was searched for clues from stem to stern. But the investigation wound up against a stone wall. The police were able to determine only that the murderer was dark complexioned, twenty-five to thirty years old, of medium height and build. And of course he wore a gray hat. As he had run around a corner he had come up against a parked car, left one thumbprint on it. A cab driver stated that he had driven a man answering the description from a point very near the scene of the crime to a certain street in Harlem. Here the passenger had alighted, asking the cabby to wait. In a few minutes he returned, paid the fare, and sent the driver away. Apparently he hadn't had money to pay the driver and had secured some in X Street.

There was quite a hullabaloo in the press about the case. The murder was so cold-blooded and senseless, the clues so hot yet useless. The police were on a spot. When this happens, an official usually announces that a break is expected momentarily.

Such a statement was now made. The police didn't really expect a break, but they got it—in Parole Officer Sydney Gross.

Syd was a remarkable sleuth. Sometimes he used roundabout methods, sometimes sheer deduction. Several times he solved crimes for the police, sitting at his desk and figuring it out by pure ratiocination.

Now he came in to see me. In his diffident, apologetic way he murmured, "I think I may have a suspect in the Patrolman Casey murder."

When Syd thought "maybe" that was good enough for me. "What've you got?" I asked.

He reviewed his deductions: The murder was committed the night before Syd's report night. So he was especially careful to note which parolees failed to come in. He conjectured that if by chance the murderer was on parole to him, he might fail to report because he feared he might be suspect. On the other hand, he might report in order not to become suspect.

Of five men who failed to come in, two were at once eliminated because one was Negro, the other a blond. Neither fitted the description of the gunman.

Of the three left, one was stricken off the suspect list because Syd, who noticed everything, recorded it all, and had a phenomenal memory, knew the parolee had never, in three years under supervision, worn any hat, let alone a gray one.

That left two men. Both fitted the description given. Both, according to Gross's record, owned gray hats. But one of them he ruled out because "he's chicken-hearted. He faints if he cuts his finger. He wouldn't kill a cop." Moreover, he wore a hat one-eighth of a size larger than the one left at the scene of the crime, so Syd recollected. That's the kind of sleuth he was.

So only one parolee remained in the running. *If* anyone on

Syd's list was the killer, this was the hottest suspect. He was dark complexioned, of medium height and build. He regularly wore a gray hat of appropriate size. He had been an armed robber, and once, Syd pointed out, had fired at a police officer.

By now I was on the wire, calling police headquarters. In no time at all, two detectives were high-tailing for our office.

Meantime Syd was musing. "But there's one thing wrong about this, one thing that doesn't add up. I can't figure it out. This man lives in Long Island, not Harlem. What was he doing on X Street? Maybe it wasn't he."

By the time the detectives arrived the unassuming Syd was ready to apologize. He believed he had gone off half-cocked. Why would the parolee be on X Street?

"Give me a little time to go over my notes," he said at last. Syd's notes consisted of a mountain of loose scraps of paper stuck under his desk blotter any which way. When the mound grew to such proportions that he couldn't write at his desk because the blotter teetered, it was time to destroy the notes. But by that time, miraculously, Syd had committed them all to memory. But before the demolition of what we called the Gross Filing System, he occasionally had to resort to his notes. Then he dipped right into the pile completely at random and at once pulled out exactly what he wanted. We always suspected he went by smell.

This time, after fishing under his blotter, he came in smiling. "I should have remembered. Guess I'm getting careless. He's got a girl friend at 1234 X Street. Name is Nancy. She's twenty-three years old, five feet tall, brown hair and eyes, went to eighth grade, lives with her parents, apartment forty-one. Should have remembered."

If the parolee was indeed the killer, he could have stopped at his girl's house to borrow money to pay his cab fare.

Gross and the detectives covered the house on X Street. After a chase they captured the parolee as he left there. The thumbprint found on the car tallied with his. He confessed. Then Gross and the officers turned the murderer over to the district attorney.

Next morning the papers carried the story: "Assistant D.A. —— announced that, after questioning a suspect all night, he had obtained from him a full confession to the murder of Patrolman Casey. This brilliant work on the part of the District Attorney's office . . ."

CHAPTER XXII

A Ghost Walked in Brooklyn

It would be nice if all crimes could be solved from a desk. There were times, though, when we were required not only to get to our feet but to defend ourselves. A parole failure doesn't always play nice.

I don't like being shot at under any circumstances, but I particularly resent being the target of a ghost. It's unnerving. You get the feeling that if you fire back, the bullet will go right through the wraith without exacting a drop of blood.

I was shot at by a ghost—in Brooklyn yet.

It happened when I was case supervisor in the New York office. Near closing time one hot Saturday afternoon, the father of a parolee I'll dub Art came in to complain that his son was on the road to further crime. He had quit his job, left home, and moved into a flat in Brooklyn. He seemed to have money though he was not working.

"Please talk to him before he does something serious," the father pleaded. "Scare him. Make him come home."

The officer who supervised Art had already left. We had only an old rogue's gallery picture of the parolee to go on. It showed him to be a powerful six-footer, about twenty-five, brutal-looking and dull-eyed.

I gathered together what men were around and we proceeded to Brooklyn, stopping at the appropriate police precinct to

ask a detective to accompany us to Art's flat. That was proper
procedure. In case we found evidence of crime, the police
should be present to take over. Almost invariably, detectives
were cooperative, eager to help, anxious for a pinch.

The detective then on duty, however, was not very pleased
at our request. Reluctantly, after I diplomatically asked if I
hadn't met him when I last lectured to detectives at the Police
Academy, he finally consented.

On the way over he expressed the opinion that Art, whom
he knew from around the neighborhood, was all right. "He's a
bum, but he ain't stealin'. Just a lazy bum, that's all."

Arrived at the flat, I suggested we surround it before an-
nouncing our presence.

"Nah!" the sleuth said. "This guy's just a bum. He ain't goin'
to take off." He advanced to the door, knocked, and called
out, "Art! Open up! Police! And parole officers!"

We heard stealthy movements inside, but no one came to
the door.

"Break it in," I urged.

"Nah! He's probably gettin' dressed. Hey, Art! Police! And
parole officers!"

"That just tips him off!" I cried, aghast. "Break the door in!"

"You ain't got a warrant, have you?" the officer challenged.
"Can't bust a door in without a warrant."

"Damn right I've got a warrant!"

The detective shrugged. "I don't want no part of this. I'll go
back to the precin't and get a skeleton key. We can get in that
way." And he departed.

All this palaver consumed at least five minutes.

I nodded to one of our better-built parole officers. With one
kick he opened the door.

Art had fled through a back window.

The apartment was stacked with loot—radios, electric fans, several dozen shiny, new golf clubs.

On a dresser we found a picture of a young man. It was inscribed, "To my pal Art. Friendlily, Harry." In a drawer there was a driver's license for a Harry K., age twenty-four. The address given was in Jamaica.

"You fellows stay here," I said. "I'll tell them at the precinct we've found this stuff. If anybody shows up, grab him."

At the stationhouse I found our detective colleague about to take off for a pleasant week end.

"Sorry," he grunted. "My trick's over. See Flannigan."

Flannigan (which isn't his true name) gladly accompanied me, listed the stolen property, tagged it, and at our request left it in the flat. To have taken it out would have tipped off the neighborhood and no one we might want would have come within shooting distance of the apartment. Flannigan offered to stay with us, help in any way possible. But since this was apparently now going to be a waiting game, I suggested he return to the precinct; we would call him when something happened.

We sat in the steaming hot, filthy flat for several hours before we had a bite. Then someone knocked gently and called softly, "Art?" We flung the door open, grabbed the caller, and yanked him into the room. He blinked at us, confused, apprehensive. He was a young man, the chap in the picture standing on the dresser.

"What do you want?" I rapped out.

"N-nothin'. I was—I was—lookin' for a fellow. Must have the wrong apartment."

"Whom were you looking for?"

"Fellow named Max."

"Then why did you call for Art?"

"I didn't!" he cried, innocent-eyed.

We often used our better-built man for dramatic effect. Bill now stepped forward. "You didn't?" he asked.

The youth paled.

"Sit down here, you bastard!" the better-built officer commanded. "And talk!"

This, too, was a calculated approach. I grieve to relate that we did, on occasion, use rough language; we did act tough. But I have never known a parole officer to strike a parolee except in self-defense. We played for effect. By seating his man, Bill was able to tower over him even more. Bill not only weighed two hundred and ten pounds; he stood six feet, two inches in his stockinged feet. Add to that a fierce expression and a choice armament of vicious expletives, and you get the idea. The general effect can be terrifying.

"What's your name?" Bill snarled.

"P-Pete."

"You're a liar," I broke in. "Now listen! We've got no time to waste. We've tailed you all day; we know all about you. Your name is Harry K. You live at —— in Jamaica. You were born on ——, 19—. We know you're a partner of Art's. You're a thief! Now will you talk?"

"Yeah!" said Bill, raising a paw, to swat a fly, no doubt. "Now will you talk?"

Harry was pale, his brow sweaty. "Whatcha wanna know?" he whispered.

"Where's Art?" I demanded.

"Jeez! I dunno! I t'ought he'd be here."

We questioned him closely. He really tried to help, for by now he was ready to sell out Art in return for a kind word at his trial—for the burglaries he confessed pulling with his so recent bosom companion. He conjectured that probably Art, knowing the flat was pinched, was hiding out at Molly's. She was a lady of the evening who had earned much good will among wanted felons by allowing them to bed and board with her for free until the heat was off.

We put Harry in jail, and Flannigan and the rest of us went to Molly's. The detective looked the place over and there seemed to be no rear exit. Molly lived on the ground floor of a two-family house. Her apartment faced the street. She had no rear windows, except for a small one in what must have been the bathroom. Besides being too tiny for a man to get through, it was solidly boarded up from the inside.

We knocked.

"Who is it?" sang a coy voice.

"Open up!" Flannigan demanded.

"Just a minute!" The voice sounded shocked. "I ain't dressed!"

"We don't mind that!" Flannigan yelped. "Open up, or the door goes in!"

One second later Molly stood at the opened door, a wrapper about her ample frame. I judged she had been building up good will for about twenty-five years.

"Where's Art?" Flannigan wanted to know.

"Who?" Molly asked, scratching a haunch. "Lissen! I been sleepin'. It's midnight. I don't know no Art. Yez can soich the place if yez want. Yez'll do it whether I want yez to or not!" She yawned widely.

We searched. We didn't find Art—but we did discover that the boarded-up window wasn't really boarded up. The boards swung inward on hinges. And the window was wide open. It hadn't been when we inspected the place from the outside.

We also found one complete gentleman's outfit—shoes, socks, underwear, and suit.

Disgusted, we took Harry out of stir and rode around the neighborhood, telling him to point the parolee out if he should spy him.

We hadn't long to wait. Ten minutes later Harry sat back into the shadows of the car and whispered, "There he is!"

Across the street, in a hallway, stood Art, holding up a man and ordering him to undress. The parolee was a frightening sight to behold. He was stark naked. His body gleamed white in the night. The hair on his head had been shaved off. A bedsheet was draped over his shoulders.

We braked the car to a halt and tumbled out, leaving one man with Harry. Bill fired a shot into the air.

Art lit out. I carried less weight those days than now, and I took the lead in pursuit.

An eerie sight it must have been. The streets were deserted. The night blackness was relieved by a full moon. Its glow suffused Art, floating, down the street, a white something billowing behind him, his body gleaming, seemingly translucent. He turned time and again and fired at me. I fired back. He sped across the corner intersection as a streetcar came rolling toward us, full speed. He made it. I fired a shot across the bow of the oncoming vehicle and sprinted across—the trolley missed me by no more than an inch.

Art was zooming on and around another corner. I reached it just in time to catch a flash of a white sheet fluttering down into the basement of a house. The ghost vanished.

The shooting had attracted a police prowl car. Two men jumped out and joined me. We searched the basement without success. Then we looked up the coal hole. There was Art at the top. He had somehow scrambled upward and supported himself by wedging his feet against one wall of the cylinder, his shoulders against the other.

We brought him down. I thought, as I regarded him, that he might be demented. He had a murderously cold and evil glint in his eye. His face was loutish, sullen, brute-like. He refused to say a word, then or later.

And if you are inclined to doubt there was a ghost that walked in Brooklyn, consider this:

Art was sentenced to prison. And he escaped from the toughest jailhouse in the state—Dannemora. Could you go over the wall like that without you could float in the air, awready?

CHAPTER XXIII

I Become a Crime Buster

I freely confess, although it is unstylish to do so, that I enjoyed the law-enforcement phase of our work. Not that I took ghoulish delight in cracking skulls or bringing about the incarceration of parolees. But there is, about this facet of the work, a fascination akin to what chess players experience. You figure all the possible moves; consider the personality and habit patterns of your opponent; ask yourself what he knows or suspects about your plans; predict where he is going to go and when; and you try to get there first and wait for him to walk into your trap.

This feeling for law-enforcement work has been termed immaturity by some, hardheaded realism by others. Either way, I plead guilty.

I personally, or the officer under my direction, participated in some of the most spectacular criminal investigations in New York State's history. The Murder, Incorporated, convictions arose out of a tip from a parolee whom we referred to William O'Dwyer, then district attorney of Kings County. In the killing of union leader Redwood, a parolee was a definite suspect. (A well-known businessman considered himself one, too, and called me, hysterically insisting he had nothing to do with the homicide. I could only tell him I had nothing to do with suspecting him of it.)

When city fireman Hitter was held up and shot, John

Davino, a parolee, was convicted and sentenced to death, though innocent. His sentence was later reversed, on evidence furnished in part by a parole officer.

The Rubel armored-truck robbery in Brooklyn involved parolees. In the Fried kidnaping we arrested a parolee who had the key to a safe deposit box which held a ring—all that remained of Fried after the kidnapers threw him into a furnace in a social club.

Willie Sutton, one of the most imaginative thieves of our time, was a parolee. Whitey Riordan, who broke out of Sing Sing, had been on parole. The Arsenal Mob, on which we and the police worked for months, numbered parolees in its membership. The Mad Dog Espositos were or had been parolees at the time they perpetrated the robbery and slaughter that brought them to the deathhouse in Sing Sing.

I'm not boasting, for no matter what we did to detect a parolee in crime, his arrest was bad news for parole. We might be credited with fine work, but always there remained the cold fact that a parolee had committed crime.

As parole developed in New York State, I was more or less tagged by police, press, and public as a person who emphasized the importance of the law-enforcement function in parole. As a result, many penologists and probation and parole executives secretly felt I was a tough guy, overdoing the bang! bang! stuff. They were kind enough not to say so publicly, or even privately to me. I sensed it by the coolness of some and by the scuttlebutt reported from penological conventions. This reputation involved me in a most unusual situation when I was chief parole officer.*

---

* Some of the basic facts of the case that follows have been altered, to protect certain innocent people, but all the developments are recounted as they actually happened.

In a fair-sized community a parolee shot and killed a pimp of one of the houses in the city's notorious red-light district. The parole officer supervising the killer must—or should—have known that the latter was working in a house of prostitution. This raised the question whether the officer had been dishonest or merely negligent.

Before we could lay hands on a certain ledger showing who was on the payroll of a particular house, the building was bombed and the book presumably destroyed. Other suspicions and allegations that came our way included: that gambling was protected by, and paid off to, the chief of police; that prostitution was protected by, and paid off to, the chief of detectives; that a number of parolees, other than the one already arrested, were employed in gambling houses and prostitution emporia with the knowledge and connivance of public officials; and that we wouldn't get an iota of cooperation from any municipal official or law-enforcement officer in that town.

Obviously it was not our province to investigate municipal graft and corruption. Our sole interest was in answers to two questions: What, if any, parolees were engaged in illicit activities? What, if any, parole officers were closing their eyes to this?

In a blinding blizzard I drove to this town, with a confidential assistant, Bill Drucker, a brilliant, imaginative criminal investigator. Our car was equipped with three sets of license plates, to enable us to move around a bit without being immediately identified.

We checked into a hotel and made plans. First, we must capture a certain parolee, now an absconder, whose story would be most important to us. Then we had to interview a gambler and an inmate of a house of prostitution, one Maymie. Finally, we

needed to look at certain check stubs and ledgers believed to
have been impounded by the district attorney.

In the course of the next few hours we discovered that the
public officials of the town knew we had arrived. They believed
I had been sent in by Governor Lehman to investigate the city,
after which I would be appointed special prosecutor, supersed-
ing the district attorney and ripping the lid off the caldron of
political corruption in the town.

Word had gone out to sit tight and watch out for us.

We were stymied wherever we turned. We couldn't get into
a gambling house. We couldn't get into a house of assignation.
We could hardly buy a drink!

In such circumstances it often pays to relax and go at things
the roundabout way. In a nearby town we looked up a state
trooper whom Bill knew. Who in town, we asked, could be
talked to? Who would give a straight story? He put us in touch
with a minor public official who, somehow, had been able to
remain honest yet keep his job.

From this idealistic public servant we got enough data on
certain people to capture Gerald, the parolee we wanted.

Objective one: Accomplished.

From Gerald we got information that told us at least *which*
gambler we should be trying to see. But we couldn't find him.
He was gone. After a week's fruitless search for JoJo, we had
established nothing. We decided to go home for a while.

About fifty miles out of town the car developed trouble that
would lay us up overnight. We went to a hotel, and got down-
stairs fast for a hot toddy to take the chill out of our marrow.

One thing led to another, you might say. We got into conversation with a gentleman next to us at the bar, a magnificent
chap, a jovial companion, a man one meets once in a lifetime.

We bought the lovable old coot a drink. He bought us a drink. We bought him a drink. He bought us a drink.

Right in the middle of one of the most hilarious stories I have ever told in my life (I wish I could remember it), the bartender asked our friend, "How's JoJo these days?"

"Fine! Fine!" said our pal. "Gettin' a little restless, ya know."

"Yeah," the barkeep said philosophically. "Why wouldn't he?"

I looked at Bill, uncertain whether he had caught it.

Bill slapped our friend on the back and shouted, "Hey! You a friend of JoJo's? Whyncha say so! Well whatdya know! Hey, Dave! He's a friend of JoJo's! Whatcha say your name was?"

"It was Jim and it still is! Har! Har!"

"Haven't seen JoJo around since that—uh—trouble," Bill said vaguely.

"Yeah," Jim countered. "They got him in the icebox, you know."

"Sure! Sure!" Bill answered wisely. "Let's drink up. I gotta buy a drink sometime! Ha! Ha! Ha!"

"Ho! Ho! Ho!" Jim chorused.

A while later I noticed Bill was becoming a bit lachrymose. "Good ol' JoJo," he was saying. "Ain't seen JoJo long time . . . long time . . . no, sir . . . long time . . . l-o-o-o-ng time."

"Yeah, yeah!" Jim agreed mournfully.

"Thought while I was down here, would look up good ol' JoJo. Can't find him."

Jim regarded both of us at the same time, one eye in each direction. "You know JoJo? Whyntcha say so? You wanna see good ol' JoJo? Come on! You friends of mine! Come on!"

Objective two: Accomplished.

JoJo was hiding out in jail—that is, in the home of a jail employee, on the jail grounds. He talked readily, having nothing to fear himself. He had holed up at the request of certain powerful people, he said, merely to be out of the range of certain individuals who might need him as a witness for this or that. JoJo gladly gave us information.

The next week we sneaked back into town late at night. We hoped the red-light houses might have reopened. They were shut tighter than ever.

We had a definite campaign in mind. Drucker had once been a state trooper in that area. A magnificent figure on horse, in his dashing uniform, even people he arrested had liked him. A number of young prostitutes had got to know him when they operated outside the town, where State Police had had jurisdiction. Bill had arrested them whenever he had the evidence. But if a girl was trying to make a comeback, leave the racket, the handsome trooper was always ready with a helping hand and dollar. Social workers called Bill a good social worker. The girls complimented him even more. They called him a good cop.

We hoped to capitalize on this, in one final effort to crack the conspiracy of silence against us. We had to find Maymie. And only some inmate of a house could tell us where she might be.

Dressed in dungarees and turtle-neck sweaters, we crept out of town to a nearby city, rented a horse and wagon, then drove to a high-grade grocer, where we bought a load of hothouse strawberries.

And so, through the frozen streets of the red-light district, we rode, singsonging, "Strawberries! *Straw*berries! Straw-*berries!*"

Strawberries in winter! What, outside of champagne in a slipper, would appeal more to the dreams of an unhappy harlot?

*"Strawberries! Straw*berries!"

Pop! The shutters of one house flew open. A girl stuck her head out.

"Hiya, Rosie!" Bill called.

Her eyes widened in astonishment. "Hi, Bill!" she called at last, delighted.

Pop! Another set of shutters.

"Hiya, Lavinia!"

"Hi, Bill!"

Down the lane of miserable hovels we traveled. Near the corner Bill looked up.

"Hiya, Gertie!" he called.

"H'llo, Billy! Whatcha doin' on a wagon?"

"Got canned! Gotta make a livin'."

"Too bad!"

"Yeah! Say, I gotta see Maymie about somethin'. Where's Maymie?"

"Maymie? Right here! Oh, Maymie!" she called.

Maymie stuck her head out.

"Hiya, Bill!"

"Hiya, Maymie! Hey! Gotta tell you somethin'! Meet me in Ginny's—right away."

"Okay, Bill, whatever you say!"

In Ginny's gin mill we met Maymie, spirited her out of town, got the information we needed.

Objective three: Accomplished. One to go: The records. On this we failed.

To try to get them we called the district attorney. He was only too happy to be of service, but unfortunately the records were no longer in his possession. They had been part of some paraphernalia seized in a gambling establishment. (That checked with our understanding). All that property, for perfectly legal and proper reasons (check!) had been transferred to a certain individual on the public payroll for safekeeping. We should apply there.

The D.A. was courteous. He sounded like a fine chap. (Several years later he was appointed to a state position and made an excellent record.)

We called the custodian of the records.

"Who're you?" he demanded.

I explained.

"Oh! You're the man from the Governor's office."

"No, sir, I'm not. I'm here for the Division of Parole."

"Yeah," he said, with ill-concealed skepticism. But he must have overawed himself by mention of the Governor.

"Well, I'm going to cooperate. Allus do, with all duly constituted law and order," he said stoutly. "If they ever was a special prosecutor sent in here, he'd find that's so. Now lessee. I can let you look at them records about four o'clock. They're out in the warehouse. Take a while to bring 'em in—about ten miles."

"Can we go out to the warehouse?"

"N-no. Wouldn't do no good. Place all piled up with stuff. We keep it ninety days, then burn it. I'll have it here four o'clock."

"Thanks." I put up the receiver.

"Let's go!" I called to Drucker. "It's one-thirty. Let's get to that warehouse!"

We got there an hour later. In back, on a lot, a bonfire was smoldering. All the gambling paraphernalia had been ninety days impounded. Now it had been destroyed—the records we wanted included. That's what they said.

The custodian was very sorry. He hadn't known this was the day of the burning, else he'd have called earlier and stopped it. Too bad! That's what he said.

As it happens, we did locate, elsewhere, some check stubs that told us what we wanted to know. Our case was pretty complete. We pulled out of town and left it in the no doubt competent hands of local authorities. If the Governor's office wanted to take over, it was no concern of the Division of Parole.

CHAPTER XXIV

What Causes Crime?

Everywhere I went people asked me what caused crime, in the belief that a person in the field ought to know the answers. I have asked myself the same question thousands of times, year in, year out. I can only go on some shrewd guesses, and these have to be in terms of particular offenders, not of offenders generally. We have to ask what factors in *this* person's life led *him* to do thus and so.

For example, consider Sue and Martin.

One of the earliest parole cases with which I had contact was that of a girl we'll call Sue. I was a parole officer then, but I didn't supervise Sue—in fact, she never knew my official capacity. She was acquainted with me extracurricularly, as it were. She knew me as a man doing a thesis on burlesque; she was working in that business. From my point of vantage I was able to get slants on Sue that I probably wouldn't have got as her parole officer.

When Sue appeared onstage she looked attractive in a sexy way. But she was far from good-looking, although she had a nice figure. Her face was on the scrawny side; her hair was dyed a violent red; her eyes were green; and her mouth was hard. She was not brilliant. When I first met her she was foul-mouthed, often loaded with gin, and one of the very few truly promiscuous persons I met in burlesque. Fortunately she finished parole shortly after I first encountered her, else I would have been in a dilemma between my duty to parole and my obligation to preserve the confidences of informants who were helping me do my doctor's thesis, "Burlesque as a Cultural Phenomenon."

Sue came from Pittsburgh. Her mother was Old World Polish, quite a drinker. Most of the time she, not her husband, was the breadwinner. But that didn't mean she went out to work. She had, for a generation, made a business out of demanding relief from family agencies in Pittsburgh. She was a professional pauper. Social-work organizations in town knew and dreaded her, for she was untruthful about her assets, perpetually claimed to be starving, and became hysterical or assaultive when refused help.

The father, of Ukrainian birth, was overfond of drink and gambling. He considered himself not at all responsible for his family, often drifted away for months at a time. He scrounged money here and there, relied on his wife to supply the rest of his needs, beat her regularly, and produced one new child a year for seventeen years.

Eight of those seventeen children survived. Six of the eight were girls. The two boys ran away from home as soon as they were out of knee pants. The girls stayed longer, but one by one broke away. Three got married, each when fifteen years old, and settled down into at least fairly comfortable surroundings. The other three weren't as fortunate. Amy became a prostitute. Mary hung around speakeasies with stray boys, became pregnant, left home, and was never heard from again.

Sue was the baby. From her mother she received no love whatever, for that woman was too harassed, after giving birth to seventeen children, to have much love left for anyone. The mother used Sue. She recognized that, at age five, the child was an appealing creature. She would have her stand on a street corner, a bunch of pencils in her hand, begging. Inevitably some person would be outraged at this and would question the child. At this point mama would appear on the scene, hysterical. Oh, there was her little darling! she would scream, hugging the child frantically. Then mama would explain. Little Sue had been starving. In fact the entire family of eight (or nine or ten or whatever came to mind) was starving. And little Sue, of the entire sweet brood, had set out from home obviously intent on bringing back some food for the empty mouths and stomachs.

By the time this much of the story had been rendered, mama was crying, Sue was wailing, and the stern questioner was either addressing the spectators or reduced to tears himself. A crowd would have gathered, and in no time at all a collection would be taken up for little Sue and her starving brothers and sisters, deserted by a drunken father, cared for by a loving but toil-worn mother.

Several times Sue's mother was arrested for such shenanigans. Somehow she got off with light fines, and she didn't lose control of her principal mealticket—Sue.

When the social agencies of Pittsburgh had just about completely shut down on the family, Sue's mother outfitted herself and the child in an advertising sandwich, proclaiming they were slowly dying of malnourishment because the such and such agency refused to help. The two picketed the office of the organization until police intervened.

Papa saved the day. Out of two years' desertion and a prolonged alcoholic spree he suddenly came to with a pang of conscience and a few hundred dollars which he had won at some game, he couldn't quite remember where. He wrote his wife, inviting her to join him in New York, provided, of course, he didn't have to foot the moving bill.

So, when Sue was nine, she became a resident of New York. Daddy insisted he had tuberculosis and couldn't work, so mama, naturally, headed right for the family agency and demanded money. Refused, she brought in Sue, fainted (from hunger, of course), came to, said she'd have to leave her dear, darling, adorable baby doll there. Mama didn't mind perishing from hunger, but she wouldn't have her baby dying; she'd insist *someone* feed her. Then she dashed out, and the agency had a sort of sit-in strike on its hands.

This sort of strategy was tried frequently. It seldom worked, but it assuredly had a lot to do with Sue's conditioning. At that age, the child was almost as pauperized and cantankerous as her mother.

That's the way Sue grew up. If she attended school, nobody noticed, and if she truanted, nobody at home cared. When she was fourteen she quit altogether.

By this time Sue had taken over her mother's role. It was now she who stormed into relief agencies, shrieked, cried, carried on, demanding support. Once she brazenly accused a male caseworker of having made her an indecent proposition.

Yet, subtly, Sue was changing. By the time she was sixteen she seemed anxious, for the first time, to *earn* a living. She sought work, but her father didn't approve of the idea. He wanted her at home, taking care of him.

Nevertheless Sue took a job. She met a man, went to live with him, and he made her a drug addict. When he tried to send her out on the street as a prostitute, she left him and returned home. By her own will power she cured herself of drug addiction, then ran off again, this time with a young man who turned out to be a thug. With him, Sue went on a stickup, acting as lookout. He was captured, promptly informed on Sue, and at eighteen she served a term in a reformatory.

When she came out she was a hard, bitter, unstable girl, an obvious "tramp," as she herself characterized her makeup later. She stayed clear of her family altogether. She clerked in a store, waited table, jerked sodas, then met a man who got her a job in the chorus line of a burlesque "scratch house" (a low-grade, cheaply run show without orchestra, usually only with a pianist, where the chorines double as strippers). This was just before her parole terminated, two years after her release.

When she was no longer under official supervision Sue moved to a bigger and better burley house, eventually became a stripper of sorts. She was never well known, but she ate regularly and loved her work.

When her father located her, she refused to have anything to do with him. He died shortly after this. For her mother she developed a deep hatred and contempt. She wouldn't even attend her funeral when that took place.

For her brothers and sisters she had little feeling by now, having been so long away from them. But when she ran into Amy, now a broken-down prostitute, Sue staked her, put her on her feet, and cared for her as if she were a baby.

When Sue was twenty-eight, after years on the stage, years of promiscuity and personal disorganization, she met a man, a stage technician, and the two fell in love as neither had ever experienced it before. It was one of those things no one will ever explain to my satisfaction, the kind of love I would have thought neither was capable of. Sue's face glowed

in those days. Her eyes seemed to be afloat in tears as she told
me, "This time I've met my guy!" The two began living together. Sue left the stage. I visited the couple once, and there
was about Sue something quiet, relaxed, restful, as if she were
now sure of herself.

I met her once more, years later. She looked the part of a
highly respectable, conservative matron. She had become
fleshy, but this tended to soften her face so it had very little
of its former toughness. She was still with the same man. She
had two children, she told me, "and they're legitimate! I
married Tony, did you know?" Her face was alight with pride
and contentment. I had the feeling Sue was out of trouble for
good.*

What made Sue a "criminal"? What caused her to undertake
crime? Before you try to analyze why Sue and others like
her become offenders against society, consider this case:

Martin was brilliant. That was obvious before he could talk.
He was destined to be a child prodigy, no doubt about it. His
delighted parents were determined to give him every opportunity to develop to the fullest those talents he would undoubtedly prove to have.

They were intelligent people. The mother had been a schoolteacher prior to marriage. The father was a Ph.D., many times a
millionaire, president of a large manufacturing company. The
family lived in a fashionable suburb of New York City. There
were other homes too, in Florida, Maine, Scotland.

Being highly intelligent, and loving Martin sincerely, both

---

* Sue's story is true in every detail affecting the points I have wanted to
emphasize, but a great many identifying features have been altered without
nullifying the essential honesty of the recital. Sue gave me permission to
tell her story, saw the draft of this chapter, and commented, "It's all right,
only I wasn't even as nice as you make me out those early years."

the father and mother realized they shouldn't "spoil" their only child. It would have been so easy to focus the entire world around Martin. This they determined to avoid by working out a formula. They would provide him, into manhood, with all he needed—luxuries, the finest education, everything—but they would prevent his becoming spoiled by not making themselves accessible to him the year around. That way the parents wouldn't be gushing over him as they would love to do. Martin would be raised in a boarding school, would be home summers only. That was how these intelligent, well-meaning parents blueprinted the future of their prodigy.

When Martin was in boarding school he was rated a genius in several respects. His IQ was phenomenal. He was gifted at the piano. He knew astronomy about as well as the average college instructor, it was said. He was particularly good at mathematics. He had a stupendous vocabulary. He read voraciously.

And he was a little gentleman, always well spoken, affable, even-tempered, and without a care in the world. He took his wealth gracefully, didn't flash it about, was able to help less fortunate schoolmates unobtrusively. He was admired and loved by youngsters as well as adults.

Martin grew into adolescence with never a blemish on his record, never an obvious problem in his life. He came home summers, and his doting parents tried not to smother him with love those three months to make up for the nine months they had been able to show him none. So they held themselves in check a little. Martin responded politely to the love he got; he gave his parents respect and courtesy, he kissed them at all the proper occasions and he showed them honor wherever he went.

He was entered in a fashionable preparatory school, and he

finished first in his class. He matriculated in a well-known university, and the first semester walked away with practically every prize offered a freshman. The second semester he was on the debate team and the school paper. He was a member of the dramatic society and he won several money prizes.

And immediately after the second semester he hit the front page when police officers spied him creeping out of the second-story window of a home near the university. They gave chase. Martin barricaded himself in his room and, shouting obscenities in a crazed voice, fired away through the door, with two pistols, no fewer than thirty times. When he ran out of ammunition he surrendered and walked out, hands lifted, snarling like a mad beast. Nothing about the affair made sense. He didn't need money. He had no reason to be carrying guns— burglars seldom do. He could not have expected to escape from the police.

The stunned parents were prostrated. They visited Martin in jail, and he was his old, calm, courteous, suave self. He couldn't explain what had got into him. He just craved adventure, he said, and had pulled a few burglaries for the fun of it. Of course he didn't need the loot. He regretted, more than anything else, having so hurt and humiliated his parents. He cried softly as he said this, and his mother fainted.

The entire situation was so fantastic, so without logic, that, what with psychiatric reports and brilliant lawyers and an understanding judge, Martin was placed on probation.

He left school and lived with his parents.

For a year they watched him anxiously, lovingly. They bought him a car and a speed boat. They ran elaborate parties for his friends. They saw to it he met the right girls.

Then, one night, Martin was caught sliding down a drain

pipe from the second floor of a dwelling near his home. His pockets were stuffed with jewelry, most of it relatively inexpensive.

His parents pleaded with him to explain why he did such things. He replied that he honestly didn't know. He kissed his parents tenderly and asked them not to put up any money for his defense.

He pleaded guilty and was sent to the reformatory. He was paroled in eighteen months. I was his parole officer.

Martin was impressively handsome, always immaculately dressed in a well-tailored suit. His personality was definitely magnetic. He had great charm, and his choice of words was such, his intelligence so keen, that it was a real pleasure listening to him. He never asked for a special privilege on parole. Nor did he hint that because of his wealth and position he ought to be treated differently from other parolees.

He went to work for his father, did well, and expressed satisfaction with everything. He wanted, he made clear, to make it up to his parents for all the suffering he had caused them.

I gave up supervision of Martin a year later because I was promoted, but I followed his career through the record from time to time.

He received several promotions on the job. He also came into an inheritance of some thirty thousand dollars, left by a relative and held in trust until Martin reached his majority.

Then, one night, police came upon Martin walking along the street, his pant leg torn from the knee down. They searched him and found some jewelry, which had been stolen.

Martin went to prison. He came out on parole. I lost track of his history for a long time. I still don't know much of what happened in the years between his second parole and the time

I picked up a certain newspaper. That day I read that Martin had been shot and killed when he entered the bedroom of a man, intent on burglary.

Is heredity a factor in crime causation? Sue's probably was bad, Martin's excellent. And we know pretty well that one can't inherit criminal tendencies. There used to be a theory, sponsored by the Italian criminologist Lombroso, to the effect that certain people were born with physical "stigmata" predestining them to crime. Then an inconsiderate researcher found that a group of noncriminal university students had more of those stigmata than did a criminal group.

Does inadequate intelligence play a part in crime? Martin was brilliant, Sue dull. And every police officer will testify that in the criminal population are people of all levels of intelligence, from feeble-minded to gifted.

The inevitable question is: "Isn't poverty the great predisposing factor in crime?" I don't know. Certainly it's logical to believe so. Prisons are full of poor people, but there are poor people who don't commit crime, no matter how dire their poverty. And there are rich people who do commit crime. How can Martin's crimes be explained on an economic basis? He never lacked for a thing. Sue was raised in poverty and degradation, which no doubt played some part in her later behavior pattern. How big a part? I don't know. There is reason to believe that crime is stimulated not only by underprivilege, as with Sue, but by overprivilege, as with Martin.

"Isn't education a factor?" people ask. Again I don't know. Sue had little education, Martin above the average. I have known offenders who didn't finish third grade and others who held Ph.D.s. I've known schools determined to help youngsters mature wholesomely; and so-called institutions of learning where I was convinced we were spending our money to pay teachers to make children neurotic wrecks.

Aha! Here's one that pops up all the time! Broken homes. Don't broken homes lead to criminality? I don't know. There is some evidence. But Martin's home wasn't broken, so an unbroken home is no guarantee.

Sociologists such as Thrasher insist the great need in crime prevention is wholesome recreation. Isn't that a very important item? Maybe. But Martin had every opportunity .for wholesome play. Sue didn't.

Housing then? Slums breed crime? Sure. Fine mansions do too.

No, I think it boils down to this: We know that certain conditions may yield crime, but there's nothing inevitable about it. The only way to answer the question, "What causes crime?" is to forget it and ask instead, "What caused this person to commit this crime at this particular time?" And only by individual study of offenders will we gain any insight into what made those offenders and what is needed to help them change.

I have a hunch as to what causative factor will be found most frequently. It is a psychological and emotional one. This doesn't mean that environment isn't extremely potent. I certainly agree that no one is born a criminal or has become a criminal. I concede that almost without exception environment makes the individual criminal. The factor I consider most important is produced in part by environment too. The factor is absence of family love and security in youth.

Psychiatrists say the human organism begins to be influenced by its environment at least from the first hour of birth. They also now assert, somewhat reversing an earlier opinion, that you can't give a child too much love.

These principles, to me, are all-important. They have been verified hundreds of times in my experience with offenders. I can think of very few parolees about whom it could not be said that their antisocial behavior was in very considerable measure traceable to family influences.

I don't mean that parents taught children to steal, rape, or assault. I mean that what goes on inside a family conditions a child's behavior, emotions, thinking, so that he graduates into the larger society the product of the smaller.

That's easily understood. For the first five years or so all of a child's world resides in the family. All the influences exerted over him come from the home. The family is therefore a powerful agency for good and bad. Criminals are made in the family. That goes for Sue and also for Martin.

There were many, many reasons why it was easy for Sue to drift into crime. Most of them arose out of one central fact: her family was completely demoralized and disorganized. She received no love from her parents. The home was insecure, what with poverty and the chronic desertion of the man who should have been its head. A child used and abused as Sue had been was bound to grow up a bundle of neuroses. She had to overcome all the trauma, hazards, friction, stemming from her family life before she could stabilize herself. Sue, like all creatures of the womb, was born social. Her family made her antisocial.

Martin was a victim of family too. He was economically overprivileged, but this failed to compensate for the absence of parental love. The father and mother believed they adored Martin. Were this so, they could not have cut themselves off from him by the mere establishment of a formula for his rearing. The very fact that they could arrive at such a plan suggests that their capacity for love was not great. The luxuries it was so easy for them to give Martin were merely an expiation of guilt for the paucity of love.

So Martin, recipient of little love but lots of "things," grew up emotionally stunted. Since the goods of life came to him so painlessly, he had no conception of the value of money. He grew up to be shallow because his family never gave him opportunity to exercise less superficial feelings. And he, like any other child, was aware of the lack of affection within the family. A child never fails to recognize it. Outwardly a little gentleman, Martin grew into manhood without realizing how deeply resentful he was of his parents.

How can I speak so positively about this? I talked with him enough to gain this impression. However, I can't prove what I have hypothecated; only if Martin had been psychoanalyzed might he have brought such material out of his subconscious and faced it openly.

Martin's parents thought they loved him, and they gave him many gifts to prove it to themselves. Mark's parents, too, were certain they loved their son. Only they took things away to establish the fact.

They believed in discipline. If Mark didn't do as he was told he was punished. Never spanked or beaten, mind you. No, no! The parents were too civilized for that. They simply deprived the boy of some privilege or pleasure. This is accepted as a very sensible method of control, provided it is exercised reasonably. Mark's folks used to put his bicycle away for a month, or prohibit his going to the movies, or cut off his allowance.

The boy didn't seem to take this badly. Children usually accept that their parents are quite justified in taking such disciplinary action.

As Mark grew older the punishments became more frequent and tougher, because, the parents argued, an older boy should know better, control himself better, or be punished more severely. Mark always seemed to be infracting some rule. Maybe the reason was that there were too many rules. However that may be, things became pretty tense between the boy and his parents. He was a pretty bright lad and he argued about the logic of the situation. His folks told him they were doing things for his own good, because they loved him.

When Mark was sixteen he told his mother he felt he was too old to be treated like a baby. He wanted to be certain of his allowance. If he made a date with a fellow or girl he wanted to know he'd be able to keep it, not be penned up at home as punishment for some act. The mother disagreed. There was quite a quarrel, in the course of which Mark was very rude.

"You don't know anything about raising boys!" he cried.

Mama burst into tears and said papa would have to deal with this when he got home.

When papa arrived and heard what had happened, he laid down the law. All right, he said, if Mark was so grown up, let him earn his own way. No more allowance. He'd even have to buy his own clothes.

The family was, while not affluent, far from poor. The father was a Civil Service employee, earning about six thousand a year. Yet he allowed Mark to quit school and seek employment—as a discipline.

To Mark, as he expressed himself to me years later, this was a great shock not merely in terms of what he had brought on himself. He considered that his parents disliked him, had always felt so about him, and were showing it at last. He was deeply hurt, not resentful. He blamed himself, felt rejected and unwanted, and determined to win his way back into the good graces of his parents. He wanted a place in the bosom of his family.

He got a job, earned some money, bought some clothes, tried to behave.

One morning, preparing to leave for work, dressed in his dungarees, he asked his mother if she would get his one good suit (the one he'd paid for) from the cleaners, as he had a date that evening. His mother demanded to know who the girl was, what she was like, and in no time at all mother and son were battling. Mark checked himself and fled from the house.

When he returned that evening he looked in the closet for his suit. It wasn't there. He asked his mother if she had picked it up for him. Whereupon the father, lips tensed primly, informed Mark that the suit had been picked up and, as punishment for the boy's impertinence, had been pawned. Now Mark would have to buy it back from the pawnbroker's.

Mark told me that when he heard this the room began to spin. He saw only his father's firm lips, pronouncing the sentence. He felt something like a red-hot iron creasing his skull. He saw black. He couldn't swallow, became dizzy.

He left the house without a word. Before the evening was over he had broken into a tailoring shop and stolen some suits. Holding them in his arms without any attempt at concealment, he walked down the street late at night and landed in the arms of a detective. That was his first arrest. It was not his last.

Each time he came out of jail or prison, Mark would return home. Always there would be a happy family reunion. But before long, recriminations would come out and the boy would leave in a rage.

I argued with the parents at this time, as Mark's parole officer, that they should give the boy a chance, never mention the past, stop treating him like a baby. They agreed each time I brought up the subject. But the father particularly couldn't overcome his sense of propriety. I was in the house once when he found it necessary to "talk to" Mark, who by now was a fully grown young man.

The father pursed his lips as if they were covered with alum. He put his fingertips together, like a minister about to pronounce the benediction. His voice took on a calm, objective, professorial tone that infuriated even me. He was so obviously the patient, forgiving father who had stood a great deal and now must, even though it pained him, talk to a loved but naughty child. Every word he uttered was calculated to wound, each sentence was a poisoned dart entering the heart of the son.

"Now, Mark," he began, "you know your mother and I have done our very best for you, all these years, when you were—ah—getting into—ah—scrapes—ah . . ." And so on.

The last time Mark came out of prison he was thirty-two. He came out without a parole term, a free man, having served his full maximum sentence. He came to see me for two reasons. The first was to tell me—to tell somebody—that he was not going home this time. He'd had enough of family. "They're too goddamned holy," he said.

The second reason was to pick up a small envelope he had left with me the last time he went to prison. It contained a pawn ticket—for the suit that had started all the trouble. Mark, for some reason, wanted to hold onto that ticket even though he didn't care to redeem the suit.

I'm not sure that even at the end Mark hated his parents. I think he simply felt unwanted, and it pained him.

But I knew a girl on parole whose very crime was a protest and a rebellion against the mother she hated because she considered her too severe.

When Bella had a date with a boy, her mother laid down strict rules about when she should return and how she should comport herself. Practically every day Bella listened to her mother discourse on how eminently respectable she was, how important it was that the girl should not disgrace the family. Practically anything Bella did outside the home was looked on with suspicion, and surely the young lady must have been made to feel that pleasures she considered innocent were really pretty ugly and unwholesome.

In disgust and frustration Bella finally ran away from home after a particularly severe quarrel. She had a job, which was enough to keep her going, yet she passed a series of bad checks. Arrested, she gave her real name and listed as her address a house next door to her mother's. That would cause the police to inquire there. They would be referred to the correct address, but meantime Bella's arrest would get around the neighborhood. That would make her mother suffer.

The girl asked police to allow reporters to take her picture. "I want my mother and all the neighbors to see it!" she gloated. "I don't care what happens to me now. But, boy! What a disgrace for ma!"

The stories I've told thus far are all about persons who were loved too little, or considered that they were. Surely there is a case where too much love caused a youngster, directly or indirectly, to seek escape through crime?

Possibly. But my guess would be that it was too much of the wrong kind of love, or too much of what passed for love and wasn't. I don't think it's possible to give a child too much of the right kind of love.

In the interest of the children there must be love not only between parent and offspring, but between the parents too. Carey's case illustrates that.

He was raised by parents who came to use him as a foil for their own bickering. Carey was an only child. By the time he was born the parents literally hated each other. Yet in spite of the fact that the father was a gangster and the mother a prostitute, they had enough self-respect to want to keep their quarrels from the child. In front of him they tried to create the illusion of domestic felicity. But youngsters, even infants, are extremely acute to symptoms of parental friction. They learn to interpret silences and facial expressions just as readily as open quarrels and frothing at the mouth.

Carey, from what we gathered later, was a "nervous" child at the age of five. About then the parents' quarrels became less inhibited. The mother would leave home, taking Carey with her, and go to live in a furnished room. The father would catch up with them and make a deal: if Carey and his mother returned, he would do thus and so. He was not really anxious to have the mother back, but she came as part of the package; he wanted the boy, for whom he had affection, in his manner. Thus the mother discovered that in Carey she had a shield and a buckler. When, periodically, she could stand her husband no longer, she would leave with her son, have herself a time, and wait to be "found" by her husband. Then she would dangle Carey before him, wring some concession out of him, and return to the family domicile until the next time.

This kept up for years. Carey eventually became a juvenile delinquent, then an adult felon.

I don't hold that there is a positive, exclusive relationship between the parental discord and Carey's criminality. Other conditions played a part too. But it is the opinion of at least one psychiatrist who studied him, a caseworker who knew the family for years, and myself that Carey's insecurity and "nervousness" were at least heavily contributed to by the domestic friction. I base my feeling, in part, on a letter I once received from Carey. True, at that time he was pitying himself. He was in the Tombs for parole violation. Upon me, in considerable measure, depended whether he would go back to Sing Sing or be freed. So he was trying to explain and excuse himself. But he hit upon some truth when he said, "From the time I was in rompers I can't ever remember being happy or feeling sure what would happen the next minute. My folks were always raising hell with each other. They didn't give a damn about the fact a kid wants to know he'll always find his father and mother home. . . . Sure, I've done things I shouldn't. But can't you consider what made me this way?"

There is another family hazard that, according to most students of the subject, plays a part in delinquency and criminality: the jealousy that develops between one child and another in the same family. I doubt that much needs to be said on this score, since probably every reader who has a brother or sister recalls some such feeling. It is difficult to control. Parents need to be extremely delicate in handling such rivalry. And some criminality is probably a direct or indirect outgrowth of such intrafamily feeling.

Even in families where there is great warmth and affection

there will occasionally be a delinquent child. Outside factors will sometimes outweigh the family's influence at a particularly crucial moment.

I don't mean to suggest by all the foregoing that each of the persons described was made criminal exclusively through family influences. But security, it seems to me, is the thing most necessary to each of us in this highly competitive modern world. I mean emotional as well as economic security.

Emotional security comes from being loved. And love should begin in the home.

CHAPTER XXV

The Careerist in Crime

Martin and Sue and Mark were amateurs—warped personalities made antisocial by youthful conditioning. They more or less were impelled into a way of life they didn't relish but had to pursue. The professional criminal frequently, perhaps commonly, chooses his activity not in antisocial protest but merely from circumstances that make it seem to him the most attractive way to get on in the world. To be sure, we can say he is deficient in what we choose to call the moral sense. But no neurotic compulsion need be involved. His problem is a totally different one, both for society in general and for parole in particular.

So let's talk, in this chapter and the three that follow, about typical professionals and how they operate against us. We'll begin with the confidence man, most fantastic of the lot.

If someone came up to you and offered to sell you a machine, for a mere thousand dollars, that turns out crisp, new hundred-dollar bills for each piece of newspaper you feed into it, you'd call for a policeman, wouldn't you? Because you know that isn't legal. Yet thousands of people fall for the money machine; scores buy them every month, in spite of the fact that the swindle is regularly publicized.

No matter how often the public is warned, there is always one more person to fall for the wiles of the artful bunco operator.

Take the Spanish Prisoner game. Since shortly after the Civil
War over a hundred thousand people have invested in it. I've
been approached myself.

You get a letter from a man in Spain, Mexico, or Cuba. He
is, he says, a political prisoner who could buy his freedom if
only he could get to that half-million dollars he has cached
away. You, who he understands are an honest man, can lay
hands on it for him. Get it, keep half for yourself, and deliver
the rest to him.

A quarter of a million not being chicken feed, you begin cor-
respondence with the prisoner. You meet his emissary, who for
some convincing reason can't do the job himself, and he tells
you how to go about locating the fortune. You are induced to
put up a thousand dollars, or twenty thousand, whatever you're
good for, to prove your honesty and good intentions. You proceed to the city where you are to find the money. No treasure.
No prisoner. You're victim number a hundred thousand and
one.

Con men will tell you, should you be injudicious enough
to get near one, that "you can't cheat an honest man," that the
"mark [sucker] must have a little larceny in his heart," else he
can't be hoodwinked.

This is balderdash, propaganda spread by the underworld
chamber of commerce to make victims reluctant to press
charges. The great majority of con games are not premised on
the proposition that the mark wants to make an easy, slightly
illicit dollar. Most victims are thoroughly honest.

There are only a very few, so-called big con, games that do
operate on the principle that you can't cheat an honest man.
These games take the longest to consummate and bring the

biggest prizes. Probably you're not even eligible for the big con because you don't have enough money.

One bunco man told me there are three big con games. Another said there are five. I know about four that should be dignified with the label. They are the Payoff, the Rag, the Wire, and stock and investment swindles. Bear in mind that a good con man doesn't go by the book. He can make a big con out of anything.

In the Payoff the victim is led to believe that the bunco artists are fleecing gambling clubs by fixing races, knowing just which horses will win. The mark is allowed to share the illicit profits. He loses of course.

In the Rag, stock is the gimmick. The con man meets and becomes friendly with the mark, tells him he is confidential agent of a Wall Street syndicate which is breaking the small branch exchanges and bucket shops by manipulating stock prices on the Exchange. The agent buys and sells according to orders he gets from the main office. Naturally he has a sure thing, for he is buying stocks already fixed to go up, selling some definitely rigged downward. Reluctantly he deals the victim in. The mark makes a profit time and again. In the final deal he puts all his winnings, plus every other dollar he owns, on the final operation. He is told to "handle a hundred thousand shares" of a certain stock. Because of the way it is said, he buys, let us say. And he is cleaned out. The con man explains "handle" meant to sell.

The Wire is described in the next chapter.

Stock and investment swindles are legion. Gold mines are "discovered" ever week. One well-known operator mulcted Britons of seven million dollars in the sale of stock in non-

existent oil wells and a "glass casket company." Florida real
estate and other items of merchandise were also in his line. More
recently uranium deposits have become the lure.

Charlie Gondorff, a top-ranking man, took a Connecticut
banker for three hundred and seventy-five thousand dollars in
a double take; that is, he swindled the Yankee once, convinced
him that was a slip that could never happen again, had the man
go back for more cash, which he promptly lost.

One church trustee was approached by two confidence men
with a proposition that—you guessed it—just could not turn
out adversely. In a matter of days whatever a man invested
would be doubled. There would be only one chance at it, no
more. The trustee "borrowed" three hundred thousand dollars
of church money, which he was going to return in a few days,
as soon as he got his huge profit. Result: One confidence man
was never apprehended; one received a suspended sentence; the
trustee went to prison.

You think these cases indicate incredible gullibility? Listen
to this one. Four New York confidence men discovered a
stretch of road under construction near Yonkers. Because of
shortage of materials, work had been suspended and the steam
shovels, drills, and other equipment left on the spot. The
bunco men quickly printed some gold mine stock certificates.
They approached and befriended likely prospects. Some quick
sales talks, and carloads of people were being driven out to
Yonkers to view the concrete evidence of the discovery of a
vein of gold. All that was needed was cash to resume operations. The prospect was urged to act fast. And he must not
breathe a word of this, for if news leaked out, Wall Street
would snap up the proposition. The gang took a reported hun-

dred and thirty-five thousand dollars before road construction resumed and the bubble burst.

The first-rate confidence man goes only for deals of at least this size. He won't play unless the take promises to be five or six figures. Occasionally, though, a neophyte takes a more modest flyer. We had a woman who was released on parole from Auburn State Prison. She took a furnished room in another city, became friendly with the landlady, and confided that she owned a fine piece of property at 50 Wall Street, Auburn. A fine address. For a modest amount, about five hundred dollars I believe, the parolee sold half this property to her new-found friend. The address is that of Auburn State Prison.

The confidence artist doesn't mind mulcting some relatively poor person. He is absolutely without scruples. The information booth at Grand Central Station in New York has been sold hundreds of times to newly arrived immigrants. The con man would bring the victim to the station, point out how much business goes on there, and sell him the booth as an ideal fruit-stand. And the poor immigrant had no larceny in his heart.

You don't have to be the least bit venal, either, to be victimized by the Heir Castle game, operating since 1847 and still going strong.

You receive a letter from a legal firm informing you that after painstaking research it has been ascertained you are one of a large number of heirs to the never-settled estate of Sir Francis Drake. With accrued interest it is worth fifteen billion. There are legitimate heirs, like you, and twelve thousand illegitimate claimants who must be fought in court. You are invited to furnish funds for legal fees to establish your claim. For every dollar invested, you will receive a proportionate share of the estate when settled. Naturally you'll contribute as much as you can. That's all, brother.

The confidence man even capitalizes on the religious feelings of people in a game such as the Pigeon Drop, also known as the Wipe. There are many variants of this, not all playing on religion, but here is an actual example, involving a man I once interviewed in Sing Sing. He didn't know it, but he had been working a racket originated over a thousand years ago in China. Like many other bunco men practicing the Pigeon Drop, he combined it with the Handkerchief Switch.

The inmate, Clark, struck up acquaintance with a Catholic man. As the two were walking along, one spied a handsome rosary on the ground. They picked it up and were inspecting it when Clark's confederate came along, his eyes searching the pavement.

"Is this yours?" the mark politely asked.

The man was ever so grateful. "Yes, indeed! That rosary is worth a fortune to me. It was blessed by the Pope. It's been in my family for generations. I wouldn't sell it for fifty thousand dollars!"

He offered each man a thousand dollars' reward. Before the intended victim could accept, Clark intervened and nobly remarked, "No reward is necessary. We're happy to have been helpful. We're good Catholics ourselves."

Smith, the owner of the rosary, was deeply touched. He invited the two honest gentlemen to dinner. There he revealed that he was a wealthy man, looking for some honest person to guard a large sum of money he planned to donate to the Church.

After some persuasion the mark consented to act as guardian. Besides working in a fine cause, he would be amply compensated. The philanthropist then counted out a thousand dollars in cash and tied it into a handkerchief. He gave the bundle to the victim, saying, "Here. You hold it until I'm able to turn it over to the priest."

Then the philanthropist bethought himself. "You know," he said, "just as good business practice, I suppose I ought to ask you to establish your financial responsibility."

With a little prodding the mark went to his bank and drew out a thousand dollars. The philanthropist reopened the handkerchief, added the second thousand, and tied the handkerchief up again. What purported to be the same handkerchief was given to the mark. He was told to take the money home, hide it under his mattress, and wait until the philanthropist called on him.

Not having heard from the rich donor in a week, the victim opened the handkerchief and found strips of newspaper.

By now perhaps you are saying, "Anyone so gullible deserves to be hornswoggled."

It's not our gullibility but the bunco man's plausibility that accounts for the stupendous success of the confidence game. The bunco artist's stock in trade is personality, charm, magnetism. He can hypnotize a hypnotist. He is invariably a lovely fellow whom you feel honored to know.

And he's always around, even in times of greatest stress and tribulation. There are the hearse chasers, who bilk thousands of people yearly. These gentry strike when there has been a death in the family and while the body is still unburied. That way, the ghoulish con man figures, the survivors are too upset to think straight.

One variant of hearse chasing, operated by a parolee, was to get from obituary columns the name of a recently deceased man. The day before the funeral he called on the widow.

"I've got that deed for your husband," he announced.

The widow told him her husband had just died. What was it about?

Shocked and grieved by the startling news, the visitor explained that the husband had paid forty-five hundred on a five-thousand-dollar lot. The final five hundred was now due, whereupon the property would change hands.

The widow, assuming her husband had transacted the deal, took it for granted that the land was a good investment. Not wanting it to go by default, she would pay the money—and receive title to some worthless swamp.

Another parolee made a big business out of another hearse-chasing variant. He and three associates subscribed to newspapers all over the country. Whenever they found that a youngster had died, they sent a package, C.O.D., two dollars, to the home. It contained a ten-cent fountain pen. The grieving mother or father assumed the child had ordered it; they were in no mood to argue about a little matter like that. They paid.

Cheap? Yes. But each sale netted a profit of a dollar seventy. Multiply that by twenty-five thousand and you get forty-two thousand five hundred dollars—which is about what these rascals collected before it was our joy to walk in on them, accompanied by postal inspectors.

Some con games attack given occupational groups. The Sick Engineer is tailor-made for lawyers.

In Rochester, New York, a reputable attorney received a visit from a fine-looking gentleman who introduced himself as Mortimer X. Portfroy. (We knew him by a different name, plus a number.) Mr. Portfroy was a mining engineer, staying   .

temporarily at the Y Hotel. He was very anxious to get hold of at least a thousand shares of Triple X mining stock (the name is fictitious, of course). He asked the attorney to represent him in picking up the issue.

"Why," the honest barrister exclaimed, "that stock's been off the market for years. It's worthless."

"Exactly!" Mr. P. replied. "That's what everybody believes. But I happen to know gold has been discovered there and I plan to gain control of the company. I will offer up to fifty dollars a share for as many shares as you can pick up. I will pay you for your efforts, and if you buy the stock for less than fifty, the difference is yours."

A week later the lawyer received a hurry call. Would he come out to a suburb to draw up a will for a dying man?

The attorney found a very sick man indeed. The poor fellow, a mining engineer, seemed about ready to draw his last breath. Between gasps he asked the attorney to open a safe and extract the contents, so the sick engineer might decide how to dispose of them.

As the advocate was listing various stocks and bonds, he came across a block of Triple X mining stock—three thousand shares!

"What about these?" he asked.

"Oh," the dying man replied, "they're worthless. Throw them out."

"No," the honorable counselor said, "you can sell them. In fact, I know where you can dispose of them at once. How much do you want for them?"

"Well, I'll be happy to get two dollars a share. Is that too much? Oooooh!" And he almost expired.

The attorney considered: if he paid six thousand dollars for the shares he could quite ethically sell them to his client for the agreed upon price and make a stupendous profit.

Being no fool, he first called the Y Hotel. Yes, Portfroy was still registered. Out on a mining expedition, but his bags were in his room, his rent paid two weeks in advance.

The attorney bought the stock, returned to town, called on Mr. Portfroy. He was still out. And that's the way he remained. The counselor was left in complete possession of three thousand shares of worthless stock.

More than against lawyers, confidence men operate on businessmen. The Slum Hustle is a device in which there does have to be a soupçon of larceny in the blood of the merchant.

In this game the con man sells a businessman certain merchandise which he hints—but doesn't quite say—is stolen, hence must be disposed of cheaply. In one instance a man convinced a liquor dealer that he had a truckload of bonded bourbon, hijacked, he subtly suggested. The entire load had to go at a dollar a bottle. The merchant bought himself a carload of colored water.

Shoddy men's suits are a favored merchandise in the Slum Hustle. So are furs. But anything at all may be part of such a deal. I once stopped in a swank antique shop to inquire about a locket I thought my wife would like. As I fingered it, the dealer gave me its pedigree—Vienna, circa 1790, and so on. While discussing price, I noticed a man standing out on the street, looking into the window. I recognized him as Bob, a confidence man of long standing. He was giving me the office —that is, an unspoken high sign that means, "Nix, brother! Come off it!" I don't know how to explain a high sign. The person giving it doesn't move a muscle, but you get the signal nevertheless.

I replaced the locket, thanked the merchant, and left. I knew Bob would be waiting around the corner, and he was.

He had twice been on parole, each time most unsuccessfully, and we were constantly pinching him for violation. I arrested him or ordered his incarceration so many times that we got to like each other. This is another feature of law-enforcement work difficult to explain. But it happens.

Now Bob asked, "You thinking of buying that piece?"

"Yes. Why?"

"Don't do it."

"Why?"

"What did the dealer say it was?"

I told him.

"It's a forgery," he told me. "It was made a month ago."

"How do you know?"

"Because I sold it to him in a Slum Hustle."

Small shopkeepers are at times victimized by the Glim Dropper. A glim, I should explain to the uninitiated, is an eye. The game, for reasons you will readily appreciate, can be played only by bunco men fortunate enough to possess but one glim.

In Binghamton, New York, a small, well-dressed man entered a store of the kind once called a dry goods emporium. A button had fallen off his jacket and he wanted to buy some thread and a needle. As the storekeeper was making change he heard something fall to the floor with a click. The customer cried, "Oh, damn!" and began searching frantically.

"Drop something, sir?" the merchant asked.

"Yes," said the gentleman, straightening up. "My eye."

And the startled store owner now saw that the customer, who had indubitably come in with two eyes, now possessed but one. A search for the missing orb was to no avail. The customer was very upset.

"That was a special job," he explained. "Made in England. It's so perfect no one knew I had an artificial eye. You didn't, did you?"

The merchant had to agree. He assured the man he needn't worry. When the store was swept up that evening the eye would certainly be found.

"If you find it," the customer told him, "I'll pay five hundred dollars' reward for it. The eye can't be reproduced in this country. It cost me over fifteen hundred." He gave his name and the hotel where he was staying.

Rest assured that the honest dealer, as soon as the gentleman left, searched that store cubic inch by inch. He found only some bobby pins and a dead mouse.

He was about to close for the day when a customer walked in for a pair of suspenders. As he was leaving, his foot kicked against something that went skittling across the floor. He picked it up.

"For heaven's sake!" he exclaimed. "An artificial eye!"

The merchant almost fell over the counter. "Thanks!" he cried. "I know the owner. He'll be very happy." And he held out his hand for the glim.

"Not so fast!" the other replied. "It happens I'm an oculist and I know a wonderful job when I see it. This is an English eye. It's worth at least fifteen hundred dollars. The man who lost it will advertise. He'll pay a handsome reward. I found it. I'm entitled to the reward."

There ensued a lively argument. Who rates the reward in

such circumstances—the finder or the man on whose premises the object is found? After considerable dickering, the shop-keeper, remembering the five-hundred-dollar promise, parted with two hundred for the eye. The Glim Dropper's confederate departed. The merchant phoned the hotel. That's all.

Few con men will play for such low stakes. Some, however, are forced to do so by circumstances—they are on the rocks or they have become too old to work more active games, or they are beginners working their way up.

During World War II a young, personable chap drove up to a gas station in a fancy car.

"Some water, please," he asked the attendant.

As the latter approached the radiator the driver cried, "No! Put it in the gas tank. Exactly ten gallons. Exactly!"

When he got over the shock of that, the attendant shrugged and ran ten gallons of water into the gas tank. After all, one got all sorts of customers these days.

The owner of the car now got out, extracted a pill box from a pocket, took out two pellets that looked like aspirin, and dropped them into the tank. The gentleman tipped the goggle-eyed attendant handsomely, got back into the car, started the motor, and prepared to roll off.

By this time the attendant was prepared to sacrifice himself to science. He almost threw himself in front of the wheels to get the driver to stop. It was a time of shortages. Gas was scarce. What was this? How could a car run on water?

The driver was a little annoyed by the insistent questioning. More than that, he was worried. "I suppose," he said wearily, "I'd better explain, since I was forced to stop for water. But remember—this is top secret."

He was, it turned out, a research chemist, assigned by the government to find a way of producing synthetic gas. And he'd done it. Each pellet of chemical, placed in exactly five gallons of water, produced five gallons of gas.

After much persuasion the chemist parted with a few hundred pills of synthetic gas and moved on to the next customer. The reason he *could* move on was because he had a false tank into which the water had gone. Imagine the face of the attendant later—he didn't have an extra tank.

Another cheapster devised a penny ante scheme that burgeoned into quite a profitable business. He advertised in farm journals that for a dollar he would send a steel engraving of George Washington "suitable for framing." Many a farmer had a spot on some wall that could stand some dressing up. He'd send in his dollar. Back would come a postage stamp mounted on a piece of cardboard. When thousands of people were similarly swindled and the government stepped in, it appeared that the artful rogue was not guilty of fraudulent advertising. Everything he had claimed was true. For a dollar you got a steel engraving of George Washington; it was mounted on a cardboard. Who says it wasn't suitable for framing? The gentleman finally offered to "cease and desist," but he wasn't prosecuted.

Restaurateurs will do well to look out for small-time operators who practice a number of petty con rackets. In one, a decrepit bum asks for a meal. He's starving. The kindly owner sits him in a corner and gives him a plate of food. He watches the poor fellow wolf the grub down. Then the bum heaves a sigh of satisfaction, reaches into a pocket, extracts a grimy handkerchief, and wipes his mouth. But as he does so a ten-dollar bill falls out of his pocket.

Outraged, the restaurateur walks up, takes the money, deducts the cost of the meal, gives the vagrant change—perhaps nine fifty—and throws him out. Thus the bum is in nine fifty, in good coin of the realm, and one blue plate special. The owner of the eating house is in one counterfeit ten-dollar bill.

Con men never expect to quit. They consider themselves in the safest business in the world.

One bunco man whom I got to know well gave me his story on the odds—after he was finished with parole.

"I figure it this way," he said. "I've got better than a fifty-fifty chance all down the line. Say I get pinched. I've got much better than a fifty-fifty chance I can talk the complainant out of pressing a charge. After all, I'd tell him, he had larceny in his heart, else I couldn't have taken him.

"But say he does make a complaint. I've got better than a fifty-fifty chance of talking my way out of it with the cop. If I can't, maybe I can buy him off.

"But say I can't. So I've got better than a fifty-fifty chance of getting away with it in Magistrate's Court. Plenty of judges can be fixed. If not, I put on an act. I'm outraged. I'm gonna sue for false arrest. I have an alibi witness in court. How the hell could I have committed the crime when I was a hundred miles away? Or I tell them my sick mother is dying—anything. Chances are I break the magistrate's heart.

"But say I don't. Say he holds me for trial. I've got better than a fifty-fifty chance of beating the case. But I can reduce the risk by copping a plea to a lesser offense, if I think things aren't going my way. Usually I don't have to. I stand trial. I could fix a juror, or maybe the judge—depends on the city. You've gotta know your town. I could get the complainant to forget certain things. I could pay the cop to forget what he saw. I could get witnesses to disappear.

"But suppose I can't. So I bring out what a hard-working man I've been. I take the stand in my own behalf, you understand? That always impresses a jury. I tell them how I long to go back to my poor widowed mother a thousand miles away. I want to make her last days on earth happy. Give me fifteen minutes on the stand, with a good mouthpiece feeding the right questions, and I guarantee you I'll have those jurors using crying towels!

"But say I don't. Say they convict me. I've got better than a fifty-fifty chance of being put on probation. After all, I'm not a killer. There's my mother too. She needs my support.

"All right. Suppose I don't get probation. So I go to the pen for a year. Chances are way better than fifty-fifty I'll get me a cushy job, I'll take a year's vacation, and come out. What's tough about that?"

"Suppose," I asked, "you get dropped half a dozen times a year. Your odds aren't going to be as sweet as that. The law of averages will catch up with you."

"Listen!" He cried, intent on his thesis. "I've figured this out *according* to the law of averages! Do you know, on the basis of estimated population and number of accidents a year, there's a damn sight more chance of your being hit by a truck as you cross this street right this minute than there is of my serving a term in the next twelve months? *Hey!* Watch it! Wanna get killed? Look both ways when you cross!"

CHAPTER XXVI

The Wire

My wife and I were walking along Park Avenue when we noticed a gentleman coming toward us. "*There's* aristocracy!" she said. "Upper crust with plenty of filling."

He was dressed in quiet good taste. His beautifully tailored clothes gave him a dignified yet dashing appearance. He wore a black Homburg hat, gray kid gloves, and he was leading a Scottie on a leash. He was about sixty. His face was handsome, his figure trim and supple. There was a definite air of distinction about him.

As he passed he smiled, tipped his hat, and bowed ever so slightly.

My wife looked at me with admiration and awe. "You know him?"

"Yes, my love," I replied, "he's the most convincing confidence man I have ever met."

Herb is dead now, and telling his story can't hurt him.

Like all successful bunco artists, he was magnetic. Talking with him was a pleasure, although it usually cost the listener a chunk of cash. Herb never played for pennies. He started young and performed spectacularly.

One of his earliest coups had to do with a yacht he wanted to sell a banker. It is a tribute to Herb's talents that at the outset the tycoon hadn't the faintest interest in any yacht. He wasn't a sportsman, hated the sea, and his idea of adventure was listening to the talk of co-members of his ultraconservative club. Yet he listened, in that same club, to the persuasive Herb and came to the conclusion he hadn't lived up to then and could hope to begin living only if he owned a yacht.

Herb took the banker aboard the vessel. They explored her from stem to stern. Then and there the hypnotized capitalist capitulated and wrote a check.

The only trouble was, the yacht wasn't Herb's to sell. She belonged to the governor of that state. The plausible bunco man had determined when she would be unattended, boarded her, and made his sale.

Shortly after that Herb went into the securities business. He made a fortune selling stocks and bonds—all of them strictly illegitimate. He unloaded a block of stock in a nonexistent copper mine. He talked a banker into trading him five thousand shares of first-rate Consolidated Edison for twenty thousand shares in a mythical diamond mine in Africa. Then he sold a corporation a telephone system he didn't own.

After this he became a specialist in the Wire. There are minor variations, as this game is played over the world, but here is Herb's version, as he explained it to me.

A roper, the first contact man, goes into a community to find a victim. The exploratory weeks or months necessary to discover the ripest mark and to put him into a position to be taken is known as "putting up the mark." The victim will be very wealthy, and also—a very important item—about to take a trip. Herb stated that the roper would find out "more about the man and his family than he knows himself. We would know whether he likes rum or whisky, church or women. What kind of women he prefers, blondes, brunettes, or redheads; good, bad, or very bad. We'd know how much he's got in the bank and how much of that he'd go for with us. Then we'd wait for him to take a trip."

Why? Because "when a man's traveling he takes more chances. And he hasn't got friends around to advise him."

Say Mr. Jones boards a train in Toledo, en route to New York. The roper is on that train. By chance he is in the club car when Jones enters. By sheer accident the two men sit next to each other. Conversation begins; drinks are purchased. Jones finds the roper a deucedly clever, altogether charming traveling companion. He *likes* him. And he is positively delighted when the man happens to mention being a friend of Sally Turner of Ashtabula. Sally is Mr. Jones' sister—imagine such a coincidence!

By the time the train is pulling into New York, Mr. Jones loves Smitty, the roper. He certainly intends looking him up when they both get back to Toledo. "I'm in the telephone book," each says, one truthfully.

As they disembark Smitty happens to say he's staying at the Sychansych Hotel. And, by God! so is Jones! That calls for a luncheon date tomorrow.

This part of the procedure is called "roping the mark."

At lunch the roper prepares to "steer the mark to the inside man." That's Herb.

"I'm going over to Western Union to see my brother-in-law. He's the manager there," Smitty says. "Why don't you come along and meet him? I'd love to have him know you."

Jones agrees. They go to a Western Union office. At least it looks exactly like one. Bicycles are arrayed outside. Messengers rush in and out. Girls take messages from customers. But it's fake; every person is a hired confidence operator, playing a

role which is his specialty. The place is run by a con man who
rents out time for a fixed period, on appointment. His associates
will do exactly what the roper and the inside man instruct, for
the benefit of the mark.

(This game *could* be played, less convincingly, without the
expensive equipment and actors. In that case the scene of operations would be a hotel room, perhaps the mark's. Under such
circumstances the bunco men say they are "playing him against
the wall.")

Herb is already on the premises as manager. He meets Jones,
and the men like each other. The roper induces the inside man
to come out for a quick one.

Seated in the booth of a bar, Smitty asks, "Are you about
set?"

Herb looks sharply at his brother-in-law, then at Jones.

"Oh, you can talk freely!" the roper assures. "Jonesy's a pal!
Why, this is Sally Turner's brother!"

That eases Herb's mind.

Now comes "telling the tale."

Herb has been kicked around something awful at Western
Union. He's sick of it. He will be eligible to retire within two
weeks. But before doing so, he's going to make a killing. Herb
hesitates.

"Go on! You can trust Jonesy!" the roper urges.

Well, it's like this. The race results come in over the wire.
Say they indicate that Three-Legged Pete has won the third
at Pimlico. Herb holds up the results a few minutes, calls
Smitty, who waits in a certain horse room, and has him lay
money on the horse that has already won. A few minutes later
the results get to the bookie and Smitty collects.

Simple. Foolproof. Lucrative. You can't lose. Cute, eh?

Jones is shocked yet fascinated. He knows this is dishonest. Yet bookies and horse rooms *are* illegal. Western Union *did* kick the guy around. It *is* quite a wonderful idea.

At precisely this psychological moment the con men must determine whether Jonesy has a bit of that larcenous juice in his veins. He will be "allowed in" only if he has and if he realizes he is doing something slightly felonious. This is important. Otherwise a man may call in the law later.

Herb returns to his office. Jones, merely out of curiosity, you understand, accompanies. Smitty to the horse room. It, too, is fake. Everything is staged. Bettors go up to cages to lay huge sums of money. Some collect thousands of dollars. Others lose and tear their hair and curse. Arguments start here and there. Occasionally (for an extra finif or so) a fight will start. All play-acting.

The phone rings in a booth. Smitty answers. He comes out and whispers to Jones, "He says bet on Calcium to win." The roper places his bet, and three minutes later collects five thousand dollars.

Jones is beginning to itch. This is the moment to "give him the convincer." Smitty allows his friend to bet on the next horse and win. How long has this been going on? Jones wonders. His nose is twitching. He wants more of the same. But this ends the day's work. Jones must be allowed to go back to his hotel with the convincer. He must have time for this great scheme to sink in. He must palpitate to get back into that horse room.

Jones *is* excited. Honest businessman that he is, how can he afford to miss the chance of a lifetime? The whole operation will last but two weeks. It's now or never.

He puts the proposition to Herb next day. Herb, after some

thought, decides to allow good old Jones to bet on his information. "There's plenty there for the both of us, ha! ha!" But
first Jones must be "put on the send."

This means he will be required to go home and cash in all
his securities, draw his money out of the bank, and return to
New York. He is not allowed to write, for then he'd have to
make explanations to his family or banker. Besides, federal
postal laws would enter in—and they're tough. This way,
Jones proceeds to Toledo, tells no one what he's doing, returns with plenty of cash. (One of Herb's marks brought in a
hundred and thirty-five thousand dollars.)

Jones plays and wins. He is twenty-five thousand ahead.
Don't forget: he can't lose.

Word comes through. Bet on Scrofula. Jones picks up another ten grand.

Then Herb announces that the next play will be his last. He
will retire after that. Jones is prepared to bet every last nickel
on this horse.

We are ready for "the blowoff."

Jones and Smitty are in the horse room, waiting for that last,
crucial call. Smitty has to go to the men's room. While he's
away the booth phone rings. Jones answers. Herb tells him,
"Place your money on Stinker."

When Smitty comes out Jones tells him, "Herb says place
the money on Stinker."

So they place every dollar, winnings and all, on Stinker to
come first.

And the stinker runs second.

Jones is bankrupt, ruined—also practically insane. Just then
Herb comes in, smiling, and asks for his part of the winnings.

"Winnings!" Smitty shouts. "Why, you ——! There *are* no winnings! Jonesy and I are cleaned out! You told us to bet on Stinker to win, and the fool horse ran second!"

"To win!" Herb shrieks. "Why, you crazy jackass! Do you mean to say you played him to win? I distinctly said *place* your money on Stinker! And Stinker *did* place!" (To place is to run second, in case you don't know.)

A wild argument ensues and soon becomes a melee. Smitty pulls out a gun and fires point-blank into his brother-in-law, who falls to the ground, blood spurting from his mouth.

This is known as "chilling out the mark" once the "score" has been taken. The blood is ink from a "cackle bladder," a hollow ball of thin rubber. The bunco man bites on it, and it gushes.

Jones, already financially ruined, doesn't want to be held as accessory to a murder as an added catastrophe. He is gratified when Smitty, good old Smitty, says, "Beat it, Jones. Don't get mixed up in this. I'll take the rap for it." Jones beats it. Curtain.

Herb played the Wire for a decade. He claimed he made over two million dollars in that time without a single arrest. Whether that's so or not, he was at last brought to book and given all of two and a half to five years in Sing Sing. When he was paroled he was broke.

His parole officer had no faith whatever in Herb when they first met. Two weeks later the officer would have floored any man denying Herb was the most charming guy in town. How could he do wrong?

The senior parole officer was altogether skeptical of the parole officer's enthusiasm. He spoke to Herb, warned him against reverting to crime, and dismissed him with the conviction that here was one of the most delightful and honorable gentlemen in Christendom. He wouldn't do wrong!

I spoke to Herb a number of times. It was like trying not to smell chloroform, yet being seduced into whiff after whiff until one went sound asleep. Herb was scintillating, stimulating, brilliant. He could discuss a wide variety of subjects. He knew books, music, sports, business, famous personalities. I constantly had to discipline myself against putting an arm around him and saying, "To hell with it, Herb! Let's forget this parole business!"

There seemed no question about Herb's employment as a salesman, for we saw his commission checks. I wanted to be certain the checks were real and asked the parole officer to visit the employer. He came back glassy-eyed. The boss not only verified that Herb worked for him; he was convinced Herb was a business genius and planned to go into a new business with the parolee—the employer to furnish a hundred per cent of the capital, Herb to receive fifty per cent of the profits!

The new business was set up, and it was quite legitimate. In no time at all, one of the firm's big accounts offered Herb an even better partnership in *his* business. Herb accepted.

Then we discovered that, without telling us and in violation of his parole, Herb had dissolved the later partnership, organized a corporation of his own, and issued stock—in a firm that was to put out a revolutionary toothpaste tube.

That spelled trouble.

I instructed the parole officer to bring Herb in for questioning. Although he outwitted me at every turn I believed he should be held in the Tombs pending a really searching investigation. I asked the officer to take Herb in to my superior, ask for a warrant, and lodge the parolee. I couldn't go with our man because I had someone waiting for me.

An hour later it occurred to me that I hadn't seen Herb being led out to the Tombs. I stuck my head in the doorway of my colleague's room. There was Herb, calmly smoking his pipe. There was the officer, looking dazed. And there was the head of the New York office of the Division of Parole frantically telephoning friends to borrow money to invest in the world-shattering toothpaste tube.

My colleague didn't support me in the belief Herb was a parole violator, and in the long run he was right. The toothpaste tube undertaking, whether legitimate or not, was dropped. Herb went into new and increasingly better—and thoroughly honest—business enterprises. The same affability and personableness that made him a fine con man served him well in business. He is the only confidence man I've ever known who did reform.

When Herb came in for his final discharge papers he was international manager of a big corporation manufacturing heavy steel equipment. He was concerned because a trade magazine had his picture on the cover. He feared his past might be revealed.

I asked him on this occasion whether he had any idea why he had turned legitimate. He said—and I believe him—that he was one of those few people in the con game so terrifically affected by a prison sentence as to be willing to do anything to avoid another term—he was even willing to turn honest!

CHAPTER XXVII

Maxie the Goniff

Not long ago I was walking along a dark Manhattan side street late at night when a thin, spidery little man stopped me to inquire how to get to a certain address. I told him, and he thanked me profusely.

"Funny thing about New Yorkers," he said. "They don't know their own city. You're the first person out of six who could give me directions!" He thrust out a hand, and we shook on it. I kept hold of his, tightened my grip, and said, "And now give me back my wallet or I'll bust your jaw!"

I had only sensed it, but, sure enough, in that split second, when he was distracting my attention by offering his right hand, his left had gone into my jacket and taken my wallet.

The dip handed me back my property, his eyes pleading. "No hard feelings, I hope?" he asked.

I almost walloped him for that. Then I recognized him. "No hard feelings, Maxie," I told him.

He drew back in fear. Then he got a better glimpse of me. "Why, it's Mr. Dressler!"

"I won't turn you in," I continued, "provided—"

He was frightened again.

"Provided," I said, "you tell me how you work. Do that, and I won't get you pinched—unless I see you on the street again."

We made a deal. I paid him a little money and Maxie gave

me his life story, or what he claims is his personal saga. It's pretty much the story of any pickpocket, or "cannon," as they are called in the professional underworld.

I can vouch for Maxie's story only to this extent: his recital of how a pickpocket operates is correct. His story about his early life may or may not be partly imagined, but Maxie has been on parole several times, and he knew I had seen his case record; hence he would be inclined to be a bit conservative in his statements.

Maxie the Goniff is a professional. Practically all cannons are. He is not very bright. His body is slight and springy; his fingers are long, tapering, and nervous. His face resembles a parrot's, the beak long and hooked downward. His eyes are furtive. He decided over fifty years ago that picking "pokes" was a fine way of making a living. He apprenticed himself to a master, studied hard, graduated with honors, and went on his own. He wouldn't tell me how old he was at the time we spoke, but my guess is that he was at least sixty-five.

"I'm slowing up a little," was the most he would say. "My fingers got a little rheumatism."

Like most of his kind, Maxie has a long criminal record. He has been arrested seventy-one times in twenty-two states.

"Doesn't speak so well for you, Maxie," I goaded him. "A good thief doesn't get caught, you know."

He flushed angrily. "Every one of them pinches came after a whole season's work. In fifty years I done six years' time. I'm living good—well, pretty good—for forty-four years and it cost me six years! You should have it so good!"

He claims that both his parents were alcoholics, that they put him out of the house when he was twelve, and that he has been on his own ever since. For a time he was a petty thief, then a shoplifter, and finally, while still a kid, he met a man who took him on as an apprentice dip and taught him the business.

Picking pockets *is* a business, Maxie insists. "You've got to figure a certain amount of risk in any business. Suppose I open a saloon. I'm taking a chance, no? I might go broke, I might have to pay too much protection—it's all business."

Like all commercial enterprise, Maxie's has its seasons. "Summers we work the resorts, like Coney Island and the buses and subways going to and from. Beaches are good too. Certain holidays is season for us. Before Easter and Christmas. There's lots of shopping. That's when I hit department stores. In the elevators or even on the floor."

When he has had a run of bad luck he will depart from his more accustomed beat and cover a church wedding. "You don't often find much dough on the guys, but, brother! are they easy to take! They don't expect a thief in a church."

Occasional gravy is a convention or parade. Maxie plays the crowds. He loves American Legion groups because "half the time they don't even know *the next morning* whether they've been hooked or just spent the dough!"

"Most fun I had was in a hotel where there was a convention of these private dicks—you know, going over transoms to find the wife in bed with a man? They drink considerable and they like a good time. I hit one after the other, with my —er—associates. Mostly we scored off them in the men's rooms. And they're so ashamed they was taken that not a one makes a squeal!"

Maxie takes pride in his technique. He has little use for the lone operator, although he admits there are some good ones. He considers they take too many risks. Only his dire need for an immediate stake had led him to try for my wallet alone.

He likes to work in a mob of two to four people. Say you're on a subway or elevator. "You pick your mark and try to figure where he keeps his wallet. It ain't hard to find out. You just jostle the sucker and move off. Right away he puts his hand where he's got the wallet to see if it's there. He tips you off.

"Of course, if he don't fall for that, you've got to *fan* him. You feel around, very easy, until you locate the poke.

"Then comes pratting. You prat the guy around. That means you push him around, edge him around, not hard, gentle, just enough to distract his attention. Also to get him into position —the position you want him in for the score."

The man who does the pushing is the "stall." When the victim is in position, the "duke" (hand) of one thief extracts the poke. This man is called, variously, a "hook," "tool," "wire," or "instrument." He is the most skillful member of the team. The victim's attention is directed to the stall as the hook takes the wallet. Maxie is a hook.

"Funny thing," he said, chuckling. "Some guys look for a poke in a hip pocket. They like to take it from there. I'd rather score out of the breast pocket. Why? Because the sucker thinks he's cute, see? No offense meant to you, Mr. Dressler. He thinks if he carries it in the breast pocket it's tough to take. It is, but a good thief likes that kind of meat. I always do." (I doubt it. Professional cannons are awful liars. Chances are, Maxie, good businessman that he is, will always go for the easier score when possible.)

While taking from the inside pocket, the wire "shades" the duke—covers his hand so the victim won't see it, perhaps with a newspaper. "What I do," says Maxie, "is 'put a throw' in his face. I shade my duke with a paper and annoy the guy by flappin' it under his nose. That makes 'im mad. He's concentratin' on the throw while I'm 'takin' off the score.'

"In a good crowd, on a hip job, the 'push grift' works. No shadin' the duke, nothin'. Everybody's pushing, so you push all you want, and the guy don't even see or feel your hand."

In digging for the wallet the "straight hoist" is commonly employed. The cannon puts the first two fingers, held stiffly, into the pocket. He stiffens his body, lifts up on his toes, and out comes the wallet.

The next step is "cleaning." "The stall distracts attention, say. Now the wire's got the poke. He has to get clean right away. Because why? If the sucker 'blows' (discovers his loss) he's gonna figure right away it's the wire, because the wire was closest to him. So I pass the wallet on right away to one of my stalls—the one who will be first off the car or elevator. If the guy grabs me I'm clean. I beef like hell. If he goes for the stall, he drops the poke and he's clean. Or better yet, he plants it on some bystander and we take it back later."

Maxie is proudest of the fact that he is a specialist among specialists, "a left-breech hook." That's a man who can draw a score out of a left pants pocket. "There ain't many can do that. It's hard. Try it!"

I asked him how much he earned a year by grifting. He became very evasive, even apologetic. "Oh, I had my ups and downs. Why talk about it? You do all right, year in, year out, if you're good. Some years I run five, ten thousand. Other times not so good, maybe a couple of Gs."

"Where did your money go? In the ten years I used to run into you off and on, you were always broke."

"Well, the horses got a lot of it. Craps. Cards. Women. And I had to eat too." He forgot to mention that he has a wife and two children who are dependent upon him for their support.

I have never known an affluent pickpocket. I don't believe they make as much as Maxie claims, and their money seems to go fast. They live riotously. Some are drug addicts at times in their lives. Many have wives and children. I've never known one who wasn't a confirmed gambler or who wasn't fresh out of money every time I inquired.

Maxie is hurt because cannons are generally regarded with contempt, even in the professional underworld. He doesn't like to admit that contempt is earned. But the average dip is penny ante. Moreover, he is weak-willed, often turns in a pal to save his own skin. Perhaps because he is a weakling, the pickpocket is often a stool pigeon.

Maxie insists there is honor among thieves in his game. "Sure, a guy rats now and then. That don't prove nothin'. You'll always find a few rats. But most of us stick together. We help each other. We put up fall dough for a guy in trouble."

"Did you ever rat, Maxie?"

"Like I say, we stick together. We put up fall dough . . ."

I asked Maxie the Goniff what rules a man could follow to safeguard himself against the cannon. He leered. "There ain't no way to protect yourself from a good operator."

"But there must be some precautions that help?"

He shook his head dubiously. "Well, you can try to remember not to feel for your poke when you get pratted. But that only delays it. You can carry your wallet in the breast pocket, but that don't help much. I dunno. I guess the best advice is stay out of crowds. How you gonna do that?"

"Maxie," I asked, "if you had it to do over again, what would you be instead of a pickpocket?"

"What's wrong," he snapped, "with this racket?"

~~~~~~~~~~~~~~~~

CHAPTER XXVIII

Sammy the Booster

Sammy is a friend of mine. He's also a professional shoplifter. When I say he's a friend, I mean it only in the sense that I helped arrest him a couple of times when he was on parole, and a sort of camaraderie developed between us. Each time Sammy was pinched I bought him a drink and a steak before he started back to the big house. He appreciated that, and the last time it happened he shook my hand and fervently said, "T'anks for what you done for me. If I can ever do anythin' for you, just ax me." I didn't know quite how to take that.

I pretty much lost track of Sammy until recently. Sitting in a cafeteria, I heard a familiar voice and turned toward a nearby table. It was my friend. When he spotted me his eyes lit up. He left his companion and came jogging toward me, coffee cup in hand.

"Jeez, Mr. Dressler, I'm glad to see you!" he cried, pumping my hand. He sat down, beaming at me.

"What are you doing these days, Sammy?" I asked.

His beady little eyes shifted nervously. "Not a t'ing, Mr. Dressler, not a t'ing, I give you my woid! How's tricks with you?"

"Fine. You know I'm not in parole any more."

He looked shocked. "No! What happened?"

"Nothing. I decided I'd had enough of you guys. I decided to become a writer."

He gazed at me incredulously. "On the level?"

"On the level. *Now* tell me: what are you doing these days?"

He grinned, revealing the seashell pink gums adorned by four teeth.

"Puttin' it like that, Mr. Dressler, I'll tell ya. What the hell would you expect me to be doin'? I'm on the grift."

He said it as a matter of fact, not apologetically, for he is a careerist not an amateur. Take someone who sees an item he likes, can't afford it, and can't resist it, so he purloins it. He's strictly amateur. Take a kleptomaniac who steals something he neither needs nor covets because of an inner compulsion. He's amateur too. Sammy deliberately embarked on his career and intends to devote a lifetime to it. He lives in a world about which the general run of citizen knows practically nothing.

I thought of that as I talked to him. He hadn't changed much, though it had been seven years since I had last seen him, and five of those he had spent in stir. He was a surprisingly well-preserved man for sixty-one, with scarcely a crease in his face. On his long, aquiline nose rested pince-nez, which, with his almost bald pate, gave him a rather distinguished air. Add to this that he was well but not flashily dressed, lean and tall, and you got the impression he might be a schoolteacher, perhaps even a principal. It was only when he opened his mouth and you saw those tobacco-browned teeth and the blanks in between that you suspected otherwise. Also, when you heard him talk. He could do more to corrupt the language than any parolee I ever knew. His voice was high and his IQ low.

His presence gave me an idea. "Sammy," I said, "I want you to do me a favor."

He looked downright grateful. "Sure t'ing, Mr. Dressler. Anyt'ing you say."

"I want you to tell me, so I can put it into a book, all about the shoplifting business."

He flashed me a worried look, fidgeted. "Un—uh," he stammered. "Dat's on de level, about you bein' out of the parole racket?"

"You can take my word."

He considered a moment. Then, "Okay. I told you once I'd do anyt'ing you axed me. I'll do it. Only I don't want my friends to know I'm—what you could say—givin' trade secrets away. Don't use my name." (I'm not.)

I made a date and saw him next in his shabby brownstone apartment. The rooms were cheerier than the exterior. Sammy must have been in the chips. Last time I'd visited—to arrest him—he had been satisfied with a furnished hole in the wall. Now he had four rooms, modestly furnished, but bright. He also, from the evidence, had a girl friend, who may have accounted for the decor. She failed to make an appearance then or on any of my subsequent visits.

I'd brought a bottle and Sammy and I relaxed.

"What d' ye want to know?" he asked.

"You tell *me* what I ought to know. For instance, what part of your racket does the public know least about?"

The answer came fast and with conviction. "They don't know the difference between us boosters and a snatch-and-grab."

A snatch-and-grab, it developed, was an amateur. "Us, what you call professional t'iefs, we're either heels or boosters. Some parts of the country I been in they call themselves just boosters. But what it really is—a heel, he steals without talkin' to the salesman, y'unnastand? He waits his chance, makes his grab, and lams. A booster, he talks to the salesman, holds his interest, while his pal takes off the score."

For the snatch-and-grab Sammy had only contempt. "They foul up a job, they get the heat toined on in a store so's a booster ain't able to woik."

Sammy can't understand the casual thief. No one, he insisted, should steal unless he intends to make it his livelihood.

"Look at them housewives, society women, preachers, professors—even cops. They'll steal off a counter when they don't need to. I even know an actress—she grabs herself one of them silk kerchiefs. How do you like that! A woman with a fine racket, plenty of dough—look at the example she sets for kids!"

"What about you?" I asked. "What kind of an example do you set?"

"I'm in the *business!*" he snapped. "Besides, I wouldn't go for no five-buck snotrag."

Sammy doesn't go for handkerchiefs because he is currently strictly a silkworm. He steals only bolts of silk. He walks up to the counter, examines a bolt, replaces it with about a foot protruding over the counter. Then he walks toward the far end and engages the clerk's attention. His confederate, a woman, walks past, shopping bag in hand. She delivers a smart rap to the protruding end of the bolt. It flips over and into her bag. It sounds incredible that this technique works, but it does, the operator working with the lightning speed and skill of a sleight-of-hand artist extracting a rabbit from a man's ear.

As Sammy described his activities he paced the floor, enjoying the recital. At one point he was telling me about an acquaintance:

"This chick was no snatch-and-grab. She was a booster from way back, a silkworm on the grift. But she blows the score and the badman makes her. She can't get clean, so she tries to cop a sneak, but the dick nailed her. It looked like the bandhouse for her. But the boys put up the fall dough, they squared the beef with the witnesses, they got a mouthpiece and sprung her on bail. She blows, the beef is chilled, and she's back on the grift."

To interpret:

A shoplifter was caught in a department store, loaded with a bolt of silk. The underworld went to work at once. When the woman appeared in court, a lawyer (whom she hadn't retained) stood ready to defend her. A bondsman (whom she hadn't approached) put up bail. A witness (whom she hadn't met) gave her an alibi. A shady hanger-on (whom she saw for the first time in court) tried to get the store detective to forget important details of the affair. The case was ironclad, so the thief jumped bail, took off, and is now back in business.

Sammy used this incident to make the point that professional shoplifters live in a highly organized subworld, with a code, standards, a protective organization, even its own language. Of course he didn't put it that way, but that's what he meant.

Big cities are honeycombed with shoplifters, small towns have their share, and all are interrelated by common bonds. Units are fluid. Sammy has operated alone, with several partners, and as part of a larger mob. Some aggregations remain intact for years, others for only a few hauls.

I asked Sammy whether men or women made the better shop thieves. He hesitated not at all in saying, "Dames. They got natural advantages." They have bosoms in which silk stockings can be hidden, skirts that conceal anything from hankies to medicine balls.

Sammy couldn't tell me what proportion of shoplifters are female, and since the underworld publishes no annual report, the exact figure is unknown. But it has been estimated as high as ninety per cent. A more conservative figure comes from the New York City Court of Special Sessions. In one year, of 824 defendants before the court for shoplifting, nearly two-thirds were women.

Sammy told me how he got started in his life work. (Part of his story is corroborated by the record.) "I loined from me mudder. We used to have quite a racket. I was seven years old when I started. The old lady would take me to a store. She had a system of signals. While she talked to a salesman, she'd tip me off to what I was supposed to steal. If I grabbed it off and got away with it, fine. If I got caught, the old lady would pretend to get mad as hell. She'd yell, 'Sammy! How many times I hafta tell you to keep hands off things that don't belong to you?' She'd beat hell out of me, and I'd yell bloody moider, and the store people, of course, that would satisfy them."

"Did your father mind about you and your mother being on the grift?"

"I don't know me father. Don't know even if I *had* a father.

"We woiked that way 'til I was eleven," he continued. "Then the welfare took me away and put me in a orphanage like. My sister Cassie, she was five then, so me mudder wasn't left alone. Cassie done very well. She's one of the finest boosters in the business today. She's smart!" His eyes glowed. He helped himself to a snort of whisky.

"I run away from the orphanage. I done this and that. And maybe I was goin' straight—I don't remember. Anyhow, I'm a kid, say sixteen, and I'm woikin' in a department store, a stock boy. I'm gettin' slave pay, so one day I try to walk out with some of the stock—I t'ink it was a coupla shoits. You pass by a time clock to punch out and you walk past a guy that stands at the door. This sonofabitch stops me. I got the shoits inside the one I'm wearin', see? He says to me, 'Puttin' on a little weight, aintcha?'

"So they take the stuff off me, give me a boot in the tail, and throw me out. And I ain't gone a block before a guy comes up to me, a salesman from the place. He propositions me. How would I like to woik for a mob of heels? Well, sure I would! So that's how it happened. This guy, the salesman, he's a finger for the mob. He tips them to what's good, and if he can, he lays it out where they can get to it easy."

"Is it," I inquired, "common practice to have an inside man?"

"No, I wouldn't say so. But it happens they quite often pick up a guy for a mob the way they got me. Because they knew I was a t'ief."

"So now, Sammy, you've been in business how long?"

"About fifty years, I'd say."

"Does it pay?"

"Yes and no. You get caught now and then—you should know that, Mr. Dressler. But take it year in and out, it's all right. I don't say it's fun. I ain't like those jerks who try to tell you they steal for a thrill. Thrill——! Anybody who steals for a thrill is slug-nutty. I steal to eat. And I do all right because I got larceny sense. If you ain't got larceny sense, this is no business for you."

Larceny sense, it seems, is the ability to smell out good hauls, to sense the exact moment for the kill, and to know when it is wiser to desist. Sammy illustrated with an example from the days when he was a suit thief. He and his associates usually entered a place dressed in double-breasted suits with trousers so baggy they could hold one suit in each leg. However, on the day of which he spoke, he was working alone.

He entered a department store on a definite mission, the theft of a size forty-two man's suit, gray, with pin stripes, double-breasted. He had a customer for it. In the elevator he spotted a store detective. Giving that gentleman credit for being as alert as he himself was, Sammy figured he had been "made."

To test his hypothesis he got off on the floor above the clothing department. The dick got off too. Sammy turned left. The detective turned right. Sammy shopped the counters aimlessly, then ambled down to the clothing department. No copper. Maybe he was wrong. The detective might not have recognized him.

He approached a salesman, asked to be shown some suits. Warily he noted that no other salesman was paying attention to him. Ordinarily he'd like that, but this time it didn't smell right. And when his salesman was called to the phone, leaving Sammy surrounded by a dozen suits removed from hangers, that was too much. "He couldn't be that dumb! I figgered it was a plant."

Sammy sat down, waited patiently for the return of the salesman, his itching fingers firmly clasped to avoid any misunderstanding. When his man returned Sammy decided he didn't like any of the suits and walked out.

"But next day I came back and filled my order."

"What about that order business?" I asked. "Do you steal on order?"

"Not often. Usually I sell to the fence. But I've known mobs that steal on order only. You'd be surprised what kind of people will deal with a grifter to getta bargain. I know about an actress—she's right on Broadway today, big time. She gives a pal of mine an order for a Spanish shawl she wants stolen and out of what store.

"In Chicago there's a mob of heels, you go to them and you say, 'I want a brown sheared beaver coat, size so-and-so, such and such a style.' They get it for you. This outfit grifts only on order.

"Out in Los Angeles I used to know a dame, I don't know is she still operatin', she used to call herself Queen of the Shoplifters. She used goil canvassers. They went around to people they figgered was all right and took orders. The customer would say what he wanted, the color, size—he could even say he wanted a certain stock number. The goils turned the orders over to the Queen, and she'd do the job, fill the order, and pay the goil a commission.

"But I like to woik through a fence. You get less that way, maybe twenty-five or fifty per cent of what it's really worth, but you take less chances. Before I do a job I know who my fence will be for the stuff. I know just what I'm after. I get it, turn it over, and I'm clean."

Aside from the basic essential, larceny sense, the good heel and booster must develop a well-nigh flawless technique. About this Sammy seemed proudest, the evenings we were together. He took pleasure in reminiscing not only about himself but about other grifters. With keen appreciation he told me about a group of shoplifters, women, who were chewing the fat and telling tall tales. One seasoned veteran boasted so shamelessly as to injure the feelings of the others.

"I guess," sneered one, "you figure you're just about the best in town!"

Calmly the braggart replied, "I'm so good I can steal a live turkey."

Touched to the quick, the group made up a purse and bet her she couldn't. She went into a crowded market, returned with a live gobbler, head tucked under wing. It wasn't the purse that made her do it. It was pride in technique.

Men and women school themselves to walk, heavily loaded, as if they were carrying only the clothes on their backs. No stooping, no puffing, no unusual gait. They learn the proper use of "booster equipment," most of it as standardized as a Ford coupé.

Most common, for women, are booster bloomers and skirts. The former are baggy affairs with strong elastic at the waist and knees. The skirt is held up by elastic too. The operator shoves an article through the waist of the skirt; it falls into the bloomers and descends to the knees, allowing plenty of room for more merchandise.

Conventionalized, too, is the booster box. It is wrapped and bound like a package, but one end, which looks tightly sealed, is really a spring lid that bends inward, permitting the thief to shove something into the box. The lid then snaps back into place and becomes an innocent package again.

Muffs are useful but have their limitations. They look natural only in winter, and in some sections, such as Florida and Southern California, they are a red flag to the Chamber of Commerce. The same is true of umbrellas, handy as they are for small items.

The "false bust" is a booster box placed in the bosom of an otherwise poorly endowed female. Two boosters, both heavily endowed with avoirdupois, walk into a fur shop. One wears the false bust, the other doesn't need it. The woman who is all flesh and no box is the customer. She asks to be shown some neckpieces. While she maneuvers the saleswoman to a far-removed mirror, her sister-under-the-dress pops a fine fur-piece into her false bust. The two ladies walk out before the saleslady realizes she is one fur shy.

Men and women alike use false linings in coats, slit along one side to admit articles.

Occasionally some genius invents a new piece of equipment. Sammy, who, I gathered, had recently paid a professional visit to Los Angeles, told me about a man there who was observed shopping a downtown Los Angeles store, dressed in overalls. Anywhere else that would have been a dead giveaway. In Los Angeles, where bearded prophets paddle around barefoot in Roman togas and women wear slacks in nightclubs, that was normal. Nevertheless a store detective became suspicious. The man kept putting his hand in his overall pocket, extracting his hankerchief and blowing his nose. He didn't seem to have a cold. Besides, the imputation that one *could* have one in sub-tropical California was an affront. The detective followed the man from counter to counter, finally saw him shove an expensive sport shirt down his overalls. Arrested, the heel proudly displayed his invention. Inside his overalls were sewn a pair of trousers, the cuffs fastened to the overall pants a foot from the ground. The underpants made a perfect catch-all.

The inventive genius for whom Sammy had most admiration was a New York woman who inserted an artificial arm into the sleeve of her coat and attached a handbag to the gloved artificial hand to give it a realistic appearance. That allowed her a free, concealed flesh-and-blood arm for business.

Sammy has pulled some pretty good ones himself, he feels. But he admitted he has never invented anything new in larceny.

"I always walk through a store like I'm on my way somewhere. I don't loiter. I go right to the coat department, say, walk around. I'm just lookin'. I feel the material, work my way to the back of the store, throw a coat over my arm, take the tags off, and walk out with the goods right over my arm.

"Or I tell the salesman I'm waitin' for a friend. He wants a suit. So the people on the floor stop payin' attention to me. I ain't a customer. In fifteen minutes I'm walkin' up and down, lookin' at my watch. I'm annoyed, see? My friend is keepin' me waitin'. Then I get real mad. I shake my head and walk out. I got the score tucked down my pants."

If Sammy were a more daring, imaginative fellow, he would be able to pull off some of the coups that have become classics in the underworld. He speaks of these with downright awe.

He tells about the time a man walked into a fur department in Chicago and began dressing one of the dummies on the floor. Employees paid no attention to him. He must be the decorator, they figured. He tried one fur coat, then another, adjusted a collar, pinned on an ornament. Then, looking about speculatively as if deciding on a suitable coat for a window, he selected a high-priced beaver job, nonchalantly threw it over an arm, and walked out.

Very frequently two or three thieves will operate together, one to make the haul, the others to create diversion. A man might do the stealing, a woman the diverting. As the male booster is about to complete a purchase, the woman, in the next aisle, gets into a heated altercation with a clerk. Her hysterical voice causes all eyes to go in her direction. Presto! The job is done.

Another device is to have a woman faint. Or an accomplice knocks over a child, who sets up a howl. One mob exploded a chemical that sent up a puff of smoke. Employees and customers rushed to the scene of the "fire." Presto!

"But," Sammy chortled, "let me tell you about the greatest one ever. This fellow, I used to know him, woiked with him in K.C., he's a very dignified-lookin' guy, see? Years back, when they run stores different, he walks into one of a winter. He's wearin' no coat or hat, see? He just walks down the aisle, smiling to this salesman and that one. He says hello to them, so they say hello to him. They figure he's one of the big shots of the company, maybe a vice-president, how do they know? The guy must be somebody! So he moseys up to the cash register, smiles, and waves the girl to step aside. He's gonna check the register. He takes out the dough, counts it, puts it in a bag he's got with him. He writes something on a slip of paper and puts it in the register. Then he walks away, like he's going to the head office. And, ho! ho!"—Sammy slapped his thigh and roared with glee—"when the girl opens the register to ring up a sale, she finds this slip. It says, 'Thanks.' Ho! Ho!"

The lifting of money is rare, however, among boosters. Merchandise is their goal, and only one kind at that. Each operator tends to stick to his specialty, although in a pinch he may switch over now and then. When he does he must learn new techniques.

The silkworm usually remains a silkworm all his—or her—life. Woolworms specialize in woolens, bookworms steal expensive volumes. One operator became known as Omar Khayyám because he almost always selected a fine edition of that poet to purloin. Suit thieves stick to clothes, fur thieves to furs. A few professionals are catholic in their tastes and steal anything that isn't nailed down.

Just as each careerist sticks to his specialty, so he selects one of two approved plans of territorial arrangement. He may be an itinerant, traveling the country, as most do. Or he may spend a lifetime in one large city, perhaps even in one district. Sammy has worked many other cities, but in New York, he says, he has never operated west of Fifth Avenue or north of Fifty-seventh Street. He has devoted the best years of his life to some twenty blocks.

As traditionalized as territory is the size of a man's operation. "Snatch-and-grabs," Sammy explained, "will woik anything from a Woolworth to a Fifth Avenue spot. They'll steal a tie or an egg. A real booster woiks mostly in department stores, where there's good merchandise. Or in little high-class specialty shops. In them little places you don't have store detectives and you get only high-grade stuff."

Sammy wastes no time on cheap stuff. "You take the same risk for ten bucks as you do for a hundred. Why play cheap? Besides," he wound up, a noble look on his face, "them high-class joints pay their help twenty-five a week. They're sweat shops. They *should* be taken!"

As he talked I noted that Sammy seemed to take it for granted he would be arrested several times a year. I asked him about this. Was shoplifting so hazardous? If so, why continue in it?

The professional knows this is an extremely risky business. "It's not like forgery, where you can plant your check and walk off clean, and two days later they know you're crooked," he said. "With us, you gotta walk off loaded, and if they stop

you they know right away you're a recruit for the bandbox."
He figures that a few months out of every year he will be out
of business, in jail awaiting trial or serving a term. He doesn't
like that, but he accepts it as a business risk. "This is your
business, so you stay in it. If a doctor don't make money one
year, does he go into the garbage-collecting business?"

I asked Sammy how many pinches he'd had.

"Oh, gee, I wouldn't remember. Maybe a couple hundred,
maybe more."

"And how much time, would you say, have you spent in
jails in the past fifty years?"

"Maybe twenty years. But only on little raps at a time. The
biggest one I done was when I was with you people. Two and
a half to five, and I come out in two."

To minimize the risks Sammy tries to familiarize himself
with the faces of store detectives, which is almost impossible
to do. This type of police work has become highly scientific
and hard to beat. Detectives, more often than not female, are
self-effacing. There are no types. Few resemble "flatfoots."
Some women sleuths are broad of beam, some slender. They
change costume often. The woman thief never knows when
the dainty lady in the powder room may be a store cop. That
girl at the jewelry counter, studying a bracelet, may be not a
debutante but a policewoman. Detectives constantly patrol the
shops. They know hundreds of thieves by face, are familiar
with all the tricks of the trade, and can spot a booster skirt a
block away.

Sammy knows, too, that merchants are most severe with the
inveterate thief. They may refrain from prosecuting a house-
wife who couldn't resist a pair of stockings. Given a break, she
rarely tries it again. But bitter experience has indicated that

the heel and booster rarely quit. The store will prosecute if the evidence is clear cut. If it isn't, there is danger of a suit for false arrest.

Because the stores are aware of this danger, Sammy plays on their fears when necessary. When questioned by a detective he puts up a great front at first, vehemently denies thieving. He vigorously disclaims a prior record, threatens suit for false arrest, refuses to be searched. When he is searched, and the loot is found on him, he capitulates at once, so as not to be tossed around. He knows that the underworld will go to bat for him immediately.

The wheels of the machine begin to grind. Money is put up for bail. Alibi witnesses are invented; they will swear Sammy, on the day in question, was too drunk to know what he was doing, or he had just buried his mother and was in a state of shock. Where it seems possible, a "fix" is attempted. An attorney is retained. Every heel and booster in town feels obligated to help, whether he knows the prisoner or not. "Of course," Sammy qualifies, "this don't go in every town. Only in certain places, where things are right—y'unnastand?"

Professional thieves are united against law-enforcement officers, their common enemy. A booster landing in a town will look up fellow workers to get the dope. His informant may hate him as a person, but he will feel obliged to tell what stores are hot, what the lowdown is on city hall, where the best scores can be taken off.

If one booster enters a store and finds another already on the job, the late arrival will leave at once. He believes in fair competition. Also, the first thief may be under observation of a cop. The place may be hot.

"The nut comes off the top" is a saying among the brethren.

When stolen articles are cashed in, all expenses must be taken care of before the cut is made. Debts must be scrupulously paid.

This is not done out of a consideration for ethics but as good business. There is no room for sentiment in the world of the professional. For instance, while an arrested thief will be helped, a hungry one on the loose will get short shrift. As Sammy puts it, "A guy's got no call to be broke when he's on the street. He can always steal."

Sammy expects decent treatment from detectives. "We're in the same business—at different ends, that's all." He deeply resents being treated roughly and nurtures grudges for years. He got a great kick out the experience of a girl friend of his on the grift, who had been slapped by a female store detective. When his friend got out of her legal difficulties she returned to the store and bought a flaming red dress. She sneaked into a dressing room, removed the wrappings, and bundled her purchase under her coat, a telltale bit hanging out. She patrolled the floor for an hour before her enemy grabbed her and rushed her to the office.

In the presence of the manager the heel insisted she had paid for the dress. "And this time you ain't gonna slap me around like you did the last time," she challenged in her most insolent manner. The detective reached over and walloped her again. Satisfied with the trap she had set, the heel produced her sales slip and threatened suit for false arrest and assault. The store settled for fifteen hundred dollars and fired the detective.

By the time Sammy had told me this much he was a little tired. The bottle was empty. The booster was feeling a bit sorry for himself, his hard life, the risks he takes. "Someday I'll quit this racket!" he said unconvincingly.

"Does anybody quit?" I asked.

He thought a long time. "Yeah, it's been done. I knew three guys who decided to get out. They was about my age at the time. They go to Miami and woik back to New York, griftin' in every town. They pick themselves up sixty grand among them, and they buy farms, every goddamn one! And they stay there!

"I know an old-timer, he used to be a pennyweighter, stealin' from jewelers. He took off the big one, got himself a stake, and right now, in this man's town, he's retired and in business. He runs a jewelry store.

"I know a no-good sonofabitch who used to steal women's garments. The bastard runs a dress shop now—and is he murder on boosters, the lousy crum!

"But, now you ax me, come to think of it, there ain't many of us ever do retire. We can't afford to. We gotta eat, we got families."

"You have a family? I never knew that."

"Sure. I gotta wife and kid in New Haven."

"Then?" I looked around the apartment.

"This? I woik from here. I go home week ends."

"Your—er—wife is in New Haven?" My eyes roamed to a negligee lying across a bed.

"Yeah. Oh, that thing? That's my goil's. I got a New York goil. Just a tramp, y'unnastand. She don't mean nothin'. But it all costs money. How could I quit?"

"You could get a legit job of work," I suggested.

He looked at me coldly. Then he softened, grinned. "Be yourself, Mr. Dressler! You ain't on the parole board no more!"

CHAPTER XXIX

Meet the Staff

Amateurs and professionals alike are grist to the parole mill. And some of those who make up the parole force are almost as interesting as their charges. I got to know every parole officer in the state. Being men and women of variegated backgrounds, they were a strange and wonderful crew.

I have already mentioned the remarkable Mr. Syd Gross, the man who solved the Patrolman Casey murder. If a movie were to be written about him, he would be played by someone like Donald Meek. Syd, a man with certain outstanding mannerisms, was constantly apologizing for himself, using little deprecatory shrugs and hand gestures. He laughed nervously and seemed most indecisive. He was almost femininely gentle. He spent hours of his own time finding jobs for parolees or helping them in one way or another.

This gentleness, and his harmless little eccentricities, caused some members of the staff to put him down as an easy mark. He was the butt of many a practical joke and always took it good-naturedly.

Shortly after he came to the staff two parole officers asked him solemnly whether he had his police certification for the use of a gun. (No such certification was required.) Gross said he didn't have one. "Do I need it?"

"Do you need it!" one of the men cried. "Man, don't you

know if you don't get it this week, before your probationary period is up, you'll get fired?"

Gross was in a sweat. The men told him to go see Inspector John Lyons at police headquarters.

"He won't want to be bothered," the tricksters told Syd, "but you refuse to leave without it. If he argues, flash your shield. That'll fix him."

Syd dodged out of the office and trotted over to headquarters.

Inspector Lyons, later State Commissioner of Correction, was a fine, keen gentleman, one of the most competent topranking officers in the Police Department. He was not a man to be trifled with. People who knew him didn't try, but Gross had never seen him before.

The then head of the New York office of the Division of Parole received a call from a very irate police inspector, demanding to know what madman had been turned loose on him —and it was a chagrined parole officer who returned to the office. But he joined in the general laughter at his own expense. That was his way.

In addition to being a kindly man anxious to assist any deserving parolee, Syd was an ace detective. He had a phenomenal memory; he was untiring and used original methods.

For instance, there was a drive on to locate parole absconders missing many years. An officer was lamenting his failure to apprehend one Walter, on the lam for about seven years. The officer had checked the last known address, traced down obscure clues by the most roundabout methods, to no avail.

Syd listened, then thoughtfully opened a telephone book, ran his eyes down the page, and asked, "Would this be your man?"

It was. Gross's originality lay in the fact that he was quite willing to try the simplest thing first. In this case he conjectured that a man missing so long would no longer fear arrest and might list a phone in his own name.

Once he walked in with a parole absconder charged to another officer. Gross had seen the man only once in his life, and that had been many years before.

"How did you ever locate the guy?" his astonished colleague asked.

"Just an accident," Syd explained. "I was on an elevated and I happened to look down and saw this man on the street below, so I got off at the next station and arrested him."

In the Tresca murder case, mentioned earlier, it was Syd's phenomenal memory that made it possible to lay hands on Carmine Galante, the parolee suspect in the killing at the time. When we told the police we had seen Galante in the car later called the murder vehicle, they wanted to arrest him without a minute's unnecessary delay. They failed to find him at his home or on the job. Where would he be at five-thirty P.M.? Each detective on the case aired a theory on this. Syd unobtrusively called me aside and apologetically asked, "Do you think it's all right if I tell them he won't be at any of those places?"

"Where will he be?"

"Well, this is just a guess, but twice, about a year ago, about this time of day I ran into him in a candy store at——. He might accidentally be there."

He was.

I rather suspect our organization represented a cross-section of public workers, insofar as types were concerned. You find all types in every government office, but the proportions vary according to the competence of the recruiting process.

We had our sycophants, our Uriah Heeps, and our eccentrics. We had our topnotch men and some who were lazy, considered that the job existed in order that they might be paid, not because there was work that needed doing. We had our well-trained, our undertrained, and our overtrained officers.

The well-trained, competent men were in the majority. But there was an undertrained little man—let's call him Mr. Carp—who had managed to pass the Civil Service examination by boning up. His schooling and experience were not such as to qualify him for the work. He got on the list and was appointed. He didn't last long, and after he left we found a homemade lexicon in his desk, a sort of guide to professionalism which he had prepared for himself. It contained expressions to put into case records. Under "mother" I found: "His mother is a well-meaning, understanding woman." Also: "The mother, a slatternly woman and poor housekeeper . . ." Under "habits" were such choices as: "An habitué of pool rooms and taxi dance halls, he . . ." Best of them in this category was: "The parolee has no habits."

Every office, I am sure, has the overtrained man. We had him in the person of a chap, Manuel, who had gone to all the necessary schools, read all the books. He was as professional a professional social worker as a professional social worker could be.

Once I observed a parolee of his whispering to another in the corridor. They exchanged addresses. I gave them a quick frisk and found a gun on Manuel's parolee. I put the two men under guard and, calling Manuel in, instructed him to get a

warrant and lock his man up. He stamped his foot in irritation.
"You've destroyed six months of casework treatment!" he
said petulantly. "I was giving that man intensive treatment, and
he was improving."

"Meantime he's got a gun."

"Another six months of treatment and he wouldn't have
wanted a gun!"

What I said to that it is unnecessary to go into.

There is always, too, the man who read a book. Heaven
protect us from him, because it almost certainly was a book on
psychiatry. And overnight the reader emerged out of his
chrysalis as a full-fledged psychiatrist with that little learning
that is a dangerous thing.

I suppose a Freudian might jump to some conclusions about
Conrad, a parole officer who was a bit on the delicate side. He
was fussy and fastidious and quite upset at the prospect of any
physical encounter. I could think of other officers whom I
would rather have along on a raid.

Once, however, he was with us to make an arrest of one of
his own men. This ex-felon, tough and psychopathic, went
berserk when we came for him. He ranted and roared that he
would not be taken out alive. He dared Conrad to put handcuffs on him. "I'll break your back!" he shouted. "I'll tear you
apart! Take one more step and I'll rip that fat head right out
of the socket!"

Conrad quailed—and I can hardly blame him. He looked
at me appealingly.

"Arrest him," I said.

Conrad advanced timidly.

"You sonofabitch!" the parolee began menacingly.

Instantly, as though it were reflex action, Conrad slapped the parolee in the face. "Be careful how you talk about my mother!" he cried.

The parolee stood open-mouthed and allowed the officer to put the cuffs on him. He came along quietly, a bemused look on his face.

Officer Hal rarely used force, as Conrad unwittingly had. Hal depended on a sense of humor and initiative. But there was the time the biter was bitten.

Hal had a parolee, Jimmy, who was a confirmed alcoholic and had been on a binge practically since his discharge from the Army in 1920. Hal warned him regularly to stay away from liquor, and Jimmy said he would.

One day Hal came upon the parolee, dead drunk, sitting on a curb. Jimmy, when drunk, was not affable.

"Jimmy!" Hal snapped, tugging at him. "Get up!"

"Gotohell," Jimmy mumbled.

"Get up!" Hal ordered.

"Getaway before I bust ya one," Jimmy said—and he could do it.

Then Hal remembered Jimmy had been a soldier. He barked, "Company, fall *in!*"

The parolee's shoulders straightened. He shuffled to his feet.

" 'Ten*shun!*" Hal snapped.

The inebriate stiffened.

"For'rd *march!*"

Jimmy marched—down the street, into a cab, and to the office. We sobered him up in jail and turned him loose.

Months later he swore he hadn't had a drop since his recent incarceration. He appreciated what Hal had done, he said, and he wouldn't let him down.

"Jimmy," the parole officer would say, "drink is your curse. It isn't for you. If I so much as see you having a beer, it's curtains for you."

"Don't worry, Mr. Hal. I'm through."

"Stay out of gin mills!"

"Yes, sir!"

One steaming hot summer day Hal's mind kept reverting to Jimmy. Heat waves were shimmering up from the sidewalks. The half-melting streets gave underfoot. Collars wilted and tempers were at hair-trigger readiness. This, Hal opined, would be one day when the parolee would be sorely tempted. This was the time to determine how well Jimmy kept his vow. If he wasn't drinking today, he *had* licked the urge. And if he was hitting the bottle, he'd better be locked up before he got himself into a serious scrape.

Hal began a tour of West Side Manhattan, the parolee's locale. Wearily he trudged along Eighth Avenue, from Fortieth Street to Fifty-second, peering into every bar on every block. He turned the corner and panted along Ninth Avenue, then Tenth, the very meat of the Tenderloin. At last he could stand it no longer. His tongue hanging out, he crawled into a shabby saloon and ordered a beer. He was just lifting the foaming glass to his parched lips when he heard a rapping on the window. He turned, his glass half lifted. There was Jimmy, outside looking in. He was shaking his head mournfully. He shook a warning finger at Hal, then walked sadly away.

In another district office we had a man whose devotion to the letter of the law surprised us. He was inclined to be somewhat literal-minded, liked to do exactly as instructed, no more, no less.

He encountered a parolee under circumstances that proclaimed him a parole violator. The officer informed the man he was under arrest.

"Show me your warrant!" the parolee demanded.

That stumped the officer. He had no warrant. (And needed none.)

"You wait here and I'll get one!" he said.

He returned to the office, got a warrant, and went back to where the obliging parolee was waiting.

"Let's see the warrant!" the man barked. The officer showed it. The parolee took it, tore it into bits, and walked away.

"I couldn't arrest him then," the parole officer explained. "I had no warrant."

There is a temptation to keep writing about the more unusual men we had on the staff, because they were the more colorful members of the agency. But the backbone of the organization was the majority who did a good job but possessed few spectacular qualities. They are, in a sense, unsung heroes who perform a fine service to society day in, day out. They rarely rate headlines. You've never heard their names. They serve silently.

And, too, we had a few dishonest parole officers, who were weeded out as soon as they could be detected. One, whom I suspected while I was on the staff, went to prison some time after I left the organization. This is no indictment of New York's parole system. Parole officers are subject to temptation. The weak ones may succumb. The organization can and should be criticized only if it fails to be eternally vigilant for any evildoing within its ranks. There will be a bad apple in the barrel every now and then. It's human nature.

That vigilance, the demand for high standards, will make friends and enemies in and out of the agency. I always felt that the fact certain political-club boys hated us was a sincere compliment. If the time comes when they agree parole is wonderful, the citizens had better investigate the parole system. It will mean somebody is playing ball with the politicians. Parole and politics can't and mustn't mix, even though not every politician is a rogue. Many are high-grade public servants, minor and major statesmen.

The fact remains that by fealty to standards of honesty, probity, and good practice we welded an organization that was top rank. We incurred ill will on the part, too, of some staff members, but they were the civil servants who wanted to do the job the easiest way. The hard-working men, imbued with zeal and the ideal of service, made up a core of public servants of whom one could be proud. They loved the work, hard as it was, and understood and supported the administration's aims. It has been a privilege to be associated with them for so many exciting and rewarding years.

CHAPTER XXX

Public Officials Are Many Things

Those who work in parole must come in contact with many other public officials; and public officials are many things. They sometimes have traits the public little suspects.

Ask anyone who lived in New York at the time, and he will tell you Police Commissioner Lewis Valentine was a very tough man. As an administrator he was, in that he demanded high-grade performance. Two detectives once assigned to our office spent hours tearing Valentine apart. Their complaint boiled down to the fact he would stand for no shilly-shallying and was determined to detect and fire any dishonest man on the force.

I first met Valentine in his office. Seated at his desk, he was the personification of the hard-boiled cop. His head was bulldog, his jaws solid, shoulders and chest tremendous.

We discussed a case, and his eyes flashed fire as he expressed his hatred of all criminals. Then the telephone rang. The stern look still on his face, Valentine lifted the receiver.

"Yes?" he said tersely. His facial muscles softened, his eyes turned limpid, and he intoned, "Yes, mama. . . . Yes, mama. . . . Yes, mama, of course!"

He got up to go, for his wife wanted him right away. And Lewis Valentine obviously loved "mama" and did what would please her.

His body, I noticed as he arose, was peculiarly disproportionate. From the waist up he was a giant, from his belt down, a gnome—or so it seemed, by contrast. His legs were short, his hips slight. He looked like a man with a size forty-five upper mounted on a size thirty lower.

There was the same disproportion about his knowledge of the world. In some things he appeared childishly naïve, in others mature and forceful. He knew little or nothing, so far as came out in the conversations I had with him, about world events or the arts. He was a cop, and he knew plenty about that. And he had definite likes and dislikes.

He admired and respected an honest public official and would do anything he could to support him.

He despised criminals, incompetent subordinates, and one or two world figures about whom he made up his mind on the basis of little knowledge and much common sense.

For instance, he loathed Trujillo, the dictator of Santo Domingo. When that ruthless fascist paid a visit to New York, Valentine furnished police escort and protection. He didn't mind that; it was his duty. But he deeply and sincerely resented it when Trujillo, upon returning to his own country, sent beautiful wristwatches, suitably engraved, to the Police Commissioner, one of his subordinates named Louis Costuma, and a few others. Valentine vowed he would send his back, with a letter expressing his opinion of Trujillo. Costuma, less blunt and more diplomatic where people of high rank were concerned, kept his memento, and got the proper people to urge upon Valentine that it would create an international incident to return his watch. The Commissioner growled, "All right, I won't return it, but I won't keep it. Give it away. I won't wear anything from that sonofabitch."

I liked Valentine. I admired him. A man of strong emotions and violent likes and dislikes can do a fine job for a police force—if he knows his stuff and has the *right* emotions, which Valentine, I am sure, did.

Another police official whom it was a privilege to know was Edward P. Mulrooney, who preceded Valentine as commissioner. I knew Mulrooney by reputation as a straight-shooter, a highly efficient police officer who knew the work backward and forward. I met him on numerous occasions when official business was discussed. Ramrod straight, he talked the same way, made decisions rapid-fire, kept his word unfailingly, and was able to cut through the verbiage and circumlocutions of official reports with one curt word. After he left his police post he became State Commissioner of Correction, and I saw him again in that period. He had an amazing breadth of interests, had met and *understood* many of the world's great. He loved the theater and the arts generally, and his interest was not that of the dilettante. He was a first-nighter, a friend and confidant of men like George M. Cohan, an associate of governors—and they all had high regard for him. He was one of those naturals who occasionally ornament the public service and never fail to leave their impress upon it.

It was, come to think of it, an era of great public servants in New York State, that period I was in the parole system. New York City had its Seabury Investigation. Mayor Jimmy Walker resigned and took himself a trip to Europe. Tammany was ousted. Reform waves swept city and state. Many crusaders rode to the wars against corruption. There was a ferment in the air. Everywhere I turned I saw young, vigorous men with fire in their eyes, doing a cleanup job, running clean government departments. It was the era when Austin MacCormack, as city

Commissioner of Correction, raided his own penitentiary; when young D.A.'s like Murray Gurfein and Sol Gelb and others were riding herd on racketeers; when Tom Dewey was rising to fame as a crime buster with higher ambitions. It was the period of the brash, impetuous, and often ruthless Bob Moses, who did so much toward beautifying the state and giving New York City kids decent playgrounds; of Newbold Morris and his political idealism.

But it was really La Guardia's era. For in the greatest city in the country (in terms of population) he dominated the scene, put his stamp upon it, and gave New York the most exciting, crazy, frenetic, wonderful, progressive, unpredictable government it has ever had.

The first time I witnessed one of La Guardia's performances was at a public luncheon. Crime was very much on his mind then, and he soon brought his talk around to what he was going to do about crime in New York. He had the solution. He would, he said, rising higher and higher on his toes with each word, "grab the . . . tinhorn . . . gamblers . . . and . . . racketeers . . . by . . . the . . . scruff . . . of . . . the . . . neck . . . and . . . *throw* . . . *them* . . . over the river . . . *into* . . . NEW . . . JERSEY!" By the time he got to the last ten words, he was shrieking in a thin falsetto. His voice choked up with emotion. His arms flailed. He all but frothed at the mouth. Yes, sir! He'd solve the crime problem—for New York.

He often sounded stark mad, but he was crazy like a fox. A shrewd politician, he was not at all averse to playing ordinary Grade C politics. He knew how far he could go and still preserve his honor and his reputation for being an honorable mayor. And he *was* an honorable mayor. Many times I swore

I would never vote for the irresponsible galoot again, and always I weakened, even after his asinine appeal to children to turn in their daddies who played a round of poker now and then.

He brooked no opposition from subordinates. Once he addressed a meeting at which he had been introduced by Austin 'MacCormack. The comments of the two men regarding crime were noticeably divergent. Almost immediately thereafter, MacCormack quit his job. Some said it was because he was an inefficient administrator, others that La Guardia just stopped loving him.

Fiorello never asked me to do him a favor, parole-wise. Had he wanted to, he would probably have done so through an intermediary, so that I would not know who really sponsored the request. But he did ask a group of us to suggest to him a slate of highly competent, qualified men, one of whom he would appoint to the board of his Municipal Parole Commission. This surprised me, for La Guardia hated, about equally, psychiatrists, professional social workers, and tin-horn gamblers. One of the first of his official acts had been the evisceration of the Crime Prevention Bureau—because it was staffed by trained workers, and he considered that meant they were people without hearts.

We submitted a list of possible parole commissioners to the Little Flower. He promptly cast it aside and appointed a baseball player, Lou Gehrig. I am convinced, looking back on it, that La Guardia's intuitions were a better guide than our professional explorations.

Once he came to a dinner honoring someone. Although it was entirely out of line with the general nature of the affair and the interests of the participants, he launched into a hysterical attack on parole, including his own municipal parole system. He practically called all parole workers criminal.

I boiled, but I held back until the affair broke up. Then I nabbed hizzonor, backed him into a corner (you had to hold him still to get him to listen), and rapped out, "That was a nice grandstand play you made. You've done a lot of harm to a worth-while service. What have you got against parole—or what in hell do you *know* about parole?"

His face looked tired all of a sudden, gray and sagging.

"I don't know a thing about parole," he said quietly. "But I've just come from the funeral of a cop—killed by a parolee. You can't go through something like that without going off the deep end a little. I'm sorry."

We shook hands.

"By the way," he asked, "shouldn't you understand my feeling? Haven't you been a police officer?"

"No, sir. I'm a social worker by training."

He almost spat in my face.

A man who I believe was once friendly with La Guardia represented, in my mind, a different kind of politician. He was Vito Marcantonio. I have never met him, but he impinged on my work more than did La Guardia, by far.

He wrote us many letters asking that thus and so be done for this or that parolee. His tone was usually peremptory, although very likely he wanted nothing more than to have a nice strong letter to show a constituent, something that would convince a voter that Marcantonio had his interest at heart. Occasionally he urged the appointment of certain men as parole officers. This we invariably disregarded. Once, however, we appointed a man who later told associates he had been a ward worker for Marcantonio. I don't know that this was so.

This officer, incidentally, is the only member of our staff ever to have gone to prison—for mulcting money from parolees and their families.

Commissioner Joseph J. Canavan was blazing mad over a story that came to him from two independent sources. Each informant claimed that Marcantonio had remarked, "I'm very influential with Canavan. I'm there once a week, put my feet up on his desk, and we talk cases."

Canavan hated even the imputation that he might be playing around with politicians. Early in his incumbency we used to lunch together in a certain restaurant near the office. A minor job holder, more ward heeler and errand boy than public official, would drop by our table almost every day. He knew Canavan slightly from the time the latter had been executive secretary to Governor Lehman. He would sink into a chair alongside us, comment on the weather, wait for our noncommittal replies, nod his head, and say, "Yas-yas-yas-yas-yas!" Then he would depart.

We discovered that this was a calculated bit of strategy. Our weather-bureau politico was telling people that he had influence with good old Joe Canavan. If they wanted proof, he let them see him conversing with the commissioner, then told his clients he had been discussing their case.

We moved to another restaurant. Here the big-time politicos bothered us. So we stopped eating lunch. For the next ten years I ate lunch only on vacation.

It was quite a while before local ward politicians believed there was a new deal in parole, that politics played no part. In fact, men like Marcantonio seemed never to believe it. Others appeared to have that point settled in their minds, yet, on occasion, they would try once more.

Once I was visited by a chap who wanted a parolee to have permission to get a driver's license. For good reason we wouldn't trust the parolee with one. His political emissary took the position that I was refusing him only because he had not presented the proper *bona fides*. A furtive, wiry fellow who spoke in jerky half-sentences, he finally jumped up, held up his hat, and cried, "You think I'm not—you don't want to—well, let me tell you! Look at this hat! Have you got a hat that costs ten dollars? Can you afford ten-dollar hats?"

I admitted I couldn't and bowed him out.

The same afternoon he darted into the office again, laden with ledgers. His molelike nose quivered as he laid them on the desk. "You'll see who I—I'm gonna prove to you. You can't say you won't! Why, I paid income tax on fifty thousand dollars last year! Look here!"

When I told him this had no bearing whatever on whether the parolee should have a license, he drew himself up, shook a finger at me, and spluttered, "Don't you think you can—I'm telling you—I don't have to—I'll get Sam Liebowitz after you!"

Sam Liebowitz, who no doubt never heard of the little man, was then a practicing criminal lawyer. He never interceded on any case with us. I met him only after he became a judge. I once remarked to him, "You were undoubtedly one of the greatest criminal lawyers of our time."

"*One* of the greatest?" he queried. "Who was greater?"

I'm still not certain whether he was joshing. And that somehow reminds me of district attorneys.

As district attorney of Kings County, Mr. William O'Dwyer was the little man who wasn't there, as far as I was concerned.

I never actually caught sight of him. I was supposed to meet him, on two occasions, in his office. The first time he was a day late. The second time he didn't show at all.

He had, without our knowledge, used a parolee as a stool pigeon. When we discovered this we warned the parolee and O'Dwyer's office that we could not permit a man on parole to go into the underworld, for whatever reason. When the D.A.'s office failed to keep its promise and continued to use our man, I had the parolee locked up. I heard from Mr. O'Dwyer in person, by phone. And a right charming voice it was, full of warmth and friendship. We ought to meet and talk this over. Would I come over? I did. He didn't show up.

Both on that and the second trip over I felt my time hadn't been wasted. I was entranced by the seeming lack of organization. People rushed hither and yon. Much work was done in a goldfish bowl. I could have stolen a dozen records. I waited in a barnlike room that didn't even have a chair. Maybe this was calculated, maybe I was being given the business. Every once in a while a worried somebody came out to report that the D.A. was expected momentarily. He never arrived.

Contrast that with Mr. Dewey's office when he held a similar post in New York County. Everything was organized from the moment you stepped through the outer door. At every corridor you met someone and told him whither you were bound. Efficiency was so high you could hear the ball bearings click in assistant D.A.s' brains as the wheels turned over.

Later, under Frank S. Hogan, that office was more productive of results. Study the records carefully, and you will see that the quiet, colorless, unassuming but brilliant district attorney achieved a higher percentage of convictions than Dewey did. When you entered the office in Dewey's time you felt him all over the place; employees reacted as if he were peeping through the walls. You rarely saw or felt Hogan. He never play-acted or put on shows, and he ran the most efficient district attorney's office that New York County has ever had.

He spoke quietly, without histrionics or eye rolling, when I was with him. He was a bit reserved, yet tried to be affable and informal. He didn't pontificate and he didn't have all the answers.

In other words, he was an unusual public official.

Working under four governors, I learned that the quality of state service is in considerable measure determined by the aims, ambitions, and requirements of the governor. He can make or break the career service, for he usually appoints the policy-making department heads and has full control over their tenure. He does not need to make appointments of lower echelon staff in order to control them, if he wishes to do so. His department heads will see to it that the employees act in accordance with the policy lines laid down by His Excellency.

The government worker, therefore, is directly or indirectly affected. Under a governor who will protect him against the district leader, he feels free to perform a public service divested of special privilege. On the other hand, he is, even though a "career man," to some extent at the mercy of a governor uninterested in decent standards of work.

Governor Roosevelt wanted a clean, efficient parole system for New York. A master statesman, he was keenly aware that parole can be political dynamite. He gave his first Parole Board a mandate to operate without interference, fear, or favor. He wanted commissioners of integrity who would exemplify to the staff the new deal in parole. Nevertheless he understood better than any man of his era the realities of machine politics. He would not completely rebuff the Democratic party, for it might cause the leaders to stymie his entire correctional program. He appointed one man who was undoubtedly the choice of political leaders, but that individual had independent qualifications for the post. He had had a long, if relatively undistinguished, career in correctional work.

The other appointees of FDR, in the opinion of this insider, were without the slightest political affiliation. One commissioner even carried this to the extent of refusing to vote.

Roosevelt, to my knowledge, intervened in parole only once, in connection with the case of Owney Madden, who had been paroled long before the Division came into being. Apparently the person charged with his case under the old parole system didn't read the newspapers, or didn't believe them. Everybody else in town seemed to be of the opinion that Madden was kingpin of bootlegging. To many citizens he was the Capone of New York. But he remained at liberty.

The wave of reform in the state caused questions to be asked. Why was Madden at large? What did the Parole Board know of his true activities?

The Parole Board, which had just got its second wind in setting up the new system, had a hot potato in its hands. It wasn't even certain Madden was on parole, for some records seemed to indicate he had been discharged under the old system. Now the board checked further and, finding no incontrovertible evidence of this, sent officers out to investigate Madden. Meanwhile, the press was belaboring the new board for the sins of the old system.

Reporters demanded to know what the record showed on

Owney. Where was he living and working? What was the
source of his income?

The then New York City commissioner followed a press
relations policy not uncommon among public officials. He
avoided reporters, feared them, and thought the best press was
no press. He refused to give out information. The papers, as
might be expected, became all the more suspicious about the
handling of the Madden case.

In this instance Governor Roosevelt personally telephoned
the New York office and first suggested, then demanded, that
full and accurate facts be given the press. The public was entitled to that, he insisted. He did this through no political mo-
tive, I feel. The revelations could only embarrass his adminis-
stration. And when, later, Madden fought his projected return
to prison, Roosevelt backed the board to the hilt in its legal
and ultimately successful moves to put Madden behind bars
as a parole violator.

When Herbert H. Lehman succeeded Franklin Roosevelt
as governor, the new deal on parole continued. Lehman, an
unassuming, hard-working man, devoted all his energies to
giving the people an honest, efficient government. Parole was
an undertaking close to his heart, for he had piloted the investigation and subsequent legislation that led to the creation of
the Division of Parole. In a sense it was his baby, and he
wanted it kept clean.

In his years of devoted service to the state Lehman never
once, to my knowledge, took it upon himself to suggest a
course of action in a given case. He stood ready to defend the
position of the Parole Board in every respect. He was jealous
of its integrity and appointed to it his own executive secretary,

Joseph J. Canavan, who was to make an outstanding nation-wide contribution to parole thinking. Canavan had originally given up a much more lucrative newspaper position to go with Lehman. He was infused with a fervor for public service, and he literally worked himself to death, collapsing on the job of heart failure after physicians had advised him to take a long rest.

Lehman believed in a career service. He furthered it even when such advocacy might injure him politically. I had first-hand experience of this zeal.

I was chief parole officer when the post of executive director fell vacant. The law specifically stated that this top post was in the competitive class of Civil Service. But the Civil Service Commission, of all bodies, suddenly announced that this was an exempt job, in its interpretation, to be filled by appointment of the governor, without examination.

Tammany had its candidate. The O'Connell Democratic machine in Albany had its boy. A governor could do himself a lot of good by appointing one or the other, for the position was well paid.

Lehman consulted with Canavan and Dr. Moore and made it known that if the position were indeed exempt, he would appoint me.

I refused, with thanks. The members of the Parole Board and I saw eye to eye on this. An important principle was involved. If I accepted, future appointments to the post, were I to vacate it, would be thrown to the pork barrel. Moreover, I didn't want an appointive job. I was not in politics. Should a new governor come in, I didn't want any favors; nor did I want to be beholden to anyone.

The pressure became terrific. Political and pseudo-civic and religious groups asked Governor Lehman to go along with the Civil Service Commission. He refused.

The situation became something of a *cause célèbre*. Papers asked embarrassing questions. The Parole Board wrote the Civil Service Commission, pointing to the exact section of law that made the job Civil Service. The letters went unanswered or were replied to in evasive gobbledegook. More than a year passed with the post unfilled and the politicians drooling and demanding.

Then the *New York World-Telegram* ran an editorial on the subject. Whether for that or other reasons, the Commission suddenly discovered the section of law we had pointed out to them right along. It reversed itself. I took an examination along with other members of our staff, placed first, and was appointed.

I have gone to some length in telling this story because it illustrates an important point. The Governor, by one decision, could have destroyed the morale and integrity of the career service, at least in one organization. Every man on the staff, including those who despised me, was in my corner on this issue. Had the Governor given in, parole would have gone into a decline. For no one could thereafter have convinced a parole officer that politics didn't play a part in parole decisions.

Some time later, when a commissionership fell vacant, Governor Lehman again evinced his faith in career service. He asked at least one member of the Parole Board if there was a staff member he wanted to recommend. There was little question that Lehman would have acted favorably on the suggestion. The board member would have proposed me, except that I still didn't want an appointive post.

Nevertheless I happen to feel that in the key policy-making

positions a governor should have the power to appoint and
depose at will, from within or outside the career service. He
will be credited with the good deeds of his appointees, blamed
for their misdeeds or incompetence, hence he has the right to
handpick the men who will set the policy line the way he
wants it.

Lehman resigned almost at the end of his term to head
UNNRA. Lieutenant Governor Charles Poletti automatically
succeeded to the balance of the term—twenty-eight days.

"Charlie," as he was universally known, was unassuming,
boyish, bubbling over with high spirits. It was easy to like
him. I once saw him leave the capitol in the company of some
friends. He was gesticulating wildly, grimacing, talking a blue
streak. Suddenly, as his party stopped for a red light, the Governor of the State of New York began dancing a jig on the
corner, snapping his fingers to the accompaniment of some
chant.

Poletti unquestionably had ambitions; he also had, I am willing to believe, genuine liberal leanings.

As governor he commuted the sentences of more prisoners
by pardon in twenty-eight days than Lehman had in ten years.
This might have escaped public notice had he not commuted
that of Alexander Hoffman, a union leader convicted of a
crime resulting from a labor dispute. It was alleged that in at-
tempting to unionize the cleaning and dyeing industry, or some
part of it, Hoffman had had shills take garments to recalcitrant
establishments that worked open shop. These garments contained incendiary pellets, which ignited and set fire to the
premises.

Newspapers looked into this and several other commutations. They discovered that a rather high proportion of the recipients of executive clemency happened to be former union organizers and underlings. A hue and cry was raised.

Poletti's part in this imbroglio has never been presented fairly. Prejudicial, distorted statements of alleged fact have beclouded the issue and hurt a career. The chief executive himself did nothing to help the situation, for he made contradictory public statements, then retired into silence as the hullabaloo increased. Yet there is one fact—a fact to which I can testify—that should have operated in Poletti's favor and didn't. I am not defending the twenty-eight-day governor. I didn't know him personally. But he was entitled to have one statement made in his favor—and he should have made it himself. We tried to and failed.

For years it had been a practice but not a legal requirement for governors to request the Parole Board to investigate and submit a report and recommendation on each case being considered for possible executive clemency. During my tenure, Governor Roosevelt and Governor Lehman had done this without any exception known to me. I don't recall that either of them ever pardoned an inmate against the recommendation of the Parole Board. On the other hand, we frequently gave a favorable report on a prisoner only to have the Governor decide against release.

The newspapers asked Poletti why he commuted Hoffman's sentence. He said he had received a favorable recommendation in an executive clemency report. This led to the inference that the Parole Board had conducted an investigation and recommended favorably in Hoffman's case.

A newsman telephoned me and asked just what we had said in our recommendation. I had to state the truth; that we had said nothing; had made no investigation; had learned of Hoff-man's release only when it was announced officially by the Governor.

That started a real furor. Actually Poletti had departed from tradition in this matter. Instead of asking us to investi-gate, he had, for reasons best known to himself, conducted an inquiry through his own counsel's office. Repeatedly, after the story broke, I and every member of the Parole Board told newsmen that the law did not require a governor to rely on us. He had full authority to commute even without investigation. This didn't get into print.

We ourselves considered that Poletti had acted injudiciously, to say the least, but the few crumbs of solace that should have been his were never thrown to him by an unforgiving press. Not a single paper, so far as I recall, printed our oft-repeated statement that Poletti had at least acted within the law.

To add to Poletti's discomfiture, a press release of his boom-eranged. In his original announcement of Hoffman's com-mutation he had said something to the effect that the inmate was a devoted family man and his release would make it pos-sible for him to return to the bosom of that family and to care for it properly. The papers insisted that Hoffman had left his family years before and had contributed little or nothing to its support.

Headlines ran for days. It appeared as if there was a feud between Governor Poletti and the Parole Board. Actually, we never talked to him during this period. We gave the facts as we knew them. If they hurt, they did. If they helped, they did.

This incident had many ramifications of significance to pub-lic service. Our stand impressed the public and our staff. Pa-role officers felt that if we could buck a governor we certainly meant it when we said we would support each employee, no matter what, so long as he dealt with cases exclusively on their merit.

Poletti was succeeded by Thomas E. Dewey. I had had contact of an official nature with Dewey in the days he was district attorney of New York County. He had a healthy respect for Joe Canavan, through whom we met.

On that occasion the dapper little D.A. positively floored me by his affability and deep personal regard for my welfare. Canavan and I had come to request his cooperation in connection with a parole case in which we needed some special investigation Dewey was equipped to make.

We were ushered into his private office. I expected to see a frigid, fish-eyed man. Instead we were greeted by a smiling gentleman seated at a massive desk, having lunch. In a voice as resonant as an organ's, he called to us most cordially to come down the tremendous office toward him. His speech vibrated through the room, each word carefully and portentously pronounced as if it were his last on earth. Each sentence carried authority.

"Joe, how are you?" The voice struck a rich tremolo.

Joe introduced me.

"How *are* you, Dave?" he vibrated, quite informally.

I began to state our business, but Dewey stopped me. He turned from profile to full face and sonorously intoned, "Gentlemen, whatever it is you want, you've got it already —on one condition."

"What's that?" Canavan asked.

Dewey smiled briefly and waggled his index finger from

side to side. "Dave," he intoned, "you look tired. You need a rest. Promise me you'll take a vacation."

I promised.

Dewey gave us full cooperation then and thereafter, although I received it under false pretenses. I didn't take that vacation.

I was already stationed in Albany, as executive director, when Mr. Dewey became governor. So far as parole was concerned, Dewey raised our budget, increased our staff, upped salaries. The administration even gave us things we didn't need. Once we were asked to move a branch office into spacious quarters we couldn't possibly fill. The local realtor was quite piqued when we said so. Why, he wanted to know, had he voted for Dewey if only to be treated like this?

All good things came to us on condition that we preserve peace within the parole family, peace at any price. For Dewey would not have it known that there were any differences among his subordinates—not when he was attacking President Roosevelt for the "confusion" and internecine strife within the federal government. Whether Parole Board members loved each other dearly or not, the façade of sweetness and light had to be there.

Dewey himself had a way of avoiding taking a stand. He evaded answering embarrassing questions from the press by falling back on formula, apparently thought up spur-of-the-moment. He would have someone say for him that the Governor "never" comments on this or that under such circumstances. "Mr. Dewey never replies to political criticism." "Mr. Dewey never comments on a case before the courts."

I once found this device helpful myself. When I was asked

to express a theory on why Dewey commuted the term of "Lucky" Luciano, the racketeer he had convicted as D.A., I sent out word, "Mr. Dressler never comments on commutations after eating noodle soup."

Although Mr. Dewey, when criticized, had a habit, I am told, of asking about his detractor, "Is the man paranoid?" there was a bit of oversuspiciousness in his nature. Once I was chairman of the program committee of the State Conference on Social Work. Following a set custom, we invited the Governor to speak before the delegates.

The Governor's assistant, Paul Lockwood, called an acquaintance of mine and asked, "What's the idea? Dressler invites Mr. Dewey to speak, and he also invites Lehman to talk on UNNRA and Mrs. Roosevelt to speak for UNESCO. What's Dressler doing, running a Democratic convention?"

I sent word back, also through my acquaintance, that we always asked any governor incumbent at the time to address the conference. We were sorry not to be able to have Mr. Dewey.

If testimony of others is to be believed, Civil Service fared badly under Dewey. In parole, however, there was no indication of any direct assault on the spirit of the career service. There were subtle indications that it would be pleasing if certain persons were appointed and certain things done. But I, for one, disregarded these hints, never took them to come directly from the horse's mouth, and followed the practices of previous years. No one in the administration offered to sack me as a result. Personally I invariably received courteous, considerate treatment at the hands of the Dewey boys.

CHAPTER XXXI

The Public and Parole

When Hammerhead Mike beats Six-Fingered Fanny's head into a soufflé, the avid reader of crime news cries, "See? Hammerhead was in jail once. Why did they let him out? That's what parole does!" And he writes a letter to the editor asking why something isn't done about this parole racket.

Few government undertakings have been so damaged by distrust as parole. And it has been hurt more by its adherents than its critics.

Many of those doing parole work harm it by having the facts but not using them properly. They accept parole uncritically, become emotional about it, and carry a torch for it even when the flame is out. They oversell their product, making claims they don't try to prove. They won't admit shortcomings and cry to high heaven when someone else finds them.

There is good parole and poor parole. The public pays the freight and is entitled to the facts.

Where we penologists fall down is in not giving those facts fully and frankly. We don't explain what parole is supposed to be and what it can't be; what the citizen should demand of his parole system and what he can't expect. Consequently we have spread confusion, misunderstanding, even open hostility to the very idea of having parole.

We have created the confusion because we are confused

ourselves. We don't agree, within the fraternity, on how to handle offenders. That isn't surprising when you consider how parole board members come into being. They are appointed to public office from all walks of life. Professors, psychiatrists, ward heelers, shirt salesmen, social workers, ministers, newspapermen, doctors, lawyers, farmers, policemen, bankers, baseball players—they have all sat on parole boards.

An outstandingly successful parole commissioner, such as the late Joseph J. Canavan of New York, insisted the board's first duty was to protect society by refusing to release poor risks. Another renowned penologist speaks of the "poor unfortunates" who are "impelled to crime" and "always entitled to another chance. We're working in their interests."

If you took a poll among parole administrators on any phase of the problem, you'd find some saying yes, some no, and some maybe. Is it any wonder the layman is confused?

Some common notions about parole have to do with the way in which inmates are released. Some say, "Parole boards act like rubber stamps. How could a Dillinger have been released? Why was 'Mad Dog' Vincent Coll paroled from a reformatory, to become one of New York's most vicious gang leaders? *People are paroled indiscriminately, carelessly.*"

It's true sometimes. There's no blinking the fact. Indiscriminate releases are not as prevalent as the man on the street believes, but they do occur.

In many places political influence still plays a part. District leader Jones calls Commissioner Smith, tactfully reminding him that he sits on the parole board because of the good offices of the leader. And, "by the way, I'm not asking you to do anything you don't think is right, but I wish you'd see what can be done for Elmer Zilch, who comes before you next week. Just a poor unfortunate—got himself in a silly jam. He has a wonderful mother."

Errors of judgment come less from political factors, however, than from others. When prisons are overcrowded the wardens howl, "Get 'em out! I'm sleeping them in the corridors!" It's difficult to remain adamant under such hammering. Result: More risks are taken than can be justified.

Public sentiment has a lot to do with paroles too. Generally speaking, when there is an abundance of labor or when we are in a depression, the public, newspapers, and legislators demand a tough policy on release. New York's Baumes Laws, increasing sentences for habitual offenders, were enacted in such an era. Then along came the war. Industry cried for labor. The pendulum swung the other way. It is not far from the truth to say that during World War II parole boards were assailed for manpower from so many sides that they released anyone whose body was still warm and who had at least three fingers on one hand able to work a machine. Where sentencing laws forbade this, the laws were changed.

Another handicap is that the majority of the boards don't know enough about the persons appearing before them. The candidates haven't been thoroughly investigated. Investigation is all important, but it costs money, and many states prefer to go on hunches. One parole commissioner said to me, "I don't need to know what a man did ten years ago. I look at him, I talk to him, and I know what he's like today." That sounds good, but it is about as logical as saying you can pick a doctor without finding out whether he studied medicine. If he carries a stethoscope, he is a good physician.

Sometimes the trouble is not faulty judgment but point of view as to whom parole is for.

Parole is a privilege, not a right. No one *must* be paroled.
He should be released only if he seems to be a fit risk. Yet a
parole commissioner told me, "When a man has served his
minimum sentence he is *entitled* to parole unless he has misbehaved in prison."

Nonsense. If that's all the discretion required, there may
as well be no parole boards. A clerk could study prison conduct reports and issue gold stars. Three gold stars, and an
inmate's won his diploma.

Many people believe *parole boards somehow smuggle
prisoners out in violation of sentencing laws.* "That fellow
got thirty years only five years ago. How come he's out?
There must be something . . ."

This reaction arises because there is no uniformity among
states as to when a prisoner becomes eligible for parole.

In one state, those serving less than a ten-year sentence may
be paroled when they have served half of it. In another,
prisoners, other than lifers, must serve two-thirds of the minimum sentence before becoming eligible. In a third, indeter-
minate-sentence prisoners are eligible when they have served
all of their minimum sentence. Definite-sentence inmates are
eligible after one-third of the sentence is over. Lifers may be
paroled in twenty years. In at least two states, the parole authority may release a prisoner at any time, regardless of
sentence.

Some discretion must be allowed the paroling authority,
else there is no incentive for the prisoner to change. A man
who knows he is going to do ten years of a ten-year sentence
has nothing to which to look forward. If he can get out before
that, provided his attitude improves, he will often work hard
to change. On this score the public would err if it criticized

a parole system for releasing men before they had served their
full terms. That isn't lack of discrimination. It's the theory of
parole.

What the public hasn't criticized very much is something
that ought to command greatest attention—the kind of people
who make up parole boards. All the errors in judgment would
be reduced to a bare minimum if parole board members were
uniformly well qualified for their jobs. Some are. Others are
well intentioned but lacking in equipment. A few are merely
holding jobs.

Some think the safest procedure is to parole as few as possible. If you don't release anyone, he can't be around to embarrass you by getting into trouble.

Some go the other way. They would parole every inmate
who doesn't positively refuse to go out. All they need, these
prisoners, is another chance, and another chance and another
chance, and some kindly soul to shed a tear over them three
times daily.

Many parole commissioners ride hobby horses. One I knew
would release any burglar, sex offender, or gunman. But he was
death on inmates involved in reckless driving. His wife, he explained, was once struck by a hit-run autoist.

Another would take a chance on a sodomist but rarely on a
man who lived in common law.

One man would stand for a little gun play or sex crime, but
woe to him who took a drink! A charming, convivial gentleman himself, all he had to find in the record was a history of
drinking, and that inmate got the book.

Fortunate is the parole system that boasts a man who does
not let his hobbies, prejudices, or personal experiences get in
the way of objective judgments; who can be a sympathetic

and understanding person without bursting into sobs; who understands people and therefore isn't carried away by them.

Happily, men of this type are becoming more frequent on parole boards, despite the haphazard methods by which governors appoint them. They don't need to be psychiatrists or social workers to be effective. They must, however, have the gift of understanding what makes people tick.

Another set of ideas the public has about parole concerns what happens after prisoners are released. That *all ex-convicts on the street are parolees* is a firm conviction. When the average reader sees an item such as "Ex-Convict Slays Girl," or "Ex-Felon Shoots Cop," he cries, "There you are! Another parolee!"

The great majority of men with criminal records are not parolees. Hundreds of thousands were arrested but not convicted. Or convicted but not imprisoned. They paid fines or received suspended sentences. And of those who have been in correctional institutions, less than half were released by parole. The rest came out by pardon, full service of sentence, and the like.

Maybe so, the skeptic says, but at least most crimes are committed by parolees.

Not so. Of persons arrested in any year, something over fifty per cent have prior criminal records. That doesn't mean they are parolees, or that they have been convicted. But even if half were parolees—that is, twenty-five per cent of all those arrested—that still does not substantiate the claim that parolees contribute most to the crime picture.

The critics are on sounder ground when they assert that *a good deal of the supervision of parolees is incompetent.* The complaint is: "Why was parolee Doakes so poorly supervised that he was able to pull a stickup?" The answer is that no parole system has a sufficient number of officers to watch every parolee twenty-four hours a day.

Incompetent supervision is due to poor administration, poor staff, or both. Some parole systems exist largely on paper. They don't attempt to watch parolees. A few still practice "sundown parole," the one condition of release being, "Get out of the state before sundown."

Some keep in touch with parolees only by mail, a system that might as well be operated by clerks who stamp and file the reports. I once examined the record of a parolee who had been out two and a half years. The file consisted of some hundred postcards, all reading: "Everything okay. Nothing new." The final entry was a news clipping: "Parolee Killed When Opium Still Explodes."

Unless officers see parolees personally, there is no real supervision. First-rate field work is an essential of good parole.

Why do we have such haphazard parole? Because it is inadequately financed, for one thing. While New York's parole budget is well over a million dollars, most states are not nearly as fortunate. Not long ago one system boasted as its total appropriation five hundred dollars a year.

You can't hire parole officers on five hundred a year, which is why almost half the parole officers of the country are in five states: New York, Illinois, Pennsylvania, California, and Massachusetts. The other half are meagerly scattered among forty-three states.

Parole staffs are sometimes of low quality, one reason being that officers are miserably underpaid. Eighteen hundred a year is not unusual, thirty-five hundred is amazing.

Good men don't stay in parole service long. They find better

pay elsewhere, and they get promoted faster in other organizations. In public work you wait for your superior to die or get
fired before you can step up.

If a poor caliber of staff is the rule, parolees won't be properly supervised. You get officers like the man who visited his
parolee's cigar store a dozen times and found nothing suspicious
in the fact that the stock consisted of one box of cigars and a
carton of cigarettes. The many men who walked in and out
without buying a thing were no danger signal to the officer.
The police had to close the place up as a horse room and policy
drop.

I don't want to leave the impression that all parole officers
are incompetent. I have already indicated elsewhere that one
of the gratifying observations one makes is that, trained or untrained, the great proportion of parole officers are sincere,
earnest, hard-working men with considerable common sense.
But too often there are too few officers; or too few *good* officers; or good officers aren't permitted to do good work because their bosses are not interested in decent standards.

Take a case like this one. A parole officer found his supposedly unemployed, single parolee living in a four-room
apartment. Whenever he visited there was a girl in the place—
always a different girl. Closets contained female apparel. Men
kept coming in and out of the apartment. The parolee couldn't
explain how he paid his rent or where he got money for food.

The officer wanted to lock the man up, at least for investigation. No, said the commissioner. Why? "This man lost a hand
in a prison shop. He has suffered enough."

The case closed itself when two men got into a knife fight
on the premises, setting fire to the place. It was discovered the

parolee was running a house of prostitution and gambling den, and selling liquor without a license.

On the other hand, under competent administration, this could happen. A capable parole officer became suspicious of a parolee because he was never at home, no matter how late the officer visited. He was permitted to devote his time to the case and was given other men to help him. For two weeks constant surveillance was the order of the day. Bit by bit the men pieced things together. The parolee was living in a tenement flat with other men. Officers observed the mob casing a jewelry store. They stepped in *before* a crime was committed and brought about the arrest of the group. An arsenal was found in the flat.

If the law-enforcement phase were all there is to parole, policemen might well—even better—operate it. Parole treatment also entails influencing and helping people so that they no longer want to commit crime. The good officer can do this. A poor one can't.

Many parolees, as I have tried to show by examples, have had the good fortune to meet a parole officer who knows how to influence people. This doesn't guarantee rehabilitation, but it certainly helps. Under such supervision men and women have worked their way back to decency and acceptance in the community. Former parolees have become businessmen, teachers, engineers, truckers, architects, artists, mechanics—yes, and writers.

The public has a right to demand results like this. The public will get them if enough good staff members are employed, under competent administrators.

In a sense, the public can be blamed if it does not get those results. When it has a good system it sits back and forgets about it, instead of keeping it under constant observation. Reform waves have a habit of burning themselves out in time. Gradually the zeal of the leaders diminishes. The old order returns. A parole system is created in the heat of reform, say. It does a fine job, and the citizens read about it. They say, "We've got a grand parole system at last!" They keep on saying this even when the wheels begin to slow up, when standards, bit by bit, go out the window. Long after the system deserves it, the public continues to praise it, because it has lost track of it.

When I speak of "reform waves" I don't want to be understood as favoring "reformers"—that is, reformers in the correctional field. I say, "Keep your reformers." In penology the reformers are the sentimentalists, the Weeping Willies. To me, the tough guys in the field are more palatable. I don't agree with them, but at least they don't insist so strenuously that the world owes them a following. They feel accountable to their fellowmen. The sentimentalists hold themselves answerable only to God—if God agrees with their ideas.

The sentimentalist feels that every man is entitled to another chance, and another chance, and still another chance, no matter how much harm he does to others and how much of a menace he is to society at large. Thus he overlooks and negates the welfare of the many in his zeal for helping the one.

The citizen does not want to be at the mercy of the dangerous criminal. I believe the majority of people want offenders treated decently, even sympathtically. They are willing to help the criminal who wants to go straight. But they do believe the welfare of the many outweighs the needs and the welfare of any one individual, including the offender.

The attitude of the sentimentalists is admirably expressed in the words of a famous prison warden who once told me, "If I had my way, there would be no prisons. We would wipe them all out."

"What would you do with the prisoners?" I asked.

"Turn 'em loose—every one of 'em!"

"Would they go back into society without harming others?"

"Maybe, maybe not. But prison does them no good."

"Agreed," I responded. "But what about the innocent by-standers—the people? Are they to have turned loose on them a horde of men, all patterned in crime, without any discrimination, any selection of good risks as opposed to poor ones?"

He shrugged. "These poor unfortunates are entitled to a chance."

Amen! But the law-abiding citizen ought to have a chance now and then, too.

The public, eventually, demands an end to a parole system that has jeopardized it. And sometimes an essentially good system is wiped out because one sentimentalist was able to bring about the release of one man who shouldn't have been paroled and who became a spectacular killer or sex offender upon gaining his liberty.

It is possible to serve the best interests of the offender and of society. A good parole system takes the position that society comes first, the individual second. But no public agency long remains vigorous and efficient unless the public sparkplugs it. In that sense, the public gets what it wants and deserves what it gets.

And there have been good parole systems. New York State's parole organization, under the leadership of Dr. Joseph W. Moore and Joseph J. Canavan, was the finest in the country.

New and better systems are being created right along. A modern combined probation and parole system was set up in Florida in 1941. Virginia followed suit the next year. California, under a revolutionary revamping of its correctional system, is improving its parole service and may soon lead the country.

I have tried to give an insider's honest view of parole as it really is. I have not glossed over its inadequacies or exaggerated them. If the theory is sound and administration sometimes weak, that does not invalidate the idea of parole. The public can decide what caliber of administration it wants. As one irate ex-parolee once told me, "You wouldn't have no job if it wasn't for us guys—the public!"

CHAPTER XXXII

Epilogue

I spent seventeen of the most productive years of my life in Civil Service. I don't regret a day of it, but I left it—which suggests the question: Is Civil Service a career to which one should aspire? My answer is: That depends on what you want in life.

If you're after a career that will make you lots of money, stay out of Civil Service. A reasonably competent person can always make more money in industry, business, or professional life than in public work. A talented top executive in Civil Service who earns perhaps ten thousand dollars a year could almost certainly have achieved an income of fifty thousand had he offered his abilities to the profit-making world early enough. It is a shortsighted policy of government that, while it wants the finest, most honest, and most creative workers, it offers salaries that discourage their staying.

If you're seeking a job that spells security, don't believe the fable that Civil Service gives it to you. True, there are certain safeguards surrounding the civil servant. He can't be fired without charges and an opportunity to answer them. But, without being dismissed, a public worker can lose his position on short notice for a variety of reasons. His job may be cut out of the budget—in order to get him out of the organization. The legislature could wipe out an entire agency. An executive could make it so unhappy for a worker that he prefers to quit. There can come a time when a man examines the values in life, weighs one against the other, and decides to give up his "secure tenure" for the sake of peace of mind or of conscience. It is my conviction that the normally sensitive, intelligent man will not find one whit more real security in Civil Service than elsewhere.

As a matter of fact, he shouldn't want that security. He shouldn't allow himself to become stultified by the notion that he has invested time in a job, therefore should never leave it. That way lies mediocrity and eventual unhappiness. The civil servant ought to ask himself every morning, "Do I still want to stay?" He should be psychologically prepared to leave his post at a moment's notice. He should *want* to leave it if it ceases to bring personal satisfaction.

If you want a job where incumbents are selected strictly on merit, don't go into Civil Service. The merit system recruits by examinations that often don't measure what they set out to measure. How are you going to determine, from a written test, whether a man has the temperament, ability, and personal integrity to make a fine parole officer? Tests measure acquired knowledge, not character and ability to use knowledge. A man may place first on a list yet be a very poor worker. I know at least one individual who came through his examination with great success. He was appointed, and he was a thoroughly worthless employee, a psychoneurotic who hadn't solved his own emotional problems, let alone achieved the ability and maturity to help parolees solve theirs. I know a man who passed the test all right—but it couldn't measure his integrity. He went to prison for dishonesty. I know a man who came out at the bottom of the list, barely managed to be appointed, and became one of the most valuable members of the staff.

If you seek a job where promotion will be based on merit and work achieved, steer clear of Civil Service. Examinations don't measure this well either. Personal favoritism may enter in. Executives may prefer yes men to intelligent workers.

Make up your mind you want Civil Service only if you can honestly say that in spite of the heartaches and discouragements you many encounter, you want to work at something vital, where you can perform a service for other human beings. Decide you want service work, not a fortune. Get your satisfactions out of the intrinsic excitement, challenge, and accomplishment of the service you enter. There is an immediacy about public work. You feel you are doing something right now that helps people this very day.

But hang on to your humility. One great failing of many public workers is that they develop the conviction they are not only all-powerful but downright infallible. Many public officials, particularly those highly placed, become vain, conceited, fatuous, and pompous. They brook no opposition and can stand no difference of opinion.

A man who espouses public service should stay at it only as long as it's fun. If he retains the feeling of impermanence of tenure, so healthy and helpful in public work, he will perform his functions earnestly as long as he enjoys it, thumb his nose at career and job when he doesn't, and walk off. Or he will give it everything he's got while it's enjoyable, and leave it while he's still enjoying it because he has decided he wants new experience, a different kind of life or more money.

I am surprised that after so many years I remain without much cynicism. Perhaps I am an incorrigible idealist. I'd hate to think so, for I believe the only way to face this world in an unstable generation is realistically. Yet I have basic faith in public service. I believe it will come through.

I believe in people. I believe in *the people*. I passionately accept that fundamentally the people are always right. They will make temporary misjudgments, will flounder about in the solution of a problem, but they will get there—by instinct. What the people want at any given time is what is right for them at that time. The public servant's duty is to determine and interpret the will of the citizens, to obey their wishes.

I believe that if a man works for the people he is bound to be happy and contented.

I believe crime can be prevented in considerable measure by intelligent planning on a broad scale, by vision and courage. No man or woman is born a criminal or foredoomed to criminality. No individual wants to fight society if he can gain normal satisfactions without so rebelling.

I believe an offender can be helped to become law-abiding. I believe the majority want to become so. I am convinced that public endeavors like parole and probation, properly administered, are valuable functions and the obligation of a democratic society.

And I believe, above all else, that a man in public work must follow his conscience without fear, compromise, or equivocation. His life will have been worth living if he can sleep at night; if he can regard himself in the mirror the next morning without lowering his eyes. His career will have been worth all the major and minor battles, irritations and frustrations if he can say, in the twilight of his years, "My wife, my children, know what I've done with my life and they're not ashamed. Perhaps they even respect me. For I have been a servant of the people, because I believe in the people."